COLCHESTER 1825

COLCHESTER 1815–1914

By

A. F. J. Brown

PUBLISHED BY
THE ESSEX COUNTY COUNCIL, CHELMSFORD
Essex Record Office Publications, No. 74
1980

ESSEX COUNTY COUNCIL
First published 1980
ISBN 0 900 360 53 4

Printed by Cullingford & Co. Ltd., The Vineyard Press, Colchester, Essex

CONTENTS

LIST OF ILLUSTRATIONS

The kind assistance of the Curator of the Colchester and Essex Museum and of the Essex Libraries Local Studies Department in allowing reproduction of items in their collections, is gratefully acknowledged.

INTRODUCTION AND ACKNOWLEDGEMENTS

Several volumes would be needed to do justice to the whole of Colchester's nineteenth-century history. In this single volume I have therefore confined myself to a limited number of themes, at the cost of omitting several other important topics or giving them only brief attention. I wish, for instance, that there had been space for separate chapters on the town's religious history or on the topographical developments of the period. Fortunately, so much local research is now taking place that one can be hopeful of these and other aspects receiving their share of attention in the next few decades.

My thanks to Mr. Hervey Benham for his generous help; to Mr. Victor Gray, the County Archivist; and to Mrs. Shirley Aldridge, Mrs. Cynthia Bambrick and Mrs. Daphne Woodward. The former County Archivist, the late Mr. Kenneth Newton, gave me encouragement and advice during the first stages of this project. My friend, the late Mr. Adrian Beckett, provided generous support. The staffs of the Essex Record Office and Colchester Central Library were, as ever, helpful and patient. Other acknowledgements are made at the appropriate points in the Notes and References.

Arthur Brown
October 1979

CHAPTER I

The Town's Economy

1815–60: a market town

When Colchester crowds cheered a unit of Gordon Highlanders into the local barracks on its return from victory over Napoleon, they were looking forward to a prosperous peace in which the commercial activity brought to the town in wartime would somehow be retained. They also expected that, as on previous occasions, the town's ancient cloth trade would recover at least part of its former strength. Though hostilities with France had almost brought cloth production to an end through the interception of trade with Spain, two firms had remained in nominal existence and several scores of now ageing weavers were ready to resume work. Yet no recovery occurred, so that by 1820 only Peter Devall, from his business at the north end of Priory Street, represented this once major industry. Installing spinning machinery in his Lexden and Bourne Mills and experimenting with types of cloth not previously made in the town, he continued in production until the 1830s when his business, and with it the woollen industry itself, finally came to an end.[1]

There were hopes that other textile industries would fill the place vacated by the cloth trade. In 1818 a Robert Dodson advertised his intention of starting a cotton-factory in St. Helen's Lane, large enough to give work to at least 2,000 people; he assured the public that he would use no machinery because he had no wish to injure the livelihood of craftsmen. No more was heard of this plan. Some dozens of former woollen-weavers turned to the silk trade, which was already replacing woollen-weaving as the chief male occupation in the other former cloth towns of Braintree, Bocking, Coggeshall and Halstead. Silk-weaving had been introduced into Colchester on a small scale as early as the 1790s by Michael Boyle, who, after selling London-made ribbons from his shop at the top of North Hill, decided to manufacture a similar product himself. His business seems to have been closed after his death in 1809, but four years later a firm in Wyre Street was producing silks, velvets and bombasines for local sale. In the post-war slump a group of silk-weavers formed their own co-operative to make silk materials, which they sought to persuade Colchester ladies to purchase as an act of charity. This venture apparently had only a short existence, but by 1832 two other small firms were in business, while Samuel Courtauld was sending some work out to Colchester weavers from his Bocking works.[2] A more hopeful development was the decision by the London firm of Henderson and Arundle to start a branch of their silk business in a former wartime inn, the Royal Mortar in Military Road. When in 1850 they decided to leave Colchester and concentrate all their work at Braintree, they offered employment there to their forty Colchester weavers if they agreed to move with the firm, but, owing to recent short-time working, none of the men possessed the twenty shillings which such a transfer would have cost them, and their employers would lend them nothing. A desperate search by the weavers led to the Cheapside manufacturers, Harrison and Lloyd, taking the vacant premises and thereby saving the industry for another two decades. When the Government decided to make Colchester a garrison town again and to reoccupy the Royal Mortar, the firm secured new premises in Abbeygate Street and Stanwell Street.[3]

The man responsible for bringing Harrison and Lloyd to Colchester had been John Castle, who had originally come from the silk-weaving town of Coggeshall and was later to be the founder and manager of Colchester Co-operative Society. His memoirs contain interesting information about the weavers' poverty and insecurity, but also about their struggles to make a living for their families and to keep their industry alive in Colchester. Their wages were below the London rates; otherwise the London employers would not have accepted the trouble and cost of providing work at so distant a place. With the frequent unemployment and underemployment that prevailed in the trade, they were completely dependent on the employers and frightened of offending them. Their occupation was doomed, since by the 1850s Colchester's silk industry was in serious decline. Once it had given work to 160 weavers, but only about fifty were listed in the 1851 census and by 1880 few, if any, were still employed in the town.[4]

The employment prospects for men were poor in the three decades after Waterloo, with the woollen cloth industry at an end and other textile trades failing to take firm root. While the Napoleonic Wars had continued, the town's economic weakness remained concealed by the temporary prosperity which the presence of many troops in the area and the high wartime incomes of local farmers had brought to its retail shops, workshops and minor industries. In 1809, for instance, a Magdalen Street shop had been advertised as "advantageously placed in the regular thoroughfare to the extensive barracks", and there were other commercial establishments which came up for sale or letting with similar recommendation. The departure of the troops in 1816 was long remembered as the beginning of the town's economic distress. As late as 1848 a writer recalled how "Colchester was for some time seriously affected by the breaking up of the military establishment which had for a number of years contributed to the support of the tradesmen and many of the labouring inhabitants".[5] With the military gone, the town became largely dependent for its livelihood on its services to local agriculture and its ability to attract the custom of the rural population. "Your petitioners are entirely dependent upon agriculture for support" was the reason given by the town's leading merchants, small industrialists and shopkeepers for their request to Parliament in 1820 to help restore agricultural prosperity. Deep depression had settled upon farming in 1816 and, though there were good years as well as bad, it was not finally lifted until after 1850. Evidence given by Colchester witnesses before a Parliamentary enquiry in 1821 described how the farmers' inability to buy from the town's tradesmen was obliging the latter to live on capital. A woollen-draper, who was also a wool-dealer, had wool on his hands which he could no longer sell to the now ruined cloth industry, and quantities of Yorkshire and West of England cloth, which impecunious farmers could not afford to buy. Wheelwrights and blacksmiths were often in difficulties because their rural customers could not pay them. Falling shipments of cereals at the Hythe were reported by a Customs official.[6] Agricultural output does seem to have been rising slowly in 1815–50 and the rural population certainly grew, but the consequent increase in demand for Colchester's services was insufficient to ensure full employment for its own rapidly growing population. The future prospects seemed no brighter than the current depression. The labourers, who with their families now constituted the great majority of the village communities, were underemployed and impoverished, their distress being reflected in machine-breaking in 1816 and 1830, in trade unionism in 1836 and in incendiarism in 1842–4. The landed interests were frightened by Parliamentary Reform in 1830–2 and Corn Law Repeal in 1846. This rural conflict and insecurity added considerably to Colchester's economic gloom.

Industrialisation left the town almost unaffected, except for the silk-factories and the railway. The only other industries were the small ones that processed local agricultural products. These had enjoyed considerable prosperity in the more favourable circumstances of the previous century, but after 1815 the rural depression stunted any further expansion, restricting the size of individual concerns and the number of their employees. Thus, as late as 1851, the largest watermill was Edward Marriage's at East Bridge, where, though steam power was already installed, only eight workers were employed. More characteristic of Colchester's milling was Mile End windmill, in Mill Road, with two workers, another in Butt Road also with two, and the one in Greenstead Road with only one. Maltings were specially mentioned in descriptions of the town as one of its distinctive visual features, but at the Hythe, where for nearly a century the industry had been partly concentrated so as to supply the London breweries, the leading maltster had only two employees in 1851. Breweries numbered at least seven, the largest being Charrington Nicholl's. In 1837 he had joined a small firm with a plant behind the Greyhound in St. Botolph Street, but he soon persuaded his partners to make a move to a former baymaker's warehouse at the bottom of East Hill where by 1851, when he had become sole proprietor, he employed no more than six workers.[7] The distilleries, which in the previous century had numbered half a dozen, now comprised only two concerns, though the joint capacity of these greatly exceeded that of all their predecessors. One was at the Hythe and here a boy who, as Professor Airy, was later to become Astronomer Royal, was able to study his first steam engine. Founded in 1812 by Samuel Bawtree and George Savill, this business was described by Cromwell's *History of Colchester* in 1825 as the largest of its kind in the country, paying over £100,000 per annum in duty. It owned extensive premises, including the distillery itself, able to produce 300,000 gallons annually, a wharf at the Hythe, three houses, seven cottages, and eleven vehicles, pulled by "dray horses, very clever and powerful"; the location is still commemorated by the name, Distillery Lane. The other firm, near the site of the present Public Library in Culver Street, had been opened in about 1815 and, after a succession of owners, had passed to A. T. Cobbold. It survived into the 1870s, outliving the Hythe concern by some thirty years. Of the brickyards the largest was Solomon Went's at Old Heath with seven employees, followed by one at Lexden in which three workers made pots as well as bricks, but more typical was John Bacon's yard on the Ipswich Road in which his only assistants were his two sons, one of whom made bricks and the other tiles. One of the largest of the market-town industrial concerns was East Bridge tannery, already large in the previous century and by 1851 employing 14 men. It is uncertain exactly how many people got a living from these agriculturally based industries, but in 1851 proprietors and employees together probably numbered less than two hundred, and this in a borough with a population of over 19,000.[8]

For women, as for men, the cloth trade's collapse proved a major misfortune. The several thousand women and girls who had still been spinning yarn for the woollen-looms in the late eighteenth century had poor prospects of alternative employment after the war. By then their chief hope of industrial work was in the two new silk mills. The larger of these, and the first to be opened, was Brown and Moy's in St. Peter's Street, a four-storey brick building facing the river, which was demolished only in the 1960s; with its workshops and other ancillary buildings, it contained some 44,000 square feet of working-space when it was built in 1826 by Stephen Brown. Using steam power and sometimes working round the clock, the factory in good times threw some 800lb. of silk weekly, and no body of workers in the town were more subject to unrest than the 400 or so girls employed, nor had greater cause for complaint. The other concern was much smaller; it was the branch of the Cheapside firm of Harrison and Lloyd, situated in Military Road, which had taken the premises over from another London firm, Henderson and Arundle. Besides employing male weavers, this concern had work for a few dozen female winders and warpers.[9] Other factory work was not yet available. In the Halstead rural area straw-plaiting had partly taken the place of woollen-spinning as a domestic occupation, but Colchester's only share of this trade lay in its fifteen straw-hat workshops with, at most, a few dozen employees between them. Tailoring was more important, a trade which, though not yet mechanised, was expanding and already adopting large-scale organisation. Hyams had led the way here, having moved into tailoring in 1817 when, according to tradition, their pawnbroker's shop had on its hands some baize cloth which the cloth trade's collapse had prevented its owners from redeeming. The firm had the cloth made up into clothing and then decided to remain permanently in that line of business. Though in 1845 they offered to "measure and make for the Nobility" in their "elegant show and measuring rooms next to the Theatre in St. Botolph Street" where cutters from the West End of London were employed, they were already giving increasing attention to their 'ready-made' branch, so expanding it that by the 1840s they were employing a thousand or so females at their homes both in Colchester and the surrounding rural area; this system of working closely resembled the one by which the woollen-clothiers had organised their spinning production a century earlier. Two other tailoring firms were developing along similar lines, though less rapidly, so that by 1851 a total of 532 women and girls were recorded as working in the trade within the borough, with probably many more employed in the villages. Quite the most numerous group of women workers were those in domestic and similar services, numbering

1,338 in 1851 and increasing steadily. Useful though any female employment was to poor families, all the female occupations of 1851 probably gave work to a smaller proportion of women in the town than woollen-spinning alone had done in 1751.[10]

One new industry did arise to increase Colchester's services to the agriculture of the region. Ironfounding had made its appearance in 1792 when an ironmonger built a foundry to the east of the present Albert Hall in which to manufacture some of the equipment which he had previously been obtaining from elsewhere for sale to his farming customers. Agricultural progress in North Essex had led to widespread interest in the improved implements and machines being developed all over south-east England, and ironmongers had an important part to perform in drawing these to the attention of their customers and in obtaining supplies of them for local sale. The builder of the 1792 foundry was Joseph Wallis, who besides making agricultural implements and general ironmongery goods of his own also acted as agent for Ransomes of Ipswich. From him the business passed to his son, Charles, and to a partner, Richard Coleman, yet another ironmonger. When Coleman resigned from the business in 1834, leaving Charles in sole charge, the latter issued a sort of manifesto, including the following brave promise:

> "Amidst eager competition, altered modes of business, improved taste and execution in all the various branches of an ornamental ironmongery, it will be the care of Charles Wallis not only to keep pace with the times, but to be forward in introducing improvement into his extensive assortment of goods".

He had enough confidence and energy at once to rebuild and reopen the premises after they had been burnt down by a widely destructive fire at the north-west end of the High Street in 1842. At his death in 1849, the business passed to Thomas Catchpool, whose family had been in ironmongery, tin-plate work and braziery for at least three-quarters of a century.[11]

When Richard Coleman had left the Wallis business in 1834, he already possessed twenty years' experience as ironmonger and ironfounder, not only in partnership with Wallis but probably, at an earlier date, in the business of his father who had his own foundry facing Colchester Castle. Richard possessed the energy and enterprise characteristic of the men who were then establishing agricultural ironfounding in the town. On leaving Wallis, he at once took premises, previously occupied by a brewer, at the corner of Abbeygate Street and Stanwell Street, behind the present Scheregate Hotel, and these he improved by building a foundry in the rear of the premises and a showroom facing Stanwell Street. Meanwhile, he went looking for business, exhibiting his improved implements at agricultural shows and gaining contracts for the building of Coggeshall gasworks in 1837, Colchester's new North Bridge in 1843 and Yarmouth's iron bridge shortly afterwards. Though in 1846 he became bankrupt, he surmounted this misfortune and in 1847–8 was again in business, not only at his Abbeygate premises, but also in the foundry by the Castle, which he had taken over at his father's death in about 1844 or 1845 and in which he now did all his ironfounding work; the Abbeygate foundry was discontinued but he still used the rest of the premises there. When he left in 1848 to take over a Chelmsford foundry, his Colchester business seems to have been closed. Meanwhile, yet another ironmonger, William Dearn, who had already been making nails for sale in his own shop, had by 1832 moved to new premises in St. Botolph Street, close to the later railway station, where the Britannia Works was afterwards to be built; he made the iron gates for the new Town Hall of 1844, recording his name on them. Altogether, much spirit was shown by these pioneers of what was to grow into the town's main industry of the twentieth century. They and their immediate successors were apparently all local men, and their success was due largely to their readiness and ability to meet the needs of the district's farmers. Nevertheless, seen from the standpoint of their contribution to the alleviation of contemporary unemployment, their immediate importance should not be exaggerated. In the 1851 census William Dearn is shown to be employing only four workers, while in the borough as a whole a mere thirteen ironfounders are recorded. This is certainly an underestimate of the total number of men employed — labourers were probably not included — but it is doubtful if more than a few dozen men as yet found work in the foundries.[12]

Industry, of the kind that was transforming other parts of the country, affected Colchester only to a limited extent. Large employers were very few. The most typical place of employment was not a factory, but a retail establishment or an artisan's workshop, a situation which, in its turn, was to be most influential in causing the town's social and political life to take the shape that it did until nearly the end of the century.

Colchester's shops, inns and other commercial establishments were of the greatest importance to the town's economic welfare, and their number was still growing. Whereas in 1800 there had been perhaps 70 retail shops, by 1848 there were about 230, besides about a hundred bakers, butchers and confectioners. At the west end of the High Street and in Head Street were found the principal establishments, with perhaps a majority of their large staffs living in. By 1851 Henry Woolton and H. O. Carr, High Street grocers, employed twenty and seven assistants respectively, John Joslin had seven men and three boys working in his High Street ironmonger's shop, while Edward Benham, bookseller, stationer and binder, kept three apprentices and employed two journeymen. Down in East Street, Robert Tabrum, another grocer, had nine assistants, but generally shops thus situated away from the centre were on a smaller scale. The number of inns was stationary, having changed little since 1800 when there had been some ninety, but about forty beershops had been opened by the 1840s, some in places of growing population where existing inns were proving insufficient. The Three Cups employed twelve female and five male servants, and the other leading inns also had large staffs, while less pretentious public houses had only one or two employees. There were a further hundred or so other commercial businesses, large and small, and about ninety professional firms. So, altogether, commercial and professional establishments numbered over six hundred, their employees probably exceeded a thousand and their proprietors could not fail to constitute a powerful force in local affairs.

The other chief group were the 1,500 artisans, whose number had grown steadily since 1815.[13] The 1851 census showed 476 of them in building, 310 in shoemaking, 117 in tailoring, 108 in coach-building, harness-making and similar trades, 105 in furniture-making and 104 in metalwork. The remainder were spread among a wide range of trades, including engraving, gilding, cutlery, organbuilding and pipe-making; as a regional centre, Colchester had enough customers to support such rarer trades. To the artisans should be added several hundred labourers working along-side them, so that the workshops and building-yards employed altogether some 2,000 men. Most businesses were small, but there were some larger concerns, including Samuel Lee's coachworks in Crouch Street with twenty men and a Magdalen Street smithy with nine. Three trades, boot- and shoemaking, tailoring and building, were slowly moving towards larger-scale operation. The footwear trade had long ceased to depend upon executing orders for individual customers, though it still offered this service, and was now producing for the general market; for instance, in 1813–23 one firm made 26,000 pairs of ladies' shoes as well as other types. By the 1840s Colchester was regularly supplying wholesalers in London, where wider markets were now open to those firms willing and able to expand. Large-scale organisation lay in the future, but in 1851 a High Street footwear workshop had twenty-four workers and, in Long Wyre Street, one had fourteen and another twelve. In tailoring, also about to become a manufacturing industry, there were High Street concerns with twelve, eighteen and twenty-six employees, while Hyams, apart from its hundreds of domestic tailoresses, had enough male employees to support two cricket teams. The third growing trade, that of building, was extending its operations as population rose and the first barracks were built; in 1851 Samuel Grimes in Duck Lane had fifteen regular workers and was on the eve of a rapid expansion. However, in all trades, not excluding footwear, tailoring and building, the large unit was exceptional. The 310 boot and shoe makers of 1851 included at least seventy-two masters, and 80 per cent of tailors were reported to be working at home.

The town was economically dominated by a large but diverse middle class. If farmers are included with the shopkeepers, professional men and master artisans, these small employers gave work to the great majority of male workers. Besides the 600 or more commercial and professional firms, there were seventy-three farms with 719 labourers, while there were not less than 350 artisan workshops. This situation was not without influence on the town's social and political character. Colchester's con-servatism, for instance, is easily understood in the light of the predomin-ance of these small businesses, the proprietors of which were, in general, unwilling to risk their hard-won substance by supporting radical social policies. Since the small scale of economic operations offered the lowliest journeymen some prospect of acquiring economic independence, any radicalism that did gain support among the workers was unlikely to take directions inimical to the survival of the free enterprise system into which they themselves might one day secure entry. Brooding over the whole community was the prolonged depression that had followed the cloth industry's extinction and this, besides causing deep insecurity among the mass of working people and weakening their capacity for social independ-ence, only confirmed defensive attitudes among the middle class. The town's politics, its working-class movement and its social relations generally were deeply affected by this economic malaise. Nor was this situation modified as yet by any major industrialisation. Until late in the century no vigorous group of large-scale employers arose to dominate the town's development or to shape its politics. The industrial working class, if such it may be called, consisted almost entirely of young females in the silk and tailoring industries, who, in the social atmosphere of the times, offered the least promising field for the emergence of an independent labour movement. Colchester, therefore, despite its already large and still growing population, for good or for ill failed to take its place in the vanguard of mid-Victorian urban history alongside the more industrialised and socially thrusting towns.

In the absence of industrial expansion, there was no strong demand for a railway, though, when one did reach Colchester, public interest was considerable. The London–Chelmsford–Colchester line, first proposed in the railway boom of 1834, was not completed until 1843, by which time the cost had long passed two million pounds. Though many criticised the placing of the station so far from the town centre, the opening caused such excitement that 2,000 people waited for hours to watch the directors and shareholders arrive on the first official train, only to be disappointed because a suspected fault on the Mountnessing bridge had caused a postponement. When two days later the party did alight at the station, they proceeded on foot to the Three Cups with a band at their head, while church bells rang out in welcome. For a month people gathered daily to watch the arrivals and departures, and a £15,000 hotel, named after the Queen, was opened next to the station. However, the Victoria Hotel soon ceased business for lack of custom and, in general, the railway made little immediate contribution to the town's economic recovery.[14] As the railway network spread over the Eastern Counties, Colchester remained interested more because it feared that rival towns might take a larger share of the existing agricultural traffic than with any view to its own further economic expansion. So the extension of the main line beyond Colchester was strongly contested, with Ipswich merchants pressing for a Colchester–Ipswich–Bury St. Edmunds route and their Colchester competitors wanting a scheme to circumvent Ipswich by taking the line from Colchester through Hadleigh to Bury. Their motives were openly avowed; the Ipswich aim was to win mid-Suffolk trade for Ipswich docks, Colchester wanted the same advantage for the Hythe. One Colchester merchant called the Ipswich proposal "a matter of life and death to the town . . . so completely would the trade of the town be cut up", and he also opposed the Colchester–Ipswich route because a line from Harwich could join it at Manningtree, thus helping Harwich, with the aid of the Stour Navigation, to supplant Colchester as the supplier of coal to the Stour Valley. When Ipswich won the Parliamentary battle, an Ipswich paper reported the running of the first train in 1846 with the comment:

> "The good people of Colchester did not appear as much
> moved by the opening as were their more vivacious
> brethren of Ipswich. There was no assemblage of en-
> thusiasts shouting *viva* to the undertaking."

If Colchester did lose trade to Ipswich, it soon made good the loss when the Stour Valley line linked it with Sudbury and when a branch was extended to the Hythe. For the present the railway's main economic advantage lay in cheaper coal and in its contribution to the agricultural expansion of 1850–75 which brought increased business to the town. Road traffic to London was diminished, but the local carriers and coach proprietors serving the rural neighbourhood probably benefited because they connected the villages with the railway. In addition, the Locomotive Inn and the Railway Tavern reflected the arrival in Colchester of a new occupation in the persons of over eighty railway employees.

Until the coming of the railway, the Hythe had been vitally important to the town's economy; "the town of Colchester depends very much on its port", a local business-man told a Parliamentary Committee. Its main inward cargoes were coal from north-east England, general goods from London and some timber from Scandinavia, its outward ones farm produce to London and north-east England. In one week in 1844, for instance, five vessels brought to the port of Colchester general goods from London and four brought coal from Newcastle, while two sailed with grain and flour for London and four with grain for Goole. There were carrier services with regular time-tables. The Oathwaite family, which had started business by the 1760s, now kept three ships sailing to Gainsborough and Hull, and they had at least one competitor on this route. By 1839 five firms were offering a weekly or twice-weekly service to London.[16] Commerce and industry had long been moving to the Hythe, so that nearly thirty coal merchants had yards there, besides which there were a score of granaries, warehouses and timber-yards. Malting had long been concentrated there, and its buildings, together with the two lime-kilns, remained a prominent visual feature. The eighteenth-century salt-works closed soon after 1815, but the shipyard survived amid some vicissitudes into the 1850s. The gasworks were built in 1836 and the railway arrived in 1846. Nearly 3,000 seamen visited the port of Colchester in 1844, many of whom found their way to the Neptune and Queen's Head at Hythe quay or to the dozen other inns and beer-houses nearby. The local economy therefore had much to lose if the Hythe ceased to be competitive.[17]

The further potential value of the Hythe was widely canvassed. From 1814 there had been several ventures aimed at turning the Colne into a major port for passenger and goods traffic. A succession of firms ran yachts or packets to Ostend, even presuming to challenge Dover as the main starting-point for the Continent. Local businessmen were quick to take up steam navigation. "Steam power is now almost universally adopted as the cheapest and most expeditious mode of communication from one place to another", ran the prospectus of a Colchester steamship company which included an ironfounder, a banker, a coal merchant and a leading grocer. They offered two services to London weekly, one for goods and one for passengers, and theirs were not the only steamers to sail from the port in the years following 1834. A local man, William Hale, made a contribution to the new techniques when he patented a system by which the paddle wheel was replaced by a propeller in the hold. His first trial started with the ship being towed to Brightlingsea and from there steaming on to Walton. Named the *Sovereign* in honour of Royalty's presence at another demonstration on Virginia Water, Hale's steamer was in 1835 making excursions from the Colne to Sheerness.[18]

None of these ventures enjoyed lasting success, partly because Colchester could hardly compete with Dover for Continental passenger traffic and local people travelling to London preferred the improved stage coaches. There was, however, a much more serious drawback which threatened not only the development of passenger transport but the whole of the Hythe's age-old trade in corn and coal. The poor state of the channel for a mile below the Hythe, with its winding course and its frequent shallows and turnings, prevented vessels of any size from proceeding further up the river than Wivenhoe. Trade was also being lost because captains sometimes feared to venture even as far as Wivenhoe, having been taught by experience that they might well have to wait several days for enough depth to sail out again. Some ships that did try to reach the Hythe were brought to a stop until lighters took off part of their load to enable them to proceed. So most cargoes destined for the Hythe were transferred from ship to lighter at Wivenhoe. In 1844, for instance, 54,000 tons of coal reached Wivenhoe in 424 colliers, of which 47,000 went up by lighter, 5,000 were distributed from Wivenhoe's own coal-yards and a mere 2,000 went on directly to the Hythe in the eighty-two small vessels that had brought them into the Colne. No steam ship brought a cargo to the Hythe until the summer of 1843.[19]

Responsibility lay with the Channel and Paving Commission, set up in 1811 with power to levy river dues for two quite distinct functions, the provision of certain municipal services and the improvement of the river. In the latter respect the Commission had been largely unsuccessful, confining itself mainly to removing some of the worst obstructions and to widening the channel at one particularly narrow place. Schemes had been advanced for a major reconstruction of the whole Navigation, including one by the engineer, Peter Bruff, for a separate canal from Rowhedge to the Hythe "thus bringing Colchester into the position that Wivenhoe now occupied", but in the continuing depression none of them had been adopted. "There is no heart amongst us for commencing and carrying out large measures of improvement" was the *Essex Standard*'s explanation when the Commission failed to respond to a rousing call to action from W. W. Hawkins, the largest owner of mercantile property at the Hythe. However, by the 1840s external events were threatening such trade as still remained. The railway reached Chelmsford in 1840, Colchester in 1843 and, most alarmingly of all, Ipswich a few years later. Ipswich had already in 1842 received a distinct advantage in the struggle with Colchester for the Stour Valley and south Suffolk trade, when its Wet Dock was opened. Plans were also being discussed for joint river and railway development at Maldon. Colchester's Customs receipts, which included river dues and so reflected coastal as well as foreign traffic, fell from £21,361 in 1837 to £18,531 in 1840 and, after the opening of the railway, to £14,220 in 1845. At last it was agreed in the town that only swift and expensive measures could check further decline. A leading merchant stated that only a major improvement of the channel "would be the means of saving what trade they had; otherwise they would be only an agricultural town without a port and without trade". On the positive side, the proposed extension of the Stour Valley railway from Colchester to the Hythe seemed to open prospects of gaining for the Hythe much of the south Suffolk coal trade as well as that of the nearer places on the Colchester–Chelmsford line, provided always that large colliers were enabled to make a direct link with the railway trucks soon to be awaiting them at the Hythe quayside. Nor was interest confined to the Hythe merchants, for, when in 1846 a Parliamentary Act was applied for to enable major development to take place, 1,200 'influential inhabitants' signed a petition in support. "The magistrates, clergy, bankers, in fact all Colchester are entirely in its favour, almost to a man", it was claimed.[20]

The ensuing conflict over this Navigation Bill was a remarkable episode.[21] The Commission was seeking powers to implement a £50,000 scheme of Peter Bruff's, by which a dam at Rowhedge would turn the river up to and beyond the Hythe into a deep still-water basin, access to which would be obtained by a separate ship-canal, sixteen feet deep and about a mile long, running from below the dam at Rowhedge up to the Hythe; by these means, it was claimed, large ships could load and unload at the Hythe, if necessary around the clock. At the Parliamentary enquiry opposition came from Lord Paget, acting for Wivenhoe interests, and from a Rowhedge maltster, while support was voiced by an impressive succession of coal, timber and wine merchants, including the Mayor himself. However, cross-examination showed that the enthusiasm of the plan's supporters was based on weak technical knowledge. Next, the Tide Commissioners of the Admiralty inspected the river, took expert local evidence and finally advised against the scheme on several grounds. If the whole of the £50,000 received in river dues in 1811–46 had been spent on the Navigation instead of a large part of it going to street lighting and paving in the town, they contended, the Hythe would already have had 14 feet of water at its quay. Even now, if such a course were adopted, the channel could be rendered much more navigable; it would be cheaper and more effective to remove the lock to secure better scouring of the channel and to use a steam dredger to flatten the 'points'; the proposed dam, on the other hand, would prevent the scouring by the outgoing tide, which was the key to real improvement, while the still-water canal would deprive adjacent land of its drainage and Colchester of its sewage disposal.

The Admiralty's opposition obliged the Commissioners to apply for a new bill to permit the raising of a £50,000 loan, on the security of increased river dues, to finance both the Admiralty's proposed measures and a new scheme by which a ship-lock to be constructed at New Quay would convert the river at the Hythe into a floating basin; both banks were to be wharfed at the Hythe and a compensating channel would be cut to permit drainage of adjacent land and to intensify the scouring of the river below the ship-lock by the receding tides. Meanwhile, the Stour Valley Railway Company, employing Bruff as its engineer, was proceeding very fast with its branch line from the main Colchester–Ipswich railway to a new station at the Hythe. Suspicions, already tentatively expressed, now began to grow that the chief owners of wharves, coal and timber yards, and other mercantile sites, who were also among the Stour Valley Railway's promoters, were supporting the new Bill in order to improve their own property and trade facilities at public expense and to establish a virtual monopoly in the coal trade, especially that part of it calculated to expand when the Stour Valley line had connected the Essex-Suffolk border area with the Hythe. In particular, the Vice-Chairman of the railway company, who with his brother owned all wharves on the Hythe's west side, and much of those on the east, came under criticism. One of the critics was especially formidable, being the proprietor and editor of the town's only paper, the *Essex Standard*. He was John Taylor, who at the start had served on the committee promoting the original Bill, and had given extensive publicity to the whole venture. With proper restraint he now began to open his paper to criticisms of the scheme, while himself writing editorials inviting the public to consider both sides of the argument, both the urgent need for an improved Navigation and the danger that "a large portion of the money will be consumed in the improvement of private quays and in the deepening and widening of part of the river, which is, for commercial purposes, almost private property". Another critic, having questioned those merchants who had been the river's main users in the past, discovered that so many of them now relied on the railway that the river could never recover its lost trade, however extensive the improvements made on it. Finally, after a further enquiry, the Admiralty's report on the new Bill fully justified Taylor's contentions when it noted that "it is proposed to construct a floating dock, the frontage of which is to remain chiefly in private hands, but the cost of which is to be defrayed by public dues". It added pointedly that "their Lordships will not object to the formation of a dock, if undertaken by a Company raising their own funds". As Taylor wrote, the Admiralty had rescued the town from "a bad and selfish measure".

The Commissioners had now no alternative but to resubmit the Bill in a form acceptable to the Admiralty. By the altered provisions the walls of all private wharves were to be improved entirely at their owners' expense and only when the necessary funds had been deposited with the Admiralty, and the proposed new tramway along the quay was to be subject to similar conditions; no income from river dues was henceforth to be diverted to pay for municipal services; the whole river from its mouth was to have money spent on its upkeep, not just the part between Wivenhoe and the Hythe; finally, the large, unwieldy Commission established by the 1811 Act was to be replaced by an elected body of only twenty-four members, six of whom had to be shipowners. The *Essex Standard* concluded its not ignoble contribution by urging voters to consider carefully who could be trusted to give disinterested public service on the new Commission when it was elected after the Bill's passage in 1847. The proceedings had been expensive, involving £1,361 in Parliamentary expenses, fees of £1,311 to Bruff, and £1,913 in legal costs. Some improvement followed, though slowly. A loan of £5,000 was obtained from the London and County Bank in 1854, enabling the Commission to arrange with a contractor for the removal of the obstructive 'points' between Wivenhoe and the Hythe and also, it was hoped, to achieve a depth of nine and a half feet at the latter place instead of the previous six feet. When the contractor reported the completion of this work the Commission sent a 'waller' to walk along the bottom of the channel at low tide to look for 'stanks', that is obstructions which might have escaped the contractor's attention.

Many were found, and the contractor was obliged to remove them. This done, the Commission expressed itself satisfied, one of its veteran members going so far as to declare that "he never saw the river in so good a state as at present". In the following years the Commission remained fairly alert to such opportunities as its limited income permitted it to take, thereby helping to maintain the volume of coal landings for two decades and even lowering the dues on this type of cargo. There was, however, no talk of any scheme of major reconstruction comparable to that proposed in 1846–7.

Despite the fiasco of 1846–7 the Hythe's leading merchants enjoyed financial success, social standing and civic eminence. Particularly prominent were William Hawkins and his brother, C. H. Hawkins. Sons of a prosperous timber merchant, they expanded the family business, fetching supplies from the Baltic and America in their own fleet of ships which included the largest vessels belonging to the port. In 1840 they almost obtained a monopoly of quay space at the Hythe, when William, then only twenty-four years old, bought very cheaply a group of properties that included the Rising Sun Inn, a malting, a limekiln, the shipyard, several wharves, nine granaries and eleven coalyards. Having married into the important Smythies family, William moved through a series of public positions. He was the main promoter of both the Stour Valley and the Tendring Railways. Despite adverse criticism over the Navigation Bill in 1846–7, he became Conservative M.P. for the borough only a few years later, the only man of trade from the locality to achieve such distinction from either political party; however, by that time, he had become the occupant of Alresford Hall, a County Magistrate and a Deputy-Lieutenant. He died of dropsy at the age of 52, to be remembered as "a self-made man with a strong will . . . leaving behind him a name earned entirely by his own energies". His brother had a longer but less distinguished career, sitting on the Council for forty-seven years and serving as Mayor on four occasions. He was long the Chairman of the Stour Valley Railway Company and of a local Insurance Society, a Channel Commissioner and a devoted worker for the Hospital.[22]

Between 1815 and 1860 the town's economy was, at best, a stagnant one, offering little prospect of expansion, while in the same period its population almost doubled. Employment was hard to find and to retain, nor did workers find migration easy, even after changes in the Settlement law had removed some of the obstacles. Suffolk, Norfolk and rural Essex were suffering the same depression as Colchester, while the industrial districts of the Midlands, the North and Wales seem to have offered little work; the census figures show how very few Essex men had moved to those places. Only London provided employment on any scale, mainly in domestic work; girls leaving Colchester to take such jobs were quickly replaced in Colchester itself by country girls who always comprised a large proportion of the town's domestic workers. Working-class families in Colchester were in constant fear of unemployment, there was much underemployment and wages were generally low. In most families everyone old enough to work did so, if they possibly could. Thus in 1851 William Aldous was helped in his tailor's shop on North Hill by his two daughters and two of his sons. Isaac Webb of Long Wyre Street was also a tailor; his wife was a charwoman and her two daughters needlewomen. Elijah Matthews of Brook Street was a plasterer, his wife and daughter tailoresses. These families were fortunate to find employment for their able-bodied members; other families were less well placed. Happily not too many children worked under the age of fourteen, even in the silk-factory where experienced workers were needed to handle the delicate material. A number of children were still at school at the late age of thirteen, more through absence of suitable employment for them than because of any humanitarian feelings among parents or employers.

1860–1885: a pause before industrialisation

In the mid-Victorian years Colchester remained a market-town on which the few minor industrial developments which were to assume importance later as yet had little impact. The *Great Eastern Railway Guide* commented in 1865 that "the commercial aspect of Colchester is of a limited character, there being no manufactories in the town". There were, in fact, two manufactories, the silk-mills in St. Peter's Street and Abbeygate Street, but they were soon to be closed. The periodic strikes in the St. Peter's Street factory marked the periods of depression in the industry and of the wage economies that accompanied them; in 1861, for instance, shortly after the press had reported that "the silk trade is in a very inactive state", the girls struck against the short-time working introduced by the firm. At the few busy times the number of employees rose from the normal 250 to about 400, and at the Abbeygate Street factory there were a further hundred or so men and women at work, but the 1860 Free Trade treaty with France had exposed the industry to keen competition which was soon to bring about its disappearance from Colchester. The Abbeygate Street factory was the first to be closed. The larger one in St. Peter's Street continued under the proprietorship of the Brown family, its original founders, until the mid-1870s. Durrants, a firm with works in Ipswich and Coggeshall, then bought it and kept it open till 1879, despite a slump in the industry. It was then closed and, though reopened briefly in 1881 by its former manager, it was very quickly closed yet again, never to be reopened as a silk factory. After remaining unused for some years, it was sold in 1886 to the Eagle Brewing Company for use as a warehouse.[23]

While silk declined, Colchester's only other industrial asset, the railway, enjoyed modest prosperity with the extension of its network into new areas of North Essex. The Tendring Hundred line reached Wivenhoe in 1863, Weeley and Brightlingsea in 1866 and Walton in 1867. The Colne Valley line was opened to Halstead in 1860 and further extended in the next few years; goods carried on this route, mainly agricultural produce to Colchester and coal from Colchester, rose from 8,000 to 20,000 tons in the first four years of operation. There were several unsuccessful schemes, too, including one that would have linked a new station in Crouch Street with Maldon and Tilbury. Though the local iron foundries began to make regular use of rail transport in the 1860s and the footwear industry in the 1870s, it was still as a market town that Colchester drew most advantage from this new form of transport. This is further seen in the extension of the local carrier network, which now linked rural north-east Essex and parts of south Suffolk with the town and, through its railway station, with London and beyond. There were fifty-six such carrier services in 1848, involving 187 return journeys each week, including eighteen from Wivenhoe, eight from Nayland and six from Tollesbury. Of these fifty-six services thirteen were daily. By 1878 the number of services had risen to sixty-two, involving 199 return journeys. In 1848 there had also been services between Colchester and London, Cambridge and Ipswich, but thirty years later only the Ipswich route was still in operation.

If the railway helped the local carriers, it was soon to undercut the town's other means of transport, the Hythe Navigation. Here, after the work of the early 1850s, the only important improvement was the deepening of the river up to East Mill, enabling the first sea-going sailing barge to reach the mill in 1865; other schemes succumbed to the leading merchants' dislike of increased dues. There was no sharp decline in traffic at first and, with the recovery of agriculture after 1850, some of the district's wealthiest men continued to derive their income from businesses at the Hythe. Thomas Moy, after buying Thomas Mann's already extensive coal business, so expanded it that he became one of Eastern England's leading coal merchants. Among other substantial businesses were a corn warehouse, in which Alfred Francis employed nine men, and an ale warehouse where seven men worked for John Garrad, who employed a further eight on his own ships. The Hawkins family continued to prosper. From the mid-1860s, however, railway expansion and rivalry from the recently improved ports of Ipswich and Maldon began seriously to affect the Hythe's trade, so that in the next fourteen years coal landings fell from 44,000 tons a year to 17,000, there was a drop of 60 per cent in foreign trade, and income from river dues fell to the further detriment of the channel, the depth of which was by 1879 diminishing alarmingly. A critic of the Channel Commission said at this time that "they had been working at Colchester for a free river, and they had got one almost free from dues and almost free from trade", at which one of his audience interjected "but not free from mud". A measure of the decline was the sharp fall between 1851 and 1871 in the number of those in maritime and associated occupations.[24]

Meanwhile, Colchester's economy remained essentially that of a market town serving a wide rural area. Milling and brewing saw most change. Though the windmills now began to disappear, young Wilson Marriage at East Mill built up a business of some size which was to survive into modern times. In 1872 he installed his second steam engine, in 1875 he opened at the Hythe a two-storey warehouse superior to any other commercial building ever erected there, and in 1878, after seeing roller-mills at the Vienna Exhibition, he bought two sets of these as part of a general modernisation of his equipment. He was also mainly responsible for the river improvement between his mill and the Hythe.[25] In brewing the few major concerns were growing still larger, as they superseded or absorbed smaller competitors. Daniell's, though formed in the 1820s, had expanded little until it took over the small Northgate brewery, established a close link with another plant in Rowhedge and built itself new premises in Maidenburgh Street. By 1869 it employed some seventy workers and was laying the basis for further expansion by acquiring scores of inns and beerhouses. East Hill brewery at this time was regarded as one of the most modern and impressive of Colchester's businesses. With its premises arranged around a spacious yard at the foot of East Hill, it employed some fifty workers, used up-to-date machinery including a 60 h.p. steam engine, and from depots at Manningtree, Maldon, Wisbech, Yarmouth and London sent its product all over Eastern England. The Eagle Brewery, also on East Hill, opened additional plant at Langham Moor, acquired Hurnard's brewery next to St. James' Rectory and St. Botolph's brewery north of St. Giles' Church, and finally, when its founder, Henry Stopes, handed over control to his two sons, was rehoused in an impressive modern building, still standing on the north side of East Hill. When the large concern belonging to A. T. Cobbold on North Hill had been closed, these three surviving firms of Daniell's, East Hill Brewery and the Colchester Brewing Company, as the Eagle Brewery was to be renamed, were left in almost complete control of the trade in Colchester and over a wide area of Essex and south Suffolk.[26] Nevertheless, the two expanding industries of milling and brewing between them employed less than 300 workers, while in the other market-town industries of malting, tanning and brickmaking there was virtually no expansion. The town's small iron foundries did expand during this period, but, as described later in this chapter, they mostly did so by moving away from the production of agricultural machinery and thus weakening their links with Colchester's market-town economy.

The other characteristic occupations of a market town, artisan businesses and retail shops, remained an important part of Colchester's economy in this mid-Victorian period. The artisans were still the typical workingmen of the town. Coachmakers, saddlers, watchmakers, building workers and cabinetmakers increased their number by about a half in 1851–71, as population grew, barracks were built and farmers' incomes rose. Whereas in 1848 there had been about seventy-two shoemaking workshops, by 1863 there were ninety-seven, some of them employing considerably more workers than before. In building, too, some firms were expanding; in the 1860s Samuel Grimes had about seventy men attached to his 'extensive' premises on North Hill and a decade later his son had increased this number to a hundred. Certain trades did decline, for instance wheelwrights and millwrights, but, over all, the total number of artisans increased as much as the population as a whole. Workshops were about 10 per cent more numerous in 1863 than in 1848; only after 1870 did the decline begin. Retail shops steadily increased in number; if their rural customers were fewer and poorer in the 1870s, the town's own population was rising through the presence of the army and the start of industrialisation. In the larger shops in the town centre there were hundreds of assistants employed, about half of them living on the premises; the moral welfare of this newly important occupational group attracted repeated attention through the whole Victorian period. In 1871 one High Street draper employed six men and three women, four of whom lived in, and another draper two men and ten women, eight of whom lived on the premises; a grocer in Head Street kept six assistants. In the High Street eight assistants worked in a hosiery shop. An outfitter living in Lexden Road — it is unclear where his shop was situated — had twenty

men and thirty women working for him, though some of these may have
been tailors or seamstresses. The numerous inns, beershops and other
licensed businesses gave work to many more. The Red Lion in 1861 had a
staff of three barmaids, a chambermaid, two housemaids, a cook, two
kitchenmaids, two waiters, a billiard-marker and a 'boots'. The George in
1871 had eleven servants living in, aged between sixteen and twenty-eight.
The Woolpack had six and the Castle Inn three. Moreover the number of
licensed premises rose from 154 in 1866 to 186 in 1885, when their
employees were counted in hundreds. Only in clerical, professional and
administrative occupations was the growth still slow for a centre as important as Colchester.

For most of these years the town showed few signs of impending industrialisation. A survey of offensive chimneys reads like a gazetteer of
typical market-town concerns:

> "the Water-works chimney, that of Cobbold's brewery,
> of Grimes' steam engine, the chimneys of the silk mill,
> of Catchpool's foundry; the chimneys in Culver Street
> at Cobbold's premises, at Tracey's bakehouse; those of
> Jenning's pipe kiln in George Lane, Daniell's brewery,
> Nicholl's East Hill Brewery, Francis's steam engine and
> Marriage's steam engine".[27]

Apart from the water-works and the silk-mill, then in its last years, the
offending firms were the breweries, the saw-mills, the agricultural machinery foundry, distillery, bakery, brick and pipe kiln, corn merchant's
business and flour-mill of a large market town.

Not until about 1880 did clear signs appear of impending economic
change, and even then only in engineering were those signs obtrusive.
Even before the agricultural depression of 1874–1914 had diminished
farmers' capital and partly altered the farming system, this industry was
escaping from its dangerous dependence on agricultural and milling customers, to whom it had owed its earlier success. The one exception was
the foundry of Catchpool, Stannard and Stanford in the High Street in
which the forty workers went on making portable and stationary engines
of small power, threshing machines, elevators and other farming equipment; one partner, E. K. Stanford, enjoyed some reputation as an inventive agricultural engineer, his two main achievements being a rotary
harrow and his 'acme malt and grain-cleaning apparatus'.[28] On the other
hand, Dearn's foundry, by St. Botolph Station, after its acquisition by
Joseph Blomfield in 1861, turned to the manufacture of velocipedes, and
also of sewing machines which were in increasing demand at that time in
the town's expanding tailoring and shoemaking factories. The firm
needed skilled workers for these products; "second-rate workmen need
not apply", read one of its advertisements for additional labour. It had its
own 'riding master', who in 1869 rode one of the firm's eight-guinea
bicycles from Aldgate Bull to Colchester Fleece in seven hours, including
time for rest, "in spite of the shingly state of the roads". It was equally
proud of its sewing machines. An advertisement at this time read:

> "The old Wheeler & Wilson's patents having now ex-
> pired, the Britannia Sewing Machine Company are
> making the same pattern machine at superior strength

and finish at greatly reduced prices, but they prefer recommending their new Britannia Machines as by far the most useful, prettiest and cheapest machines in the World. Depot Blomfield's, Colchester." [29]

In 1871 this firm was foremost in the industry, its 105 employees making it the largest single employer of male labour in the town. Though growing fast, James Paxman's business still had a total staff of only seventy-one. Paxman, originally an apprentice of Thomas Catchpool and later promoted to be his foreman, had opened his own foundry in Culver Street, where the Public Library stood in 1978, in partnership with the brothers Davey. His first employee rose within two years to become foreman of nearly fifty men. At first this was a typical country-town concern, competing for the custom of the north Essex farmers. An advertisement in 1867 offered a repair service for agricultural and milling machinery and a stock of portable and fixed steam-engines, boilers and threshing machines. One of the firm's earliest successes was an improved steam corn-dryer, which won prizes at the region's agricultural shows. However, a move was soon made out of too heavy a dependence upon agriculture. Within a decade of its foundation, the firm was producing for a much wider market new types of wheeled boilers, self-propelling traction engines and vertical boilers which economised in fuel; the favourable account of the last of these in *The Engineer* indicated that nation-wide recognition was imminent. A measure of success was the increase in the number of workers from fifty in 1867 to seventy-one in 1871 and nearly 200 in 1876, the year in which his increasing business and improved methods of production obliged Paxman to transfer his works to a new site near the Hythe, where there were railway as well as water facilities and room for expansion. The new factory quickly became one of the town's most impressive industrial assets. Brick-built and well ventilated, it included spacious workshops for the five main departments, in which were made every part of the boilers and engines sold by the firm. The former building in Culver Street, which James Paxman had previously shared with A. G. Mumford, was after 1876 taken over entirely by the latter who also turned increasingly from the production of agricultural machinery to that of naval and maritime equipment. [30]

Important, though less impressive, was the progress in the other two industries which had begun to grow earlier in the century. In tailoring the pioneer had been the firm of Hyams, which built in Abbeygate Street a two-storey factory with a 115-foot workshop to house its modern cutting and sewing machines. By 1861 there was concern that, with so much mechanisation, unemployment was growing in the industry, but a succession of London firms now began to establish branches in the town. One of the first was that of Moses which in 1852 was employing Colchester women in their own homes on work cut out by London tailors, but by 1863 had opened its own factory in Priory Street where, in the sewing machine department alone, 180 women were working. Hammonds started their business in 1854 and by 1871 had some 500 employees, some in their Stanwell Street factory and others at home in Colchester and nearby villages. Alfred Hagg's Works at No. 1 St. Botolph Street employed fifty women and twenty-four men. Altogether there were reported to be six large firms in 1865, giving work to 2,500 women and girls and to 200 men. Many of the women worked in their own houses in Colchester and in the rural vicinity, especially the Colne Valley.[31]

The other trade to expand was shoemaking, though mostly it still remained organised in workshops as it had been before 1850. It already had a London market, but its more enterprising firms began now to use the railway to reach a wider area of south-east England; by 1887 the trade claimed to have become the Great Eastern Railway's chief commercial customer in the town. The tradition is that mechanisation began when a leather-seller, W. Warmington, began to interest local shoemakers in the new machines then becoming available and even lent some of them money with which to buy them. The pioneer was probably S. G. Knopp who from a small concern in Hythe Street, started in 1860, was obliged by his own success to make a series of moves, first to Long Wyre Street, then in 1866 to Osborne Street and finally in 1868 to the corner of Portland Road and Mersea Road, close to the present roundabout on the south ring-road. There he so prospered with his 'Time Will Tell' products that he had to carry out a series of improvements, culminating in a three-storey factory with its own tall chimney, bearing the title 'Knopp & Son, Wholesale Boot Manufacturers'. In 1861–71 the number of his workers rose from twelve to sixty-one. In the 1860s T. Harbour, already established in the High Street, acquired a second workshop in St. Botolph Street, increasing his employees to about fifty in the process. W. Warren, whose family was in business for most of Victoria's reign and claimed in the process to have developed a range of footwear specially suited to local needs and tastes, was in 1871 employing forty-five men and three boys in his Short Wyre Street works. Other establishments were expanding, though more slowly.[32]

The establishment of barracks in and after the Crimean War, besides affecting Colchester both socially and politically, had important economic consequences. The population figures, showing a rise of 9,000 between 1851 and 1881, representing a 46 per cent increase, were largely due to the influx of soldiers and their families and also to the trade which their presence generated. The largest population increase in any decade during the century was one of 23 per cent between 1851 and 1861, the time when some 2,400 men were occupying the new camp. The building of cavalry barracks along Butt Road in 1862 brought many horses, too, and a further considerable increase in trade. One of the earliest press reports of military building noted with satisfaction that "contracts for coals, straw etc., have already been entered into" and by 1869 it was estimated that £80,000 was spent annually in the town by the army.[33] Keepers of inns, beerhouses and brothels, almost every kind of shopkeeper, the suppliers of corn, hay and coal, stable-proprietors, coachmakers, saddlers, wheelwrights, blacksmiths, farriers and domestic servants were some of the principal occupations to benefit from this unexpected access of customers, an asset that was to prove all the more valuable to the town when, after the onset of agricultural depression in 1875, the north Essex rural population was falling and had less money to spend. To an appreciable extent the continuing presence of the Garrison helped Colchester's market-town services to survive in the middle of a languishing rural neighbourhood.

1885–1914: the growth of industry

In the 1880s calmness gave place to uncertainty in the town's economy. The agricultural slump had started in 1875 and was quick to affect Colchester's market-town services. "There are numerous instances of farms, which are now on hand and could not be let on any terms", Colchester Town Council was told. Severalls Farm commanded only one shilling an acre in 1882, and Monkwick Farm at one time could not be let at all. A Colchester magistrate wrote "Corn growing is undoubtedly doomed in Essex. It has been carried on at a loss for some time, but the market prices now settle the matter beyond all dispute. To continue it means ruin to landowners, farmers and labourers alike, besides the serious consequence to trade, which towns like ours, depending a great deal on the spending power of agriculturalists, must feel." [34] Village population was falling as young people moved away, Great Tey's from 781 to 563 and Great Bromley's from 754 to 585 in 1871–1901, to take but two examples, and every departure caused some loss of trade to Colchester. The number of artisan workshops in the town was reduced to about a half by 1900; though competition from mechanised factories in Colchester and elsewhere was partly responsible, decline was also observable in trades which were as yet unaffected by mechanisation. Among the agriculturally based industries there were many closures, too. Of the dozen windmills only two, a wooden one in Butt Road and Seaborn's next to the Six Bells in Greenstead Road, were left in operation by 1900. By the latter date there were fewer maltings, while only one of the three tallow-works was still in business. The last of the distilleries, A. T. Cobbold's, close to Mumford's in Culver Street, was closed in 1881 and its building let to the Brush Company, then making the first attempt to run an electricity concern in Colchester. One tannery had survived, Warmington's in St. Peter's Street, but, though it had been prospering in this shoemaking town, it was not rebuilt when in 1898 a fire caused £13,000 of damage and threw its sixty tannery workers and shoemakers out of work. [35]

The only important market-town industry to survive in any strength was brewing, which gained from the growth of the town's population and the presence of the Garrison. The three largest concerns steadily bought up inns and beerhouses in the villages and small towns of the region, closing down any attached breweries, and by 1900 they together owned some 500 licensed houses, most of them in north Essex. The Colchester Brewing Company, besides acquiring the former silk-factory in St. Peter's Street, built substantial new premises near the bottom of East Hill, adorned with an eagle in memory of the former Eagle Brewery, which had been the largest of the firms making up the new company. With its capacity of 40,000 barrels at Colchester and a further 50,000 barrels from its other plants at Eye and Halesworth, the firm supplied the 250 licensed houses which it owned in Essex, Suffolk and London. Also situated on East Hill, Charrington Nicholl's had remained a family firm, specialising in its trade with the armed forces, including troop ships and foreign stations, but also supplying its own licensed houses. Its premises were enlarged in 1884 and a mineral-water factory was opened next to the brewery. About sixty workers and draymen were employed there and a further forty worked in the firm's timber-yard and saw-mills in Culver Street. The third of the large firms, Daniell's, which in 1887 became a Limited Company with a capital of £300,000, owned 134 licensed premises, including Colchester's Red Lion, and by 1912 it had increased this number to 150. Meanwhile it bought and closed the Crown Brewery at Tiptree and the Donyland Brewery at Rowhedge, concentrating all production at its Colchester and West Bergholt plants. Its fortunes fluctuated with the general state of trade in the neighbourhood, but its over-all prosperity was such that, when in 1912 a merger with Colchester Brewing Company was proposed, its shareholders, who included some of the town's wealthiest citizens, rejected the proposal because they felt they might lose by it.[36]

Besides the three leading breweries, Marriage's flour-mill also survived from the economy of 1815–80, undergoing further mechanisation, especially in 1885 when a new mill was built to accommodate the larger machines. Yet by 1900 there were no more than a hundred people employed there, while the brewing concerns had hardly more than two hundred workers between them. With the artisan workshops declining in number, the town would have become as economically depressed in the 1880s as it had been a century earlier during the cloth trade's collapse, if there had not been rapid industrial expansion at this time. As the *Essex Telegraph* noted in 1896:

> "Colchester is becoming a considerable manufacturing
> centre, though we are not where coal and iron abound
> — yet through the skill and enterprise of its leading
> men, our industrial concerns are constantly extending.
> In our engineering works there are now three times as
> many employed as there were eight years ago, our boot
> factories and clothing establishments, our flour mills
> and breweries have all quite recently enlarged their
> bounds and are now in a state of lively prosperity. Agri-
> culture has declined but the people of Colchester have
> sought other industrial pursuits and the result is, instead
> of a decaying agricultural township, we see a growing
> commercial community." [37]

The three emerging industries referred to, engineering, footwear and tailoring, were by 1900 employing some 4,000 men and women in Colchester factories as well as thousands of tailoresses in neighbouring villages.

In the footwear industry Knopp's had at first continued as the foremost firm, enlarging its premises three times between 1877 and 1895. Using steam-driven machinery and employing about a hundred men, it made shoes of some quality, particularly ladies' light shoes and men's shooting-boots which were advertised widely. It also specialised in "welted boots. Do not creak when walking . . . well adapted for the office or shop." [38] By 1890, however, it was overtaken as the largest employer by John Kavanagh, a newcomer to the trade who had started his career as a regular soldier and had then become a Great Eastern Railway worker before setting up in Magdalen Street, near the Camp, as a clothier and outfitter with a special line in soldiers' greatcoats. He was thus well placed for the next stage of his career, when he bought rejected army boots and repaired them for resale to the public. He next won contracts for the mending of army footwear and by 1887 at his Stanwell Street factory he was dealing with 2,700 pairs weekly from camps all over England, having become the largest repairer for the army in the whole country. Meanwhile, his manufacturing branch had grown from a minor undertaking into his chief concern. He made all major types of footwear in a variety of styles, but was becoming known particularly for his men's heavy boots, made on the latest Standard screw machines. Much modern equipment was used, including machines for rough-cutting, sewing, heeling and lasting. In 1887 he employed 237 men at Colchester, and others in his thirteen retail shops in Reading, Liverpool and London, and he was planning a new factory in which he hoped to double both his output and the number of his 'hands' as he called them. He did not quite achieve the latter — he employed 370 men in 1892 — but he probably more than doubled his output with the improved machinery and organisation in his new factory, opened by the Mayor in 1890. It was Colchester's first large modern factory and made a great impression. The *Essex Telegraph* wrote:

> "On Wednesday this lofty and spacious structure was formally dedicated to the uses of the business in the presence of the Mayor and Mayoress, who had the pleasure of inspecting what is believed to be one of the largest and best appointed boot factories in the world. An idea of the magnitude of the concern . . . may be gained from the fact that it gives employment to some 300 persons, who manufacture 170,000 pairs of boots yearly, of all kinds, in addition to the re-manufacture of 100,000 pairs of Army boots. . . The building consists of a basement and five floors, and each of the lofty and spacious apartments is well lighted, ventilated and furnished. Communication all over the building is established by telephone and the several floors connected by a lift. Hot water pipes have been laid for heating purposes. The stair-cases are absolutely fire-proof. Mr. Kavanagh has had the whole of the new factory filled with electric light plant, and at a given signal the Mayoress switched on the light and instantaneously illuminated the whole of the capacious apartments. The motive power is supplied by an Otto gas engine of 12 horsepower, and there is a second and similar engine for driving the machinery." [39]

The third most important footwear factory was A. C. George's; the building still stands at the corner of Kendall Road and Charles Street. George, like Kavanagh, was a newcomer and no less vigorous and enterprising. In the 1880s he was opening fresh markets for his products in the South and West of England and by 1890 had begun to penetrate the Midlands and the North; he also kept two shops in Colchester High Street.

His employees increased in number from about fifty to a hundred in the 1890s. He steadily mechanised his production and kept abreast of current demand, offering in 1900 "latest novelties in ladies' dress shoes, a great variety of boys' and girls' useful school boots for rough hard wear, athletic boots and shoes". Both W. Warren in Short Wyre Street and Thomas Harbour in St. Botolph Street employed about fifty men. They were local artisans who had gradually transformed their fathers' workshops into small factories in response mainly to local demand. There were other small manufacturers who also seem to have emerged from the artisan-staffed trade of the 1860s. One of these, Warmington, the tanner and leather merchant in St. Peter's Street, specialised in the making of footwear uppers and increased the number of his employees from eighteen in 1871 to sixty in 1898, the majority of these being in his footwear department.[40]

By the early 1890s boots and shoes had become at least the equal of engineering as the provider of male employment. In 1887, at the annual dinner of Colchester's railway staff, the Trade of Colchester was represented by the Hythe coal-merchant, Thomas Moy, and by John Kavanagh, who said in his speech that he was presumably being thus honoured because he was the largest employer in the town's chief industry, for "the boot trade was the staple trade of Colchester". There were then about 750 men in the industry, he believed, and between them they earned close on £35,000 a year.[41] Within a few years the number of employees had further increased. Yet, remarkably, between 1897 and 1908 this apparently vigorous and diversified industry dwindled to a couple of small concerns, comprising Samuel Buckingham's large workshop in Head Street and a new factory opened by Potter and Fisher in Moses' former clothing factory in Priory Street; only about 200 people were listed by the 1911 census as working in the trade, and some of these were only doing repair work. Kavanagh seems to have closed by 1898, Warmington by 1905, Knopp in about 1909 and Warren at about the same time. A. C. George had reduced his once considerable scale of operations by 1905 and some three years later he closed his manufacturing business altogether, though he kept his Short Wyre Street warehouse open until at least 1913. On the eve of War the collapse had proved so final that the *Essex Standard* regarded the industry as a thing of the past. "Time was" it wrote "when Colchester was a thriving centre of the boot manufacturing industry, but, as the outcome of the specialisation of industries, it was allowed to fall away to nothing . . . Its place has been taken by the wholesale ready-made clothing manufacture which has developed and absorbed the premises previously occupied by the makers of boots and shoes. No further proof is required of the versatility and capability of Colchester people." This reference to specialisation is not illuminating, as it fails to explain why so strong and technically progressive a centre as Colchester failed to emerge as one of the beneficiaries rather than one of the victims of the footwear industry's development. Nor does the writer note the economic loss suffered by the town when almost a thousand men lost employment at nearly a living wage, to be replaced in the same buildings by women and girl tailoresses, paid little more than a third of the shoemakers' rates.[42]

The clothing industry was certainly expanding. By 1907 some dozen firms were employing 1,500 people, mainly women, in factories, besides sending work to the villages in a fleet of sixty vehicles. Hyams remained the leading firm. From their earliest years they had their cutting carried out in London and in 1903 they built a new factory for this purpose in Southwark, while employing 300 workers at their Abbeygate Works at Colchester and sending out work by motor-car to Ardleigh, Langham, Tolleshunt D'Arcy and other north Essex villages. They claimed at that time to have the largest sales in the country. Of the other older firms Moses had closed before 1900, but Hammonds, renamed the Colchester Manufacturing Company, continued in Stanwell Street with over a thousand employees working at home or in the factory. There were a number of newcomers, some attracted from London by the cheap labour available both in the villages and among the fast-growing female popula-tion of Colchester, to whom, with the agricultural depression in rural north Essex and the closing of the silk mills in Colchester, only domestic service and shop work offered alternative employment. One of the most important of the new firms was Hollington's, which took over Kavanagh's former boot factory in Stanwell Street in 1898, re-equipped it thoroughly and was soon employing 200 workers there. Increasing orders, including one for the supply of all Great Eastern Railway uniforms, caused it to become one of the town's principal employers. Another expanding firm was Hart and Levy, who had premises in Magdalen Street from the 1890s, but, finding these too small for their increasing business, ceded them to yet another London firm and built themselves a very modern factory a few doors away, "so roomy as to make the old place diminutive by com-parison". Here a reporter found "a hive of industry, a regiment of young women in long rows, each having her special machine, in another part of the room rows of male workers, pressing, packing and doing the heavy work . . . An electric motor drives a series of ten machines, yet each machine is controlled separately by the individual operator with the mere touch of the foot . . . The very seats are a novelty; for they work on a swivel arm, so that, as soon as the operator rises, they automatically swing under the machine out of the way. The machines are a revelation." Though most of the output was for the colonial trade, the home demand was considerable, and the reporter was told that an order, received by telephone, could be met within seven hours. The firm of Senior, Heap & Co. had started in 1890 at a former ropery in Osborne Street, but soon moved to George Rickword's old premises next to the Castle, where they used the ground floor for cutting and packing, the first floor for fifty or more sewing machines and the top floor for storage. Finally, they moved again to St. John Street, by which time the firm had become Heap, Osbourn and Piton. They specialised in corduroys and moleskins, chiefly but not entirely for the British market. Other firms were Trent and Upsdale in East Stockwell Street, Richmond and Lewis in Magdalen Street and later in St. John's Street, the Monkwell Street Warehouse Company in Priory Street and the Magdalen Clothing Company in Osborne Street. One local firm which rose with the general expansion of the industry was that of Henry Leaning, who in 1878 was a tailor and clothier at the corner of Eld Lane and Long Wyre Street. By 1899 the firm was Henry Leaning and Co., 'Wholesale clothiers', and, after the closure of Knopp's boot and shoe factory in Portland Road, it took over the building as a clothing factory.[43]

The clothing industry employed mainly women and, with the disappearance of the footwear industry, there was need for more employment for men. This was to a large extent supplied by the expanding engineering industry. The latter was dominated by four firms, only one of which remained committed to the production of farm machinery. This was Catchpool, Stannard and Stanford and, probably because of the continuing depression in local agriculture, it was by now the smallest of the four firms. Blomfield's, near St. Botolph Station, had already added velocipedes and sewing machines to its range of products and after 1880 it turned increasingly to the manufacture of oil engines, lathes and machine tools, being successively called the Britannia Manufacturing Company, the Britannia Machine Company and the Britannia Engineering Company. At one time it housed a motor-car manufacturing enterprise. It shared in the industry's pre-war expansion, increasing the number of its employees from 160 in 1904 to 300 in 1914, but, shortly before the death of its senior partner, Joseph Blomfield, it was suddenly closed on the very eve of the 1914 War. The Labour Exchange sent some of its former workers to similar work in Erith, but Paxman's took the plant over and were soon using it on war contracts.[44] The third firm was A. G. Mumford's, situated in Paxman's original premises in Culver Street. Its proprietor, a latecomer to the town, had also started as a manufacturer of farming machinery, but by the 1880s had turned to making marine pumps, compound engines and other nautical equipment for the British, Russian and Italian Navies, as well as for merchant vessels and yachts, including those launched from Wivenhoe's shipyards. To cope with increasing business, he gradually acquired a number of additional buildings in the immediate vicinity of his works and was contemplating building an additional factory at the Hythe, but in the end he remained in Culver Street where by 1914 he had over 400 employees.[45]

James Paxman's Standard Ironworks in the 1880s was still employing fewer workers than Kavanagh's boot factory or Hyams' clothing business, but the proprietor's energy and inventive zest were already taking the firm away from agricultural machinery manufacture into that of gas and benzine engines, electrical machinery and new types of vertical boilers. On his convenient new site at the Hythe the fitters' and turners' shops had each 10,000 square feet of floor space, the smiths' shop 5,000, the boiler shop 10,000, the foundry 6,000 and the woodworkers' shop 5,000. Steam was used to drive "a large number of self-acting tools". On average one boiler and one engine could be completed each day, with every part of the product being made on the premises. By exhibiting at agricultural and electrical shows, a method he had favoured ever since visiting the Great Exhibition of 1851, Paxman had already secured nation-wide sales and a national reputation. A London office was soon opened to deal with both his British and international sales. His foreman could claim that "Mr. Paxman had made Colchester well known all over the world". Exports included electrical machinery for South African mines, refrigerating equipment for the ships in the South American meat trade and carbon-dioxide compressors for the British and Japanese fleets.

When in 1898 the firm became a limited company, it already employed 600 men and was taking on extra workers every year. For twenty years there had been no short time, strikes or lockouts. By 1903 over a thousand were working on premises which covered fifteen acres. The works, now much larger than any other local factory, had become the pride of industrial Colchester, with its 120 h.p. steam engine, its overhead travelling cranes and its drawing-office with thirty draughtsmen, and James Paxman was the most influential man in the town's local government and public life. However, in 1910 the firm experienced its first strike when it introduced American methods of work organisation in its attempt to increase production, an event which, in several ways, marked the approach of a new phase in Colchester's industrial history.[46]

There were some new ventures in Colchester engineering in the pre-1914 period. In 1899 F. W. Brackett, with three men to help him, started his business in a former five-stall stable in Hawkins Road, with such success that he had soon to take new premises in Hythe Station Road, where the firm is still situated today. The Pasley Engineering Company began in 1908–9, also in Hawkins Road. Maurice Woods, a London electrical engineer, in 1909 took over a small electric-motor works, situated next to Colchester Lathe Company at the Hythe, in which to make coiler fans, propeller fans and fractional horse-power engines. Within five years his six employees had been increased to about forty. In 1907 Colchester Lathe Company started in Hawkins Road with five employees and by the early months of the War was employing over eighty men and boys in a 100-foot-square gas-lighted building. For these new firms, as for the older and larger ones, the years immediately before the War were busy and prosperous, overtime working was frequent and extra labour was often needed. The engineering industry as a whole gave work to nearly 2,000 people and had become the mainstay of the town's economy, rivalling the cloth trade of two centuries earlier and ready to cope with further expansion in the years of war.[47]

There was a variety of other enterprises at this time, some of them small-scale as yet but destined to expand later. Printing had developed very slowly from the eighteenth century, at the end of which there had been two small firms, into the nineteenth century when the publication of newspapers led to the industry's first expansion; by 1870 Benham's had twenty-five employees. Wiles had opened a business in 1862 in small premises behind his house on the east side of Trinity Street, where after extensions in 1900 and 1910 he employed about forty men. Cullingford's started in 1885 as a stationer's on North Hill, but the growth of the business led to two successive moves to larger premises in High Street. The firm also developed a printing branch in the basement of its first High Street shop, then in a two-storey building in Nunn's Road and finally in a gas-powered plant behind its present Stockwell Works. Rose's had been calendar printers on North Hill, but when their business expanded, they took over a former shoe factory in Kendall Road. Both the newspaper firms expanded their general printing in these years. In 1905 Mrs. E. M. Mason began copying architects' and engineers' plans by electric arclight, though as yet on a small scale. A significant addition to the printing industry at the time was the arrival in Hawkins Road in 1908 of the 200-

year-old London firm of Spottiswoode's, which by 1914 was employing at
least 180 workers.[48] There were two other developments of importance. In
1912, when the Post Office took over the telephone service from the National Telephone Company, Colchester was made the regional centre,
with the exchange situated at the corner of St. John's Street and St. John's
Avenue; between thirty and forty people were employed. Finally, the
Town Council was itself becoming quite a large employer, as it developed
an ever wider range of services. In 1897 it had about 200 employees and two
years later some 280. By 1907 it was paying out £45,000 a year in wages,
about half of it to the 200 teachers in the town's twenty-one schools.[49]

The town's increasing trade required expanding transport services and
it found these in the railway rather than the river. In 1880 a new attempt
was made to rescue the Hythe from the decline of the previous decade,
when two businessmen, Wilson Marriage and E. S. Sanders, carried out
a successful rebellion against the sitting Commission which was generally
considered to be too complacent. The *Essex Telegraph* noted that it met
only four times a year and added, "So far as we are able to ascertain, the
greater part of the income is spent in salaries — an agreeable arrangement which it seems unkind to disturb". The outcome was the replacement of older Commissioners by Wilson Marriage, the brewer Charrington Nicholls, J. N. Paxman and other critics, but the remedies proposed
were not on the scale contemplated in 1846-7, since the time had passed
for Colchester to be transformed into a port for modern vessels. Instead,
the Wivenhoe–Hythe stretch of the river was to be straightened, deepened, and widened, a 'bay' was to be made at the Hythe to enable vessels
to swing around and a steam dredger was to be employed. The whole
scheme could not be carried out, but, as a result of improvements then
made, traffic did increase. Figures given to Colchester Borough Council
after it took over responsibility for the river in 1892 showed that, whereas
in 1881 only 905 vessels of 60,000 tons had entered the port of Colchester,
by 1882 the figure had risen to 3,091 vessels of 162,000 tons, at which level
it had remained fairly constant during the following decade. However,
the vessels involved were mostly around fifty tons and the cargoes rarely
included raw materials needed in Colchester's factories nor the products
leaving them. Thus in one week in 1895 five vessels arrived with wood
from Harwich, no doubt timber already imported from northern Europe
and Scandinavia, while five others brought grain from London, probably
originating in America; there were also seeds and general goods brought
from London, granite from Guernsey and stone from Mill Head. None of
these cargoes presumably was destined for use in the town's main industries, nor were the latter using the Hythe for sending out their finished
goods; for, of the nineteen vessels leaving, no less than fourteen sailed
light, two carried oil to London, one oilcake to Ipswich, one wood to
Harwich and one malt to London. The oil did come from a local works,
Parry's Oil Mills at the Hythe, and the malt possibly originated from the
Hythe's surviving malting, but neighbouring factories, such as Paxman's
on Hythe Hill or George's in Kendall Road, sent nothing. That week's
figures were quite characteristic. Agricultural produce leaving the port
had so shrunk in volume because of the depression in farming and the
competition of the railways, that it was sometimes less than the amount of

foodstuffs being brought in, while the cargo which had once predominated in the inward trade, coal from north-east England, was now only of minor importance. Schemes for improvement of port facilities continued to be proposed. The Mayor declared that "everybody must acknowledge the great value that the river was to Colchester and the much greater value it would be, if it was dredged and the channel made navigable for ships of a fair size". The Corporation took some measures to this end and, in particular, improved the quayside and its equipment, but agricultural depression continued to curtail traffic in farm produce. In the years preceding the 1914 War the voyages in and out of the port, and the tonnage of the vessels involved, had fallen to about a quarter of what they had been two decades earlier. Sailing boats far outnumbered steamers, by 676 to forty-five in 1911. In 1910 the Corporation borrowed £9,000 to build new quays and carry out other improvements for the benefit of "the new factories which they hoped would be built there". Four years later, however, the *Essex Standard* noted that "not sufficient work is done at the new quays to prevent the grass from freely growing under the feet of those who frequent them". This decline of maritime trade led to a decrease in the number of Colchester seamen and dockers, and the latter were further reduced in number by the development of mechanical loading.[50]

Perhaps the Hythe's chief contribution to Colchester industry was that many years earlier it had caused the railway to be extended to the riverside; Hythe Station remained the chief goods depot for the town through the century. Since the vicinity also afforded space for new factory development, industry had been moving to it from the time when Paxman's established their new plant there in 1876. Another engineering firm, Mumford's, almost decided to set up a second branch there to relieve the pressure on its cramped premises in Culver Street. The Corporation itself encouraged the process in 1908 by helping to improve Hawkins Road along the east side of the Colne below Hythe Bridge. A local reporter, visiting the scene, was impressed by the industrial activity already to be observed there, including Spottiswoode's gas-lighted and motor-powered printing works, Colchester Lathe Company's gas-powered plant, Brackett's pump-making factory, Gray's electrical works, Moy's Flare Lime Kilns, Owen Parry's Oil Mills where a hundred men were employed, the Gas Works and, stretching up Hythe Hill, Paxman's Standard Ironworks. "The Hythe is not a place to look for decaying industries", he wrote, and he looked forward to the years when there would be a continuous line of factories stretching down the river. Less development followed than the reporter had hoped — there was a new gut factory, a sausage factory and little else — but existing firms, with Paxman's in the lead, continued to expand, so that by 1914 the area between St. John Street and Greenstead Road had become Colchester's main industrial area and the place of residence for many of its industrial workers. The river itself, however, contributed little to this activity.[51]

The last census before the War showed Colchester to be, economically, a very different place in 1911 from what it had been in 1811 or 1861. True, it was less industrialised than scores of British towns. It still remained an important market town and an Army town, so that inns numbered 107, beerhouses forty-one and beershops thirty-three, making one licensed house to every 206 of the population, compared to one to every 618 in Cardiff. Its 235 shops and similar retail concerns had at least as many employees as had those of 1861; the Co-operative Society's total staff was over two hundred. Within the borough 838 men were still in farming and market gardening. There was observable, too, an increase in the number of those in non-industrial middle-class occupations, including 231 women teachers, 212 nurses and midwives, 429 in other professions and 314 in clerical work. Other non-industrial workers were the 2,128 women and 448 men in domestic service, laundry work and similar occupations, and the 574 women and girls making hats, stays and dresses in places of work other than factories and large workshops. Yet by 1911 so much of the town's economy had been industrialised that a majority of male workers, probably over 5,000, were working in factories, building and transport. About a dozen factories had more than fifty workers and there were other large concerns like building firms, the railway, the Post Office and the borough's electricity, road and tramway departments. Though a smaller proportion of the 5,800 gainfully occupied females could be termed industrial workers, most of the 1,400 tailoresses in the town worked in factories or large establishments. In half a century the local economy had therefore changed in important ways and with significant social consequences. The outburst of trade unionism in 1891–4 and its revival on a sounder basis in 1908–14 emphasised the extent to which, in the process of economic change, 'the poor' of the town had become its 'working class'.

By 1914 there was much less poverty than there had been fifty or a hundred years earlier. Real wages had been rising, if spasmodically, for most male workers, whether skilled or 'unskilled'. There was some unemployment in building from time to time, and the threat of it arose even in engineering when in 1914 Britannia Works were suddenly closed, but breakdown was averted by Paxman's decision to take over the plant, along with many of the workers. Nor did the footwear industry's collapse cause prolonged distress, such was the demand for labour at the time both in Colchester and elsewhere in the country. Women workers were paid much less than the men, yet they did enjoy better opportunities of obtaining employment of some kind than women did in most other parts of Essex; only Halstead, with its silk industry, had a higher proportion of its female population at work. In Colchester, though only 11 per cent of married women were in employment in 1911, the figure for unmarried females over ten years of age was 57 per cent and for widows 31 per cent. In general, in 1910–14 the local press gives a picture of a working population with some money to spend in shops, at the cinema and on occasional summer outings. Photographs show most people warmly, if drably, clad, while working-class houses of this period, however dismal to modern eyes, would have seemed warm, dry, clean and comfortable to older people who had grown up in Colchester's courts and alleys in earlier years. Working people now shared the amenities increasingly supplied by Local Authorities, such as better schooling for their children, parks, swimming-facilities and a free library. Many of these various improvements had been made possible by Colchester's belated and limited industrial revolution.

CHAPTER II

The Town's Government

From Waterloo to the 1835 Municipal Reform Act

In 1815 Colchester's local government comprised several different authorities, the most ancient of which, the Corporation, was exclusive, ineffective and, its critics said, corrupt. It had lost its Charter because of its corrupt practices in 1742 and, when this was restored in 1763, it quickly resumed its old ways. Its 'Select Body', composed of the Mayor, Aldermen and two other grades of Councillors, became so exclusive that in 1834 it consisted of forty-eight Tories and only two Whigs, all fifty being Anglican in denomination.[1] Because of the Corporation's ludicrous oligarchic constitution, no reversal of this situation was possible, even in the rare event of a change of sentiment among the several hundred townsmen who possessed the municipal franchise; when in 1820 the Whigs won a temporary majority among them, this victory had no effect whatever and in the following years the Tories recovered their control.[2] Consequently the Select Body never hesitated to act in an unashamedly partisan and sectarian manner, especially when the French Revolution and the rise of a Reform movement in Colchester itself made its members feel insecure in their privileges and therefore ready to resort to any method of defence. It was quite a normal event when at Parliamentary elections they rode out to the Lexden Borough boundary, in company with numerous local gentry and clergy, to escort the two Tory candidates into the town to open their campaigns. An unsuccessful Whig Parliamentary candidate, addressing voters after the poll, identified the Corporation leaders as "a junta, formed by a few, who have too long assumed the right of dictating to you the men who are to be your representatives".[3] Nor did the Select Body shrink from indulging its denominational preference. In 1825 it passed a resolution opposing any concession to Roman Catholics, while contributing from public funds towards the new Chapel of Ease being built by Anglicans in the centre of Brightlingsea.[4] It remained consistently partisan to the last. When in 1834 it saw in the brief Peel administration the possibility of a reprieve from municipal reform, it passed a resolution of thanks to the King for his "paternal regard for the best interests of the country" and expressed its hope for "salutary measures whereby the hallowed institutions of our forefathers may be protected from the innovations of revolutionary principles". It petitioned against the Municipal Reform Bill of 1835 and, after the Bill's passage, gave a defiant banquet, at which the guests applauded speeches against democracy, nonconformity and Temperance.[5]

The Select Body was also accused of various forms of corruption. The publicans and tradesmen among them were said to be using their position to their own financial advantage, while the Select Body as a whole was criticised for over-indulgence in feasting at the Corporation's expense. The money spent on official feasts was small, only £115 in 1830–1, but critics saw it as helping to finance the strengthening of the bonds linking the town's rulers with their rural patrons, the landed gentry. Select Body members were often guests at fashionable gatherings in the neighbourhood. In July 1826, Sir G. H. Smyth, Tory M.P. for Colchester, "gave an entertainment in his Park at Berechurch Hall, where a large marquee was erected, under which three rows of well stocked tables were placed. At 4 o'clock the Corporation of Colchester, the clergy, gentlemen, farmers and tradesmen of the town, forming together an assemblage of the highest respectability, in number 260, sat down to a collation that did honour to the worthy baronet. The bottle circulated freely to loyal and personal toasts." On this and other occasions the mingling of the Select Body with the well-to-do of town and neighbourhood did much to build influential support for the old system. Reciprocally, the Mayor used his £80-a-year salary "to extend the invitation to his inaugural dinner to the respectable inhabitants".[6]

There was some nominal provision for public control of the Select Body. Those of the burgesses who lived within the borough and paid "scot and lot" rates were entitled to take a somewhat ineffectual and indirect part in the choice of men to fill vacancies on the Select Body. The majority of these burgesses were Tory, though there was always a Whig or Liberal minority. The burgesses' tolerance towards the Select Body's expenditure on entertainments was in part secured by their own receipt of small emoluments like the annual gift of 16s. from the proceeds of the sale of their grazing rights on borough land. Since the advocates of municipal reform wanted such doles to be ended and the proceeds used to help lessen the borough rate, most burgesses remained zealous upholders of the existing municipal system.

The Select Body's duties were few. The most expensive was the suppression and punishment of crime in collaboration with the borough magistrates; in 1833–4 about £960 was spent on this out of a total expenditure of £1,310.[7] The borough police force was small and the constables appointed by each of the sixteen parishes were unpaid, so that propertied ratepayers sometimes persuaded vestries to provide special night watchmen or even paid for their own nocturnal policing. The Courts were active in maintaining their system of social discipline, harassing pedlars, regulating innkeepers' hours and prohibiting the sale of fireworks. All such measures were inadequate to combat the heavy incidence of crime in the distressed years after the war, when increasing population and greater mobility made detection more difficult. The prison, next to the Moot Hall, now proved to be too small, so that some prisoners had to be sent to the county gaol at Chelmsford at the borough's expense. There was no attempt to train the inmates of Colchester gaol for productive employment, only occasional schemes to discipline them, such as the one devised by one of the Mayors, by which the sixteen inmates, most of them juveniles, were chained to a post in the yard in such a way that they could be forced to march twenty-five miles a day in silence within a narrow circuit, a punishment claimed to be more effective than the treadmill in Chelmsford gaol. Feeling the need for further deterrents, the magistrates used transportation as punishment for minor cases of theft. In the single year 1822, seven years' sentences were inflicted on three men for stealing a silver watch, 5s. in money, and a looking-glass, on two men for stealing wheat from a barn and on one man for stealing a pair of shoes and a coat from the Barley Mow Inn. There were not a few sentences of fourteen years, for instance in 1829 on a man for two burglaries in which he stole articles of no great value. Public flogging was still imposed. For stealing candle-ends and some beeswax a man was flogged for 200 yards down High Street before spending six months in prison. Altogether, the maintenance of order was a sorry business. At a time of deep poverty and economic insecurity the people of property, acting through the borough authorities and courts, ruthlessly punished offenders for quite trivial offences and did so very often in a spirit of self-righteousness and vengeance.[8]

The Corporation's second duty, and one of central importance to a town with Colchester's post-war economy, was the regulation of markets and fairs. In this connection the Select Body made some attempt to balance the interests of farmers, shopkeepers and the public, and also to provide better facilities. When some farmers requested an earlier opening time for the Saturday corn market in winter to enable them to return home in daylight, the Select Body agreed to advance the time to mid-day, but, when a weighty counter-petition opposed this change, the arrangement was reversed. Because of its offensive nature, the pig market was moved from the narrow west end of the High Street to the wider area near the Obelisk, and its hours of opening were reduced. The Green Market, where fruit and vegetables were sold, was also directed to the same eastern end of the High Street, and a permanent building was afterwards built for it by subscription next to the Three Cups. It had been felt also that there should be an indoor corn exchange, and in 1803 the Corporation had erected such a building at the north-west end of the High Street. In 1819, to pay the cost of some of its litigation, it was obliged to sell the building to the Essex and Suffolk Insurance Society, which allowed the ground floor of its new Doric structure, which still stands in 1978, to be used as a corn market.[9]

Other important services the Corporation was content to neglect altogether or to leave to other agencies. It had always refused to take over the water supply, which had originally been provided by a private benefactor in 1707, and, when in 1808 it was proposed to restore this service, it was happy to yield responsibility to a private firm which established works at the bottom of Balkerne Hill and from there brought water by steam power to the top of the hill for distribution to central Colchester.[10] Road maintenance and improvement, as well as street lighting, was fortunately not the Corporation's responsibility but that of the Channel and Paving Commission. This important body, originally established to improve the river channel, had acquired additional powers of Paving, Lighting, Cleansing and Improving. Its income was very small and it had to meet opposition from influential ratepayers fearing higher rates and from parish vestries resenting the Commission's supervision of some of their activities; All Saints' vestry, for instance, asked the Borough M.P.s to oppose renewal of the Commission's powers in 1811 because this "will be very oppressive to the inhabitants and give most arbitrary and alarming powers to the Commissioners, and will also, from the great expense, be attended with the most pernicious consequences". The Commission was obliged to forgo a number of improvements it would have liked to undertake, for instance the widening of North Bridge at the prohibitive cost of £500. It also, for financial reasons, declined to develop the gas supply, initiated in 1817 by Firmin and Harris, High Street chemists.[11]

Within its limitations the Commission showed a zeal and persistence of which the Corporation was quite incapable. As soon as a private firm took over the gas supply, the Commission began to instal gas-lamps in the central streets of the town. In 1818 it erected "handsome cast-iron fluted pillars" to carry the new lighting down High Street to St. Nicholas's Church and, a year later, to St. James's and up Head Street. By 1821 the foot of East Hill had been reached and by 1823 Priory Street and the eastern part of Crouch Street. By 1829, when North Hill and East Street had been added to the system, £525 was being spent on lighting for eight months in every year, mostly by gas, though still partly by oil. In 1834 there were 143 public lamps. The Commission also pursued an active policy of road improvement. Numerous accidents on North Hill caused it in 1823 to widen the thoroughfare there by the purchase and demolition of part of a house projecting beyond the frontage, despite the high compensation awarded by the magistrates. A year later it was investigating the desirability and cost of macadamising the 'pavements' as the thoroughfares were called, and, having satisfied itself, it proceeded to introduce the system into the central part of the town. Nor were the sidewalks neglected. Cromwell's *History of Colchester*, published in 1825, noted:

> "To the credit of the present Commissioners, both the foot
> and carriage ways are now everywhere in very sufficient
> repair; in particular the footway of the greater part of the
> High Street is remarkably broad, commodious and hand-
> some".

The Commission exercised some control over new building, on one occasion requiring an artisan to remove two new bow-windows which encroached upon the Eld Lane passage. It watered the streets in the hot weather, using special carts which had been purchased after some of the Commissioners had gone to Romford to see similar ones in use. All this work was carried out with the utmost economy. In 1823–4 total income was £1,542 from dues levied on ships using the Hythe and £1,209 from rates on Colchester residents, while expenditure included £1,347 on maintaining, watering and improving the streets, £428 on lighting them and only £95 on the salaries of the surveyor and the clerk. On improving the river channel, the service for which it had originally been established, it now spent a mere £480; and this was its main failure. Otherwise its record was by no means a bad one, at least by the standards of public service then prevailing and by comparison with the Corporation's indifference. Furthermore, the Commission's members included some able Liberals and Nonconformists, like the Tabors, Richard Patmore and Joseph Wallis who were effectively debarred from service on the Corporation's Select Body by the latter's Tory and Anglican exclusiveness, but could automatically take their place as Commissioners by virtue of their high property qualifications. The Commission also included *ex officio* most of the Select Body and the Justices of the adjacent rural areas, yet the two elements, Whig and Tory, seem to have co-operated in its work without partisan rancour.[12]

Of even greater importance in the local system were the vestries of the sixteen parishes within the borough, because, in administering poor-relief, they held responsibility for the local service which affected the great majority of the population. Expenditure on poor-relief in 1815 was £8,560, much more than the total amounts spent by Corporation and Commission put together. In that year the vestries gave regular relief to 523 adults, mainly widows and old people, living in their own homes, and to a further 101 adults and children, lodged in the small workhouses maintained by nine of the borough's sixteen parishes. The latter were insanitary and boring, but not brutal, places to live in, where the food compared favourably with that eaten by the town's able-bodied workers and their families; the average expenditure was £13 a head per year, a figure higher than average expenditure per head in most Colchester working-class families.[13] Since the collapse of the cloth trade the inmates, who had once spent their days in spinning, had little work to do, so that the workhouses had mainly become hostels for the old and disabled, together with some sick people, orphans and illegitimate children. The vestries also showed willingness to alleviate some of the distress arising for able-bodied people from the post-war economic crisis. St. Mary's at the Wall gave allowances to a number of unemployed people, while St. Botolph's, besides helping its even more numerous unemployed, gave occasional help to gardeners, bricklayers and farm workers, who, though in employment, were earning 10s. a week or less. Critics of these practices alleged that poor people knew more of their supposed entitlements to such relief than did the officials and were able, if refused assistance, to win their claims by an appeal to a Justice's arbitration.

There were attempts by some vestries to economise in the economically bleak years after 1815. They discussed the possible centralisation of poor-relief under an inter-parochial authority with a view to saving money, and the imposition of a hard 'labour test' on all able-bodied applicants for assistance, but such proposals came to nothing through disagreements between the parishes and the unwillingness of the busy tradesmen, who comprised the majority of the vestrymen, to spend their scarce time supervising such schemes. Instead, all the central parishes appointed full-time Assistant Overseers to supervise the payment of relief and investigate suspected frauds. A few vestries, including St. Botolph's and St. James's, also elected special committees to check all expenditure.[14] These attempts at economy were made without any fundamental erosion of the rights of people in need and, above all, without the abrasive, even brutal, measures of the New Poor Law of 1834. Another merit of the pre-1834 system was that in any one year several hundred of the town's ratepayers played some part, supervisory or deliberative, in the relief of poverty, besides finding from their own number over a hundred people to serve as Overseers of the Poor, Churchwardens, Constables and Surveyors of the Highways, offices which had to be performed without pay. This activity by the town's middle class counteracted to some extent the decline in civic morality that otherwise would have resulted from the Corporation's laziness, exclusiveness and dubious honesty.

The Parliamentary Reform Act of 1832 inexorably hastened the end both of the old Corporation and of the parochial administration of poor-relief. Colchester Liberals had sought a middle-class Parliamentary franchise partly in the hope of bringing about middle-class control of municipal affairs and effecting major economies in the poor-law. Both these issues had been given prominence in the Reform struggle of 1830–2. Chignall Wire, chief Liberal organiser, had made municipal reform the main issue when he addressed Colchester burgesses living in London and, at a Colchester meeting, one of the only two Reformers on the Select Body referred to D. W. Harvey, the Liberal candidate, as "a rocket let fly from the corruption of the Colchester Corporation"; D. W. Harvey confirmed this judgment in his Nomination speech at the 1831 election. Harvey's successor as Liberal candidate, Tufnell, said in his declaration of candidature:

> "I am an independent and uncompromising Liberal, anxious that a searching enquiry should be made into every department . . . One of the first objects is the reform of Corporations which, in their present exclusive state, are completely at variance with the spirit of the times and totally inadequate to secure good municipal government."[15]

When in 1834, as a prelude to municipal reform, Commissioner Hogg arrived to investigate the old Corporation, he won the approval of the expectant Liberals for his quite unconcealed dislike of the old system. Allegedly they primed him in advance of each sitting about the questions he should ask, causing the *Essex Standard* to write, "Is it true that Messrs. Wire, Barnes, Rouse, Dennis, etc., attended his soirées at the Three Cups every night during his enquiry?" Certainly, at the open hearings, the Liberals were present in force and were quick to applaud or jeer at each controversial point, turning the proceedings into a rowdy mass meeting; when the town's education was being discussed, the Liberal leader shouted "Education! Why, there are some members of the Corporation who can neither read nor write." The Tories attributed the rowdiness to the Commissioner's "ungentlemanly conduct", but there was cause enough for excitement in the actual proceedings and in the evidence given. Though the Select Body made a great virtue of its having allowed the Commissioner to use the Moot Hall for the enquiry and of having promised to hand all the accounts over to him, the vital book recording the sale of some of the town's estates proved to be missing. When the Commissioner pointed to this omission, the Mayor stalked out of the meeting, followed by the Town Clerk. The Commissioner then used his power to summon them to return, but they refused to come, sending the Recorder in their place to say that they felt insulted by the Commissioner's insinuations and required an apology. No apology was forthcoming and the Commissioner, when at the end of the proceedings he made his final statement, said, "There has been nothing but concealment and evasion throughout, and it has been the least satisfactory enquiry I have ever met". The Town Clerk then wrote to the press, justifying the Corporation's conduct and making the remarkable comment that the Commissioner "is now reaching Mrs. Hog and the little Hogs, having, vermin-like, been crawling over the country to fatten and gorge upon filth wherever he could find it and make it where there was none".

The Commissioner had indeed been aggressive and the Corporation had tried to present some sort of case, but, amid all the vituperation and innuendo, there had emerged, at the very least, a strong impression of evasiveness by the Corporation over the sale of town land, of general inefficiency on the part of the Corporation officers, and of the Select Body's indifference to any interests but their own. Furthermore, it had become clear that only Tories and Anglicans could enter the Select Body and that the system was resented by many of the town's most active citizens. The ensuing Municipal Reform Act, by firmly giving the municipal vote to the borough's ratepayers, remedied these and other middle-class grievances and gave power in municipal matters to those who possessed it in economic life.[16]

Local Government after Reform, 1834–1873

At the first election after the old Corporation's abolition the newly enfranchised ratepayers, consisting mainly of shopkeepers, master artisans and professional men, were generally expected to vote for the Liberals as the authors of their enfranchisement. This they did to the extent of giving the latter a majority, but a small one because, in normal times, the middle class in this market town were mainly pro-Tory and a very strong change of allegiance was not to be expected. The Liberals, once in power, made a clean sweep of the old Tory officers, replacing them with men of their own party, but, when the Tories regained a majority at the next election, the process was exactly reversed. Nevertheless, the Municipal Reform Act had changed the situation in important ways, as the Liberal paper noted when it wrote that the Town Clerk appointed by the Tories after their return to power "will find his office very different from what it would have been in the snug days, when, in a closed chamber, the public excluded, the Town Clerk was wont to act as dictator to the corporators, who dared hardly say their ears were their own". This was true. The new Council's activity, limited though it was, had now to be discussed in public and was open to comment in the press, while every Autumn one third of its members retired and, if seeking re-election, had to face an electorate of ratepayers, with the press directing its readers' attention to what it regarded as the important issues. At their resumption of power the Conservatives found it hard to shed their old partisan exclusiveness and were still inclined to look upon the Council as the preserve of their own party. The Town Clerk, though a public officer with a salary paid from public rates, could say at a Mayoral dinner in 1842, "I cannot let this opportunity pass without congratulating every gentleman present on the results of the labours of the Conservative party on the first of November".[17] By the 1850s, however, such comment was reserved for non-official occasions.

Meanwhile, parish control of poor-relief had been ended by the 1834 New Poor Law Amendment Act, a far less desirable change than municipal reform for the great majority of Colchester people. In place of the sixteen separate parishes a new single authority, the Board of Guardians of the Colchester Poor Law Union, was set up for the borough as a whole, consisting of representatives of all the parishes. Paid Relieving Officers were given the task of maintaining an economising system of relief in strict conformity to the code laid down in the Act and interpreted by a new central government body, the Poor Law Commission. The latter ruthlessly forced the Colchester Guardians to proceed with the implementation of the Act's harshest regulations when they sought to mitigate them. The most hated change was the one stopping outdoor relief to able-bodied men in need, such as the unemployed, who, to obtain relief, had to enter the new 'Union' workhouse, built in 1836 near the Balkerne Gate and still doing service in 1978 as St. Mary's Hospital. Worse, they had to bring with them their wives and children, who, on entry, were sent to separate wards. The régime was made hard and bleak in order to deter entry, and this purpose was largely achieved. The small number of recorded able-bodied inmates strongly suggests that, in the years of unemployment and underemployment up to 1850, many Colchester families endured privation and malnutrition rather than enter that grim building. Hatred of the New Poor Law was general among the whole working population, because even employed workers never ceased to fear that they might be dismissed from their work and be faced with the Union workhouse; furthermore, the old and disabled were also subjected to the new economising system and often found themselves lodged for the rest of their lives in the workhouse. Yet another disadvantage of the new administration was that, by employing professional Relieving Officers, it gave ratepayers no opportunity of public service such as the amateur Overseers of the Poor had enjoyed under the old parochial system. Without poor-relief to administer, the parish vestries had lost the main reason for their existence as civil authorities, and when their modest policing and roadmaking responsibilities were eroded by the growing Borough police and the Paving Commission respectively, they no longer had any important work to do. Except as the scene of occasional denominational conflict over the church rate, the vestries attracted little interest after the 1830s, as the rather formal press reports of their occasional meetings make clear. This decline of the vestry, combined with the ending of the old municipal burgess meetings, meant that popular participation in local government actually decreased in this era of Parliamentary Reform.

The Town Council, though it took its place in the centre of the town's public life, for some three decades did not extend its range of services very far beyond those performed by the old Corporation. For instance, in 1852 its total income of £3,369 came from three sources, rent for town lands, the sale of licences to fish in the Colne and rates amounting to £923. The expenditure included £427 in mortgage interest on town lands, £466 in salaries, £409 on public works and £1,347 on law enforcement, the last item including £650 for policing. The police force grew steadily in number, more or less in step with the population, until in the 1870s there were twenty-eight officers, costing in salaries £2,028.[18] Another function taken over from the old Corporation was the maintenance of the three main bridges, the North, the East and the Hythe; the new Council replaced Hythe Bridge when it collapsed in 1839 and four years later rebuilt North Bridge in cast iron. It continued to manage markets and fairs, in particular seeking to free the High Street as much as possible from their often tiresome presence. St. Dennis's Fair was moved to the Fair-field, near East

Bridge, and the horse-market to Head Street, though not without protests from horse-dealers. In particular, the Council was eager to find for the cattle market some alternative place to the High Street where its stench was regarded by the residents as "a foul blotch" but, at first, it could find neither the site nor the money. Time passed, gentility grew and, by 1860 there was enough support for a fresh attempt. After a bitter controversy which nearly dominated the municipal elections, the Council decided to acquire the site of a former tannery at the foot of North Hill on the west side. This place, though criticised as too far from the shopping-centre, was preferable to the two others suggested, the ground round Colchester Castle and some land opposite Balkerne Gate; in the latter case the extension of the High Street westwards to reach the new market could well, in those days, have involved the destruction of the Balkerne Gate itself or the breaching of the Roman Wall. When opened in 1863, the new Cattle Market had cost £4,633, necessitating further mortgaging of the town's remaining property since the Council had no power to raise a rate for the purpose and Government loans were not yet available.[19]

The Council's other major decisions in the three decades after 1835 numbered only two. The old Moot Hall urgently needed replacement and a scheme was drawn up for a new building that would combine accommodation for Council business and for a Museum. The latter purpose was soon abandoned and architects were invited to submit plans just for a Town Hall. The seventy-three plans submitted were open to public inspection, a procedure quite novel in Colchester, and two architects were selected by the Council. In 1844 the new building began its half-century of unsatisfactory service, having cost £6,666 to build, of which the public subscribed £4,666 and the Council gave £2,000, raised from a further sale of town land.[20]

The other important undertaking was almost forced upon the Council against its will. When the new Town Hall was first projected, its advocates envisaged that it would accommodate a museum. In the outcome no such provision was made, but the energy of John Taylor, proprietor of the *Essex Standard*, kept the issue alive, despite the Council's refusal to adopt the 1845 Museums Act and raise a rate to run a museum. All he achieved at the time was an arrangement by which donations could be received of articles to form the nucleus of a future collection. When in 1852 Henry Vint's collection became available to the town as a legacy on condition that it was kept in fire-proof premises, it was not the Council but the new Essex Archaeological Society that resolved to provide the required accommodation. Its treasurer, C. G. Round, offered the crypt of the Castle, of which he was the owner, and within the stipulated time the Museum was established there, though it was not until 1859 that a curator was appointed and the public admitted. Many donations of valuable articles followed and a large part of William Wire's earlier collection was also acquired. The Council had now set up its own Museum Committee and, with some hesitation, began to improve and extend the facilities at the Castle. By 1872 visitors were already exceeding 10,000 annually.[21]

Apart from the Museum venture, the Council in these early Victorian years undertook little that the old Corporation would not have done,

though its honesty and openness were in refreshing contrast with its predecessor's shady proceedings. By the 1860s the range of Council activities
remained so narrow that the annual expenditure was only £6,400, more or
less. Most of the important services were left to other bodies. Private
enterprise provided gas, water and public baths; the last of these were
opened in 1847 in Osborne Street, where, in a new building in the Ionic
Order with a frontage of 112 feet, two large tepid swimming-baths, as well
as individual baths, were available. The local traders and agriculturalists
paid for the new Corn Exchange, opened in 1845 next to the Essex and
Suffolk Insurance office in the High Street and later named The Albert
Hall. [22] Those wanting the amenities of a reading-room or a good-quality
library had to pay to belong to the Mechanics' Institute, in Queen Street
and later in High Street, or to the Literary Institute in St. John Street;
Liberals preferred the former and Tories the latter. The parks then available were the Botanical Gardens behind Greyfriars, until the land was
taken over for house building, or "Mr. Jenkin's Pleasure Gardens" in St.
John Street, but entrance to either place was open solely to those paying
for it. The only publicly financed education until the 1860s was that provided in the Workhouse. The Hospital, built in 1820 by subscription,
remained entirely voluntary, the only medical aid available from any
public authority being that grudgingly given by the Board of Guardians.

The important matters of street maintenance and improvement, of
public lighting, and of sanitation and health could hardly be left to voluntary action or private enterprise but continued to be the province of the
Channel and Paving Commission which, until superseded in 1873, remained quite the most useful and creative force in Colchester's local
government. In retrospect its omissions are glaring, but it was the ratepayers' unwillingness to pay for improvements that often crippled its
efforts. In any case, its effectiveness was dependent upon the unpaid
effort of a very small band of public men, the twenty-four Commissioners
who, after the Commission's reconstitution in 1847, were elected from
the local shipowners and the £30 ratepayers. Before 1847 any large ratepayer had been eligible to sit on the Commission if he so desired, but very
few did so desire, so that the change to an elective system gave responsibility to those interested enough to accept nomination, without depriving
any significant number of people of the chance to serve. Outstanding
among the Commissioners was J. B. Harvey, who joined in 1848, became
chairman in 1860 and found there the most convenient scope for his sustained pursuit of town improvement. The limited success of this very
small band of Commissioners deserves to be seen as one of the worthiest
achievements of the town's middle class in mid-Victorian times.

The Commission's income was very small, about equal to that of the
Town Council, averaging £4,200 in the 1850s and £5,000 in the 1860s, and
part of this had to be spent on the river. With these inadequate resources,
it took on one task after another within the limits of its powers. The ten
miles of main roads under its jurisdiction were gradually improved, North
Street and Maidenburgh Street being macadamised in 1842 and 1844
respectively. North Hill was further improved when the railway was
opened, and a few years later it was the turn of Head Street. The Commissioners themselves felt that the 1840s had been a time of considerable

achievement in this department and, during the next two decades, they went on to metal and otherwise develop Balkerne Lane, St. Peter's Street, the Roman Road estate, Osborne Street, St. John Street, the Essex Street estate, Crouch Street and Maldon Road. Annual expenditure on street watering was quadrupled between 1841 and 1863. Street lighting was further extended, reaching well up Lexden Road by 1870. Whenever it could afford it, the Commission replaced oil lamps by gas lamps, while frequently testing the quality of the lighting supplied by the Gas Company in both the streets and private houses. The Commission seized various opportunities to promote general welfare; for instance, on the pretext of being the Highways authority, it laid down maximum fares for cab hire for different distances "within one mile of the obelisk".[23]

Much to the disappointment of some of its members, the Commission found itself powerless, legally and financially, adequately to deal with the appalling sanitation, made all the worse by the growth of population in central Colchester and the addition of the Camp's sewage to that of the town. The Commission had shown awareness of the need for action when it identified the causes of a cholera outbreak in 1834 as lying in the neglect of public and private drainage, the pigsties in populated neighbourhoods, the rubbish and waste matter thrown into the streets, but, above all, the blocking of drains for the purpose of obtaining manure for gardens. Lacking other means of compulsion, however, the Commission could only threaten individual house-owners with prosecution for creating nuisances, and the results were disappointing. For instance, in a cottage-garden near East Bridge there was an open cesspool, for which the Commission's Inspector had long demanded a proper cover, but no action was taken until the occupant's daughter, aged five, was drowned in it. As for improvements, the Commission did what lay within its legal and financial competence, for instance building a new brick drain down North Hill in 1842 and extending barrel drains down Hythe Hill in 1849, but, until the 1847 reorganisation, it found itself powerless to run a sewer over private property south of Crouch Street in order to drain a stagnant pool, formed of the efflux from houses in Crouch Street, Butt Road and Maldon Road.[24] After 1847 it was able to remedy the latter abuse and to complete a network of public sewers throughout central Colchester; to the original 2,402 feet it added new lengths each year until by 1854 there were 28,080 feet. The cost had been £2,808, which the Commission was able to meet only because the work had been extended over seven years.[25] Ratepayer resistance precluded further major reform and in 1865 a house-to-house survey by a committee of doctors revealed how many abuses remained unabated. Their report showed that the water supply was inadequate for the growing population and that many poor people used contaminated wells or bought water also obtained from impure sources. Courts and alleys away from main roads were mostly unpaved and filthy; "in no other town . . . of corresponding size is so much manure or straw and filth lying about". Foul pigsties, stinking slaughter-houses and smoking factory-chimneys abounded. "There are plots of land honeycombed with cesspits to an extent utterly incredible", the worst abuses being in the old Dutch Quarter. The state of the sewers and their outlet into the river were considered particularly dangerous, especially with the growth of the Camp.

"At the east end of the town . . . a very grave nuisance exists in the over-flow channel of the sewer, and at the time when we visited it, there was a deposit of many tons of inconceivably filthy stinking-black mud, which the storm of about a month ago had brought down. And this disclosed another fact, that our sewers are nothing but elongated cesspools, and contain at all times many tons of solid matter ready for flushing, if there were in existence any system of flushing . . . The outlets of the sewers at North Bridge emit foul effluvia . . . The sewer at the foot of Maidenburgh Street had so contaminated the water at King's washing place as to inter-fere with the comfort, and probably the health also, of the bathers."[26]

The Commission continued to do what it was in a position to do, threat-ening prosecution for nuisances and seeking voluntary co-operation from house-owners. Its excuses of inadequate income and legal impotence were firmly upheld a few years later by a Government Inspector who came to investigate cases of dysentery in Balkerne Lane and of cholera in Priory Street. He pointed to the same abuses as the doctors had identified, and absolved the Commission because it lacked effective powers, had borrowed to its permitted limit and had persuaded 500 householders to instal water closets.[27] Within a few years new legislation armed local authorities with the necessary powers and income, but by that time the Town Council had been invested with the Commission's sanitary duties and the Commission had been disbanded. The latter's most valuable service had been its sustained surveillance of those aspects of the town's welfare with which the law permitted it to concern itself. In the absence of any social-reforming zeal on the Council's part, the Commission was the only body to perform this important duty. At almost its last meeting, on the very eve of its extinction, it was still earnestly discussing the current problems within its jurisdiction. On that occasion it discussed and ap-proved the addition of the buttresses that still stand against the north side of St. Mary's at the Wall, it recommended that the west side-walk of Queen Street should be paved with blue Staffordshire paving-blocks and, most importantly, decided to require all new houses to be connected with the nearest main sewer. There was also a long discussion about the best material to be used in the future making of side-walks so as to combine durability with convenience to the public. By then the Commission had almost acquired the structure of a municipal council, with sanitation, highways and lighting committees, and was spending annually some £7,300, as much as the Council itself. Its shortcomings had been numer-ous, but its total record was far less inglorious than the Council's.[28]

The Town Council takes charge, 1873–1914

In 1873 the Town Council assumed responsibility for all the services pre-viously provided by the Commission, except that of river maintenance. Within a few years its sanitary powers were further strengthened by na-tional legislation and, within a decade after that, it came under increasing pressure to do what it could through municipal action to meet the needs of the town's fast-growing and increasingly industrial population. There fol-lowed a series of changes that left Local Government in complete or partial control of services previously provided by voluntary bodies or private enterprise, including elementary, secondary and technical education, electric power, libraries, fire prevention and local passenger transport. Exceptions were the gas supply and, notably, the Essex and Colchester Hospital, as it was originally called. It would have been difficult for the town to take over the latter, if only because the institution had always served Essex as a whole and even parts of Suffolk. Subscriptions and legacies, too, had come to the Hospital from many places and among the strongest supporters had been county magnates like Lord Braybrooke of Audley End and Viscount Maynard of Easton Lodge.

The idea of this 'General Infirmary for the Poor' had been advanced in 1818 during that busy era of charitable initiative.[29] The first scheme was for the purchase of the south wing of the wartime military hospital, but the owners of the land found that they had no power to sell the site, so that much of the building and its equipment had to be moved to the present Lexden Road position, where a three-acre piece of ground was bought. Sufficient contributions were obtained from the well-to-do of Colchester and Essex for the Hospital to be able to receive its first patients in September 1820. It was at once recognised as one of the most useful and successful local charities, and its charitable character was strongly emphasised. Subscribers were entitled to recommend for treatment every year a number of poor persons proportionate to the size of their subscription; this rule confining admission to poor people was vigorously upheld. Annual donors of two guineas or more were eligible for membership of a twice-yearly Governors' meeting. Despite its small income the Hospital's record was an impressive one. In the year 1846, for instance, only £1,863 was received and, if the senior doctors had not given their services free, the Hospital could not have coped with its ever-expanding work. At the start there were about 150 in-patients on average each year, but by 1836 the figure had risen to 293 and by 1876 to 338, while outpatients had increased even more.

During the nineteenth century the recurrent accommodation problems were met with the help of the voluntary contributions of well-to-do supporters. When in 1837 a temporary ward had to be set up and every bed was being filled as soon as it became vacant, £2,000 was raised, mainly by a bazaar, for the addition of wings to the original building. In the 1870s the number of in-patients rose sharply just at a time when national standards of hospital equipment and sanitation were improving. In 1878 the Governors commissioned an expert survey and accepted its conclusion that a major scheme was needed "to bring the Essex and Colchester Hospital into accord with modern sanitary science and render it complete for its important work". For improved sanitation, proper outpatients' accommodation, a nurses' dining-room, a larger dispensary and the other improvements now planned, the estimated cost was £5,000, a formidable sum at a time when the voluntary schools needed continual help to meet the demands of the 1870 Education Act and when the town was also in the middle of an expensive programme of church and chapel rebuilding. Yet, though the final expenditure exceeded the estimate, the deficit was quickly paid off by voluntary effort. At the same time a Medical Board was instituted to govern admissions and the régime was made less bleak for the patients. The Queen's sixtieth year on the throne was celebrated by further major improvements and the £6,000 needed for these was again raised from well-to-do supporters. By the early 1900s it was the running expenses that were causing most anxiety. With the growth of population in the town and with higher standards of care, annual expenditure rose to about £6,000 by 1914, when there was an accumulated deficit of £7,000. The problem would have been greater had not support now been forthcoming from the public at large. Hospital Sunday, inaugurated as early as 1871, and Hospital Saturday, introduced a little later, together with collections in the streets, in the schools, from door to door and at Friendly Society church parades, enabled the Hospital to survive, while making it more dependent on popular goodwill. Workers gained the right to admission by paying a penny a week from their wages, leading to a complaint in the press that this and similar developments "seem to have given rise to a sort of impression that the Hospital is public property and that the public have a right to dictate to the Governors as to the terms on which they shall dispense the benefits of the Institution". However, the Hospital retained its voluntary standing in these years, while losing much of its early character as a charity provided for the poor by the public-spirited members of the affluent classes.

Though so many services were eventually to pass under its control, in the years following the transfer of 1873 the Council was content to feel its way while it was still learning to operate its newly acquired Improvement powers. It did in 1878 borrow as much as £5,000 to buy certain private houses obstructing main roads at various places. It also started a Fire Brigade, manned by volunteers, commanded by the head constable and equipped with a fire engine purchased by subscriptions; the Brigade distinguished itself by its prompt turn-out at the 1884 earthquake. It appointed a Medical Officer of Health, whose regular reports provided useful reinforcement for the continuing local movement for sanitary improvement. However, it was not until the 1880s that the Council entered upon a major undertaking. J. B. Harvey had now transferred his energies to the Town Council, becoming Mayor for two successive years in 1881 and 1882, and he set about using his greatly increased opportunities to bring about a decisive improvement in the water supply. It was during his Mayoralty that the Town Council agreed to buy the Waterworks for £82,000, a sum fixed by arbitration, and to spend a further £10,000 on building a water-tower on the site of the old cistern at the top of Balkerne Hill, for which purpose it obtained the largest loan in the town's municipal history up to that date. 'Jumbo', as the new tower was immediately called after the elephant so well known to the mid-Victorian public, at once became the subject of acute controversy, partly because of its cost, but ostensibly on the grounds that it was out of scale in its conspicuous domination of the High Street. Harvey, however, had achieved his greatest success in a lifetime of public service. At the official opening of the tower in 1883, undaunted by the concerted absence of the local gentry, he turned on the water with the words, "a wholesome stream of water is flowing through a thousand channels to the homes of the population". [30] After Harvey's death in 1890, his fellow-Liberal, James Paxman, replaced him as the leading advocate of sanitary progress. In 1894 and in 1896 major improvements sufficiently increased the volume of supply to make possible the extension of the service to outlying parts of the borough. By 1901 a total of 37 miles of water mains and 47 miles of sewers had been connected, and in 1906 a further important step was taken, when Lexden Springs were acquired.

'Jumbo', which distinguished itself by its complete invulnerability during the Colchester earthquake to the surprise of the crowds who rushed to view it within minutes of the occurrence, was the first brash precursor of a series of modernising ventures undertaken by the Council. A more cultured building was the new Town Hall, which replaced the by now insecure and inadequate structure of 1844. There had been talk of such an undertaking when the Queen was approaching the 50th anniversary of her accession but, though fully aware of the need for a building large enough for its increasing business and expanding staff, the Council could not then face the issue of the expense. When a decade later the next Royal anniversary approached, there proved to be much more support and at the 1897 municipal elections, where the issue was made the dominant one by the opponents of the scheme, those advocating a new Town Hall won handsomely. The decision once made, the town's leaders showed imagination and vigour during the three years of planning, preparation and construction. The Council secured a large loan, engaged an architect of national repute, John Belcher, and employed specialists for the different parts of the building and its decoration. Every effort was made, notably by Gurney Benham, to ensure that episodes and personages from the town's history were correctly represented in the sculpture and other embellishments; the *Essex Review* called the new building "a storehouse of local history". Among the donors of statues, stained-glass windows and other embellishments, the town's industrialists were well represented; James Paxman, for instance, paid the whole cost of the tower. The happy blend of civic vigour and learned good taste, embodied in the building, reflected both Colchester's new industrial power and the well-informed regard for the past to be expected in such an ancient town.[31] Local industrialists had by now become prominent in public life — James Paxman, Wilson Marriage, Gurney Benham, George Knopp, John Kavanagh and Joseph Grimes sat on the Council at this time — and they saw themselves as a progressive, yet enlightened, influence in the town's modernisation. The *Essex Telegraph* also attributed municipal progress to the recent industrialisation when it wrote editorially at this time:

> "In the matter of improvement it would seem as though Colchester has now taken a decided step forward and has developed a spirit of progress that is very satisfactory, though rather startling when the conservatism of the Borough is remembered. The cause of this is easy to be seen. With the extension of the town and the introduction into it of a large increase in the industrial population, there has grown up that demand for progress in municipal affairs that is making itself felt in all centres of commercial activity."[32]

It was a confident period and, in opening the new Town Hall in 1902, Lord Rosebery said of the building: "With the extraordinary growth of public business and municipal departments, it will not be surprising if, in a generation or so, it is altogether inadequate to the requirements of the time".[33]

Other improvements, major and minor, followed one another at a rate unthinkable a few decades earlier. The idea of electric lighting was not new in Colchester. As early as 1849 an experiment in its use both in and out of doors had attracted much attention from the public and in 1878 the *Essex Standard*, with some satisfaction, warned the Gas Company of the competition likely soon to confront it from Edison's discovery. Indeed, four years later, in 1882, the Council discussed whether to start its own electricity service, but in the end gave the concession to a private company. The latter took over the former Distillery, situated at the west end of Culver Street, and from its plant there proceeded to supply lighting to several businesses in the town centre. Large crowds stood in the streets, admiring the bright light that made adjacent gas lamps look weak and yellow, but some local supporters of the new venture seem quickly to have lost confidence and in the end only fourteen householders agreed to become customers. Perhaps the Gas Company, with its influential directors, was too strong an opponent; the *Essex Standard* referred to the electricity company's "always ineffectual struggle with the powerful Gas Company". Subsequently the Council gained confidence enough to apply for powers to provide its own electricity service. In 1892, despite 1,500 signatures of protest, it sought and obtained from the Army a promise that the Camp would use the new service, borrowed £15,000 and made a survey of the likely response from the public. The survey proved disappointing, but the Council hesitated only briefly and in 1898 began operations. When the High Street was first illuminated, large crowds walked up and down it until a late hour. Gas prices were reduced to 9d. per unit, the lowest ever. Electricity customers numbered only 150 when indoor lighting became available in 1900, but by 1909 there were ten times as many. Between 1900 and 1913 output rose by about 600 per cent, and at the latter date the Council was making over £7,000 profit annually from the undertaking.[34]

After an electricity supply came electric trams. A private company had earlier tried to run steam trams. In 1887 the cab-drivers were alarmed, and the public delighted, to learn that, as a local newspaper put it, "men should for a mere copper ride up the weary slope of North Hill or glide down dingy Magdalen Street". However, after spending £1,000 on tramlines between North Station and High Street, the company abandoned the scheme. In 1901, with electricity now available, the Council obtained Parliamentary permission to start its own service, though it was three years before the trams started out on the first routes to be opened, from North Station to East Street and from Lexden to the Hythe. The opening coincided with August Bank Holiday when, reported the *Essex Telegraph*, "the stay-at-homes had a new toy which they patronised freely. The cars were crowded and the takings tremendous. On Saturday night the street scenes were remarkable. There was a great rush for every tram." An attempt to prevent Sunday working was defeated, new routes were added, and the number of passengers steadily rose. Unlike electricity, trams were not a financial success. By 1912 the annual deficit reached £2,400, but the public verdict was that the service had proved too useful to be abandoned.[35]

In these years the Council became a major provider of educational and cultural facilities, a field which it had not previously entered except for its somewhat reluctant acceptance of responsibility for the Museum. By the 1902 Balfour Act it was given control of the town's elementary education and, with commendable zest, continued the policy of expansion and improved provision initiated by its predecessor, the School Board. Adult education, long an area of voluntary enterprise, became in part a municipal responsibility when in 1896 the Council took over the Albert School of Science and Art from the voluntary committee hitherto running it, though in 1902 it was obliged to yield control to the Essex County Council. After several unsuccessful attempts to overcome ratepayer resistance to the establishment of a public library, in 1894 it took advantage of a £1,000 legacy made specifically for the purpose and built a Library in West Stockwell Street at a cost of £4,000; it also set up additional reading-rooms in the suburbs of Parson's Heath, Mile End, Lexden and Old Heath.[36] A start was also made in the provision of athletic facilities, when in 1884 a bathing-place was constructed by the river near St. Paul's Church, an undertaking which proved very popular. A year later the Recreation Ground was leased from the Army, and here too the Council's initiative was rewarded by increasing public use of the new amenity.[37]

Local opinion was both favourable to these changes and amazed at them. The *Essex Telegraph* had written in 1896 that "Colchester was reckoned at least 50 years behind the times, now it is getting very much the other way" and it went on to count the recent municipal achievements. In 1912, in a similar survey of the local scene, it could give an even more impressive list:

> "The institution of the Electric Light and the Power Station, Tram services, Free Library, Castle Park, Recreation Ground and many public schools, gigantic improvements for the supply of water, widening of the river, building of the Town Hall, General Post Office and new Corn Exchange and the construction of the Cattle Market are so well within the memory of young Colcestrians that there is no need to detail. Even for a decade there is much of interest, while in a quarter of a century or more the advance is of considerable magnitude."[38]

For all the impressive new buildings and large municipal undertakings, perhaps the most important part of the Council's work was its sustained attention to the day-to-day efficiency of the whole of its widening range of local services. A typical routine meeting in February 1903 noted the Fire Brigade's success in mastering a serious fire at Lucking's stores, decided to borrow £2,000 to improve the corner between Head Street and St. John's Street and resolved to widen the road between the foot of North Hill and the railway station at a cost of £2,586. It discussed, but did not decide on, changing the market day from Saturday to Thursday, it insisted on modifications to plans for a new theatre about to be built in the High Street, and it resolved to demand £50 in rates from a gentleman who kept his steam yacht permanently moored in the river. It took note of the thinning of the lime trees in Creffield Road, the increase in the output of electricity and in the number of its consumers, and the use of the Bathing

Place during the previous season by 8,620 males and 900 females. A Council meeting four years later had an even more crowded agenda, including reports from no less than sixteen committees, those for Finance and General Purposes, Policing, Markets, Roads, Sanitation, Water-works, Fisheries, Museum, Lighting, Library, Harbour, Electricity, Tramways, Parks, Town Hall, and Education.[39]

The cost of the expanding services was made a subject of continuous controversy. A Liberal paper, reporting a loss of £532 by the tram service in its first two years, solemnly warned that "a loss of three or four hundred pounds a year is a high price to pay for a public boon". By 1907 the town's debt had risen to £405,000 and its annual bill for wages and salaries to nearly £50,000, four times the 1899 amount and still rising. "It is generally admitted that nothing can be done to check the flowing tide", wrote a local journalist, and it was generally, if grudgingly, accepted by both parties, the newspapers, industrialists and the trade unions, that twentieth-century Colchester had to have services and amenities which could not be provided without expense. Significantly, when a Ratepayers' Association tried to resist the rise in expenditure, it quickly acknowledged failure. The Council's expansion had also made it a major employer, so that its work could not be curtailed without resulting unemployment; it had nearly 300 employees by 1900, even before it took over elementary education and launched its electricity and tramways services.[40] The Town Hall was now the centre of public life, and the Council's record was made the focus of controversy every year at the November municipal elections. Evidence of the prevailing interest was the space given every week in both Conservative and Liberal papers to detailed reports of Council meetings and to comment, letters and gossip about municipal matters. Such was the Council's standing that to gain a seat upon it was the chief political ambition of the youthful labour movement, and Tim Smith's success in doing this was for long regarded as a landmark.

CHAPTER III

Education

Elementary education

In 1800 the town's educational provision for working-class children was not extensive. The Anglicans' Blue-coats school, situated behind All Saints' Church, and its Nonconformist counterpart, the Green-coats school in the former Independent Chapel in Priory Street, with perhaps 150 pupils between them, were the only centres of public daytime education; a third charity school, once run by Presbyterians, had probably been closed by then. Of more value were the Sunday schools, established in the 1780s and subsequent decades by Anglicans and Nonconformists, which gave some elementary schooling to 500 or more children. However, opinion among the well-to-do was becoming more favourable to a renewed charitable effort and in 1812 a committee was elected of sixteen clergymen and seventeen laymen, including the Mayor and the Grammar School headmaster, for the purpose of opening a day school in which hundreds of poor children were to receive an elementary education and learn Anglican doctrine. Called a National school because it was connected with the Church of England 'National Society for Education', the new institution set out to use the Monitorial system of teaching by which monitors were to help the teacher to pass on instruction to hundreds of pupils instead of merely to the scores whom he could reach when working on his own in a classroom. The prospectus claimed that "the leading feature of this method is economy, as by the excellence of its mechanical contrivance 500 children may be educated at nearly the same expense as a fifth part of that number formerly was". This topical reference to factory techniques proved persuasive, for subscriptions worth £1,200 were soon received for the acquisition and conversion of a former cloth-warehouse in Maidenburgh Street to serve as the new school building. The Blue-coats charity and the main Anglican Sunday school were merged with the new institution, the denominational character of which was emphasised by the requirement that candidates for its headship "be members and communicants of the Church of England, of sober life and conversation".[1] At almost the same time the Green-coats charity and Lion Walk Congregational Sunday school were linked with the newly founded British School, which also proceeded to use the Monitorial system in the former Green-coats' building in Priory Street; officially at least, this institution was not a denominational one, but it always remained closely connected with Lion Walk Congregationalists.[2] The two Monitorial schools were soon claiming a total of 600 pupils between them, and by 1830 the attendance at the National School had so increased that St. Helen's Chapel was taken as an annexe.[3] As other denominational schools were established and new private 'dame schools' came into being, the total number of schools grew from twenty-two in 1818 to sixty in 1833, by which time 2,548 pupils were said to be attending, just under half of them at denominational schools.[4]

Though the effective school attendance probably fell far short of the number claimed in 1833 and though the quality of the education was very poor, the building of these schools and the enrolment of so many pupils in them was a considerable achievement at such a time and it was made possible only by the participation of numerous laymen who now contributed their personal influence and financial resources with a zeal not apparent in the previous century when the clergy had carried the main responsibility for such work. The motives behind this effort had to be powerful ones. They arose from the deep anxiety among the well-to-do about the security of the social order in those troubled years between 1789 and 1850, when the French Revolution, D. W. Harvey, trade unionism and Chartism seemed to present a never-ending series of incitements to the poor to throw aside old loyalties. To counteract these influences among the adult poor a network of charities was brought into being, but it was considered equally important to train the minds of the young to attitudes of obedience to the social order. These calculations were unreservedly voiced in speeches, in sermons and in the press by leading citizens from various parties and denominations. Culver Street Methodists recommended their new schools because they would promote "social security" by means of "sound scriptural instruction". The Liberal *Essex and Suffolk Times* wrote that "the inattention of the upper classes to the education of the working classes leads to the disassociation of the lower classes from them and they are led to adopt the doctrines of physical force, insubordination and infidelity"; the remedy, the paper concluded, was to build more schools. Churchmen went further, claiming that, to be fully effective in combating social disaffection, all teaching should be imbued with Anglican doctrine; the aim of their central National School in Maidenburgh Street was the "securing to our enviable constitution in Church and State the best affections of the rising generation". The utility of education in habituating poor children to obedience was usually the main inducement offered to well-to-do supporters to pay for new buildings. William Wire, describing an appeal for funds for a new church school in Holy Trinity, commented that "the Rev. D. F. Markham pleaded the case well, but the inculcating passive obedience was the chief doctrine". On the other side of the political conflict, some radical workingmen criticised the new education for much the same reasons as Churchmen and Nonconformists recommended it; one Chartist urged his comrades to teach their children at home rather than allow them to be indoctrinated in schools paid for by the wealthy.[5]

The political threat to the established order faded as the Reform movement and Chartism subsided in their turn, but, with a working class growing in numbers and gaining little in prosperity, the continuation of deep social division still gave cause for anxiety and, in particular, all disregard for current morality was seen as a sort of rejection of the social order itself, one remedy for which was the education of the rising generation in a religious atmosphere. The Rector of St. Leonard's at the Hythe wrote that "my people are of a class that specially ought not to be left without sound education, as a wharf population is proverbially of a low type" and thought a new building for his girls' school to be the best corrective to "the increasing immorality of the young females of our neighbourhood". At the same time, those seeking financial help for education had to guard against the suspicion that a too-well-educated working class might disturb the social order in a different way. So the Rector of Mile End phrased his appeal in 1844 with some care:

> "The Revd. P. Strong having found the efficiency of his
> Sunday School sadly impeded by the idle interval between
> Sabbath and Sabbath, feels constrained by a sense of duty
> to appeal to his Parishioners to help him in obtaining a
> Weekly Establishment for the children of the labouring
> Poor. His object is, not to educate overmuch, but to train
> up both sexes, with such principles and information, as
> may make them diligent, useful and religious Members of
> Society in the Class to which they belong. And he does not
> desire to keep them under Tuition, the Girls after 14, and
> the Boys after 9 years of age, except on Sunday."[6]

Strikingly absent at this time was any claim that elementary education should be expanded or improved because the new industrial economy needed better-trained workers; had such a feeling been widespread, the curriculum would presumably have been different, and the quality of the teaching higher. Vocational needs were to some extent met in Colchester's middle-class schools and, to a small extent as yet, in adult education, but not in the schooling of the children of the poor. One exception, however, was the desire of the town's growing middle class for more and better domestic servants. The Rector of St. Leonard's believed that his new school would help remedy "the constant complaint that scarcely a good servant is to be met with in Colchester" and the headmistress of the central National School took pride in reporting that out of seventy recent girl leavers no less than forty had entered domestic service.[7]

Following the early struggle to establish the first schools, their further expansion is equally impressive. In central Colchester the original National School in Maidenburgh Street was receiving so many entrants by 1861 that it was replaced by a larger, purpose-built school in St. Helen's Lane. Anglicans opened other schools in the central area. There were two in St. James', for instance, one of which, in East Street, was for infants and the other, on the north side of East Hill, for girls. In St. Peter's also there were two, one in a building still standing in the churchyard, the other in Crispin Court, now demolished. The British School was rebuilt in 1853 on its existing site in Priory Street at a cost of £1,300, mostly met by Lion Walk Congregationalists. In Culver Street the Wesleyans turned their Sunday school into a day school in 1835 and, as more pupils came, succeeded in expanding its accommodation despite its somewhat cramped situation. The Roman Catholics opened a school in the basement of their new Priory Street church in 1838.[8] Even stronger evidence of religious and denominational zeal was given by the sustained movement to found schools in the outlying parts of the borough, often alongside newly established places of worship. When churches were opened at St. John's, Ipswich Road, and St. Paul's, near North Station, each had a day school attached. In Mile End a National school had already been started in 1840, but, when in 1854 a new parish church was built, the materials of the old church were re-used for a new school building. The growth of population at Shrub End led Anglicans to build a church there in 1845, and the establishment of a school followed fifteen years later, by which time Lion Walk Chapel had opened both a preaching-station and a British school in the same vicinity. Among the growing community at the Hythe the Anglicans opened an infant-school in 1836, which they changed into a girls' school nine years later, and during the same period Lion Walk Congregationalists and Culver Street Wesleyans each started a chapel and school there. Another British school in East Street seems not to have continued beyond the 1840s. During this expansion into the outlying areas denominational rivalry gave strong incentive, with the Anglicans enjoying more success than all the other denominations put together. By 1860 the Anglicans had a school of some kind in every parish in the borough and were able to pursue the policy of sending older children to their central establishment in St. Helen's Lane, while keeping juniors and infants in their local parish schools. Meanwhile, this expansion of denominational schools restricted the private and dame schools; between 1833 and 1870 pupils at the latter decreased from 1,382 to 801 while those at the denominational schools increased from 1,166 to 2,625.[9]

Standards of schooling remained poor for many years, except in St. Helen's Lane National School, which for a time acted as a training-centre for intending church-school teachers and won the commendation of an Inspector for giving, not a narrow drilling for examination success, but a varied and enlightened education. At St. Peter's National Infant School, on the other hand, one untrained mistress was found teaching seventy-four children, while, of the forty-nine girls at the Crispin Court church school nearby, only nine could read and the instruction was mainly by rote. At Lexden church school a teacher, though declared to be respectable and hard working, was able to give only "elementary" teaching. The best that could be said of Greenstead church school was that "it is a nice village-hamlet school, and as much is done as circumstances permit". Overcrowding was normal. In the tiny church school, still standing in St. Martin's churchyard, forty-four children were attending in the year of its opening and as many as seventy in 1851, it was claimed, though, even by standards then current, this figure seems an impossible one.[10]

From the 1830s the denominations had to face the conflict between their desire to keep their schools free from public and secular control and their need for financial help from the state. Government building grants were obtainable in places where local effort and contributions were also forthcoming, and from the 1860s small annual grants towards running costs could be received on certain conditions. Towards the £3,500 cost of the St. Helen's Lane National School in 1861 a Government building grant of £754 was made. Among other Anglican schools to benefit in the same way were those in St. Mary Magdalen, St. John's and St. Paul's. Congregationalists and Wesleyans seem at first to have feared that their voluntary status and freedom would be prejudiced by the acceptance of such help, and this fear was shared by some Anglicans, including the Vicar of St. Peter's, who, writing when the Whig Government was still in office, stated that he had long suspected that "our present rulers, influenced as they are said to be by unprincipled men, may ere long, seize on all the schools, to which grants have been made, and render them subservient to some system of education independent of our national Church. God forbid that our Colchester Schools should be liable to such a visitation."[11] However, financial necessity overcame most such fears. Building grants were obtained, where possible, and by 1870 several schools, including the central National School, were receiving annual grants towards running costs.

A more challenging situation arose in 1870, when the new Education Act required that all children of school-going age should thenceforward be taught by trained teachers in a satisfactory school building. The denominational bodies, if they were able, were allowed to provide the additional accommodation needed to meet this requirement, but, in the event of their failure to do so, the Act laid down that a School Board should be publicly elected, with power to supply the deficient places in non-denominational Board schools by means of a rate. Anglicans were seriously worried. One of their newspapers, the *Essex Gazette*, opposed the establishment of a School Board in Colchester because "A School Board implies a School Rate, and a School Rate is an unknown something, a *nescio quid* of expenditure and disturbance . . . School Boards are armed with a power of cramping the religious element in teaching, in fact eliminating from Education its vital principle and leaving its power to do mischief unchecked."[12] When, as required by the Act, an official survey of Colchester's educational provision was made, the town was found to contain twenty-three satisfactory schools, mostly denominational, with 3,204 places, and twenty-five unsatisfactory ones, mostly private, with 600 places.[13] The deficiency was estimated at 1,000 places, which Anglicans proceeded with some determination to provide from their own resources. First, they had to persuade the Nonconformists, who, as their paper, the *Essex Telegraph*, made clear, preferred the establishment of a School Board, not to close down their British Schools and so make the deficiency even larger. That accomplished, they started new schools at Old Heath and St. Paul's, changed the Ragged School in Stanwell Street and the Sunday school at the foot of St. Mary's Steps into day schools, and improved several existing schools. Though they received increasing Government grants, they faced an impossible struggle. The deficiency of school places steadily grew, as education was made compulsory, the town's population grew rapidly, and the Education Department kept redefining what it meant by adequate accommodation. Anglicans found it more and more difficult to pay for the series of extensions and improvements demanded of them after 1875 when the agricultural depression made subscriptions more difficult to obtain. This was in spite of the steadily increasing financial help received from public funds; grants to Colchester schools rose by two-thirds between 1876 and 1881, amounting to more than their patrons' voluntary subscriptions and their pupils' 'school pence' put together. In 1889 a total of £1,422 was given by the Education Department to the town's church schools.

In the 1880s Colchester's elementary education moved towards a crisis. Several schools were officially condemned, while others could not be satisfactorily enlarged and provided with playgrounds because they were on restricted sites, including those in St. Martin's churchyard and at the bottom of St. Mary's steps. The central National School and Culver Street

Wesleyan School had not the required cubic capacity to accept would-be entrants, and St. Leonard's church school was obliged for the same reason to discharge seventy pupils already enrolled. The one successful effort at this time was the building of a new church school in Kendall Road to serve the fast-developing New Town area. By 1891, when elementary education had become both compulsory and free, children could be seen on any morning roaming around the streets, many of them presenting anything but a favourable impression because the schools rejected the less prepossessing children in order to win the maximum grant with those whom they thought likely to perform best at the annual inspection. The chairman of the School Attendance Committee, on whom the immediate responsibility fell, issued a statement that "they could not let a thousand children run about the streets without any education" and, in the course of a few weeks, the completely voluntary system, so long and so laboriously maintained, was abandoned amid general agreement that a School Board was inevitable. A speedily conducted survey revealed an absolute deficiency of 528 places; a further 1,062 places were far below the required standard and, in addition, it was likely that 450 places would soon be needed because of continuing population growth; almost every school building was deficient in one or more important respects. A second survey raised this estimate of deficient places from 2,040 to 3,000. The Anglicans admitted that they lacked the resources to remedy the situation — a recent appeal for funds by them had failed — and they proceeded to close their three worst buildings, in Stanwell Street, Osborne Street and East Street, while the Nonconformists declared their inability to repair any of their existing schools. The newly founded Trades Council pressed for a School Board, too.[14] In a matter of months a Board was elected in 1892 and it at once, as a temporary measure, took over the main British School in Priory Street and the church schools at the Hythe and in Osborne Street. It then started upon a steady programme of replacement and expansion, building new schools in North Street and Old Heath in 1895, at St. John's Green in 1897 and in Stockwell Street in 1898. Wilson Marriage School, opened in 1898 as Barrack Street School, was regarded by the Board as its greatest achievement, embodying as it did some of the most modern ideas in school design and also containing facilities "eminently suitable for the class for whom we cater" — an interesting description from a public authority elected by householders' suffrages. As these new buildings arose, the older ones, which had been temporarily taken over by the Board, were closed.[15]

In 1902, through the passing of the Balfour Act, the School Board was replaced by the Borough Education Committee as the authority for elementary education. The latter continued the building programme with equal vigour, opening Canterbury Road School in 1903, Mile End in 1906 and East Ward in 1908. Thus, in thirteen years, eight new schools had been built from local rates, grants from national funds and loans of about £75,000. By 1911 their annual cost had risen to £27,000, two-thirds of which comprised the salaries of over 200 teachers; "alarming cost of education" was the headline in one local paper.[16] Meanwhile, the voluntary schools, which survived the establishment of the School Board, now relieved of much of their financial responsibility by the 1902 Act, still retained an appreciable share of educational provision; in 1909 they numbered twelve and had about 2,400 pupils. Culver Street Wesleyan School had never enjoyed a higher reputation than in these years. It had already in 1884 been singled out by an Inspector as one of "the four absolutely best schools in the district" and in 1890 had won the highest possible grant for its success in the annual examination. It easily survived the coming of the School Board and, under its veteran headmaster who was also an active N.U.T. member, it submitted pupils for the new public examinations with some success, enjoyed the support of an active Old Pupils' Association and gained a place for itself half-way between the elementary schools and the Grammar School. All this it accomplished despite its dark, overcrowded classrooms, but these bad conditions led to a threat of closure which was averted, though only temporarily, by the intervention of the 1914 War.[17]

The new buildings of the Council schools impressed the public, but their chief importance lay in the encouragement and scope which they offered to the new generation of teachers who, with their improved qualifications and growing self-confidence, were now in an unprecedented position to shape the town's elementary education. Colchester's teachers, like those elsewhere, had been very cautious previously, partly because they had been open to summary dismissal by the denominational school committees, composed of able, zealous and doctrinaire men, to whose tenets unquestioning conformity was required. Teachers had been all the more reluctant to jeopardise their own position, when they remembered the long and gruelling process by which they had gained it. For instance, a successful career had begun for one teacher when, at the age of six, he had been admitted to the National School in St. Helen's Lane. "He remained at the school till he was 15, when he gained a top leaving-scholarship of £10 and he then served another four years as a pupil-teacher at the same school. He had to be ready for his pupil-teacher lessons at 6.30 in the morning, and then it was his duty to take classes throughout the day. His evenings had to be devoted to study, and the rest of the time he had to himself. Ninety-six boys were not considered too large a class to crowd into the gallery in those good old days. Mr. Houghton added to his duties membership of the school band and he had to study drill for inspection by the Colonel of the Garrison." Mr. Houghton had then to go forward towards the acquisition of his certificate. This he obtained and he found it, as did his colleagues, a source of economic security and professional self-confidence. The number of teachers so qualified now rose steadily as the denominational bodies and the School Board were both obliged to employ trained teachers in order to obtain financial support from public funds. These were the men and women who took the lead in contributing to public debate on educational policy, as well as working towards more enlightened methods in their own classrooms.[18]

Teachers had been invited to engage in discussion of teaching-methods as early as 1850 when the Essex and Suffolk Church Schoolmasters' Association was holding regular meetings in the town, but these always took place under the supervision of the clergy. By 1857 the Essex and Suffolk

Teachers' Association, evidently a Nonconformist rival society, was also using Colchester for its meetings, to which schoolmistresses as well as schoolmasters were invited. Not until 1869 did anything like a trade union arise; in that year the Essex and Suffolk Certificated Teachers met in the town to hear a paper on "whether the schoolteacher's work is more detrimental to health than that of other callings". The increasing number of teachers in the vicinity enabled an early branch of the new Elementary Teachers' Association to be formed, which in 1874 was discussing not only pedagogic problems but issues like teachers' holidays and superannuation schemes. In the trade union upsurge of 1892 members of the Colchester branch of the National Union of Teachers, which was now the main organisation representing elementary school teachers, were confident enough to write to the press during the public debate on the desirability of establishing a School Board. They complained that nobody had consulted teachers on this issue, interested and expert though they were in such matters; a Board would be the best means of securing for the town "good well-furnished buildings and a liberal supply of efficient teachers"; they themselves needed greater freedom to experiment in teaching-techniques and they should also be liberated from the cramping control they underwent in voluntary schools, since "no man works well in fetters"; if a School Board were established, parents should press all candidates seeking election to it to promise a maximum of sixty pupils in each class, because the teacher "cannot do justice to more . . . Though a teacher may, and is in fact often compelled to, *cram* 70, 80 or even 90 or more children, it is utterly impossible that he should *educate* such a number". These were bold words from such a source in 1892, but in the next two decades the teachers' right to advise on educational policy and the need for more enlightened teaching methods were often to be asserted. In 1907 a letter in the *Essex Standard* began:

> "Sir, I am surprised to see that our Council cannot understand that teachers and school mistresses are in a position to judge better at what age children should be sent to school than any grandfather on the Council . . . Many children's minds are much more active than older people think."

Another spokesman went straight to the main deficiency in the old system of teaching, when he said that "genuine intelligence was at a discount, and the pupil who was able to disgorge a large amount of unassimulated mental food was preferred".[19]

By the eve of the 1914 War, when the East Essex branch of the N.U.T. had enrolled over 200 members, teachers had become an influence not to be ignored, although their salaries remained very low, rising in Colchester Council schools from an average of £75 in 1904 to only £103 in 1913.[20] In addition, at the secondary level there was a smaller group of mainly graduate teachers, employed by Essex County Council in its Grammar and technical establishments or working in private schools. Teachers were becoming more prominent in local life generally and education was being given increasing attention in the press. By 1914 the progress in the elementary schools, the foundation of the High School for Girls, the powerful recovery of the Grammar School, along with the development of technical and art education, were combining to make education one of the town's most impressive modern achievements.

The Grammar School

In 1800 the Grammar School was still situated in a cramped and decaying building at the east end of Culver Street, and its existence was nominal, because instruction was not at the time being given. In 1806 a clergyman reopened it, but proceeded to conduct it in the same manner as the dozen or so private schools then in the town were conducted. It was, indeed, little different from them, since in the 1820s only three free scholars attended; poor parents, who alone were eligible to apply for free places for their sons, could not afford to buy books and stationery and, in any case, thought a mainly classical education of little use to people of their class. As a private school, it was not unsuccessful, giving some seven boarders and thirty day boys an education that, by contemporary standards, was quite well balanced. The future Professor Airy, later to be Astronomer Royal, who was a pupil in 1814–19, was taught Geometry and advanced Mathematics in addition to Classics, though he had to pursue his interest in steam engines by private reading and visits to the steam-driven Hythe distillery belonging to the father of one of his school-fellows. The headship was still in the direct gift of the town Burgesses, but 1835 was the last year in which the new master was chosen by popular election; in the fiercely reforming atmosphere of that year, the Rev. Mr. Sanders, candidate of the Liberals, defeated by 200 to nine the Rev. J. Henderson, standing for the Tories and the old Corporation. When four years later a vacancy occurred again, under the provisions of municipal reform, the Borough Council itself chose the new master.[21] By then the school had relapsed into an even worse state, with three fee-payers and only one free scholar in attendance. The latter's father, the archaeologist William Wire, complained to the Bishop of London, the official controller of the curriculum, about the limited range of subjects taught and secured the addition of History, Geography and more Mathematics, together with a promise that other subjects could be included, if approved by the Bishop. The number of free places was increased to twelve and, after other improvements had been made, the local paper could claim that "a most excellent education is within the reach of the inhabitants of Colchester".[22]

William Wire's initiative had arisen from a sustained movement by the Liberals and Nonconformists for a radical change in the school's constitution and teaching. In this increasingly middle-class town there was strong criticism both of the Anglican control and of the Classical curriculum. A leading Nonconformist "could see no possibility of its becoming a great school while there remained this monkish illiberality". A Liberal councillor, having noted that "we have become a nation of shopkeepers", went on to urge that the training should therefore be made a utilitarian one, while another wanted "to have the school thrown open for the admission of 100 boys to receive a commercial education". It was generally envisaged that, if any such change took place, the sons of the middle-class townsmen would be eligible for the commercial training thus made available and that the system of free scholarships for poor boys would be ended.

Twice the critics arraigned the school, first before the Commission on Charities and then at the 1835 Municipal enquiry. Despite a campaign of meetings, their sole success was this reform achieved by Wire in 1844 and the school was not changed into a commercial college. Indirectly, however, the sustained criticism helped to hasten the school's major reconstitution in 1851, when the master resigned and the school was reported to be "at a standstill".[23] The Corporation's Grammar School Committee urged the trustees to rebuild the school, even if this were to cost £500, but almost at once an alternative proposal for a larger building on a completely new site gained wide support; it was felt that only in this way would a headmaster be obtained, who would bring the qualities needed. Efforts were started to raise a large sum and, with this assurance, the Rev. William Wright, the successful principal of Huddersfield and Leamington Colleges, accepted the appointment. The trustees, after rejecting a High Street site because of its proximity to urban temptations, settled upon "an elevated plot of ground on the south side of the London road, affording ample accommodation for a large establishment and extensive exercise grounds for the pupils". It was designed to accommodate sixty day pupils and twenty boarders, and, consistently with contemporary methods and school design, its teaching accommodation comprised one forty-one-foot hall, with only one additional classroom. The architect was Henry Hayward of Colchester, a man associated with much of the town's mid-century expansion. The £3,600 cost was met by a grant of £1,200 from the estate and £2,400 in subscriptions. A collective effort by the town's leading Anglicans had thus provided Wright with the means of building a modern school, imbued with Victorian Christian morality and able to offer secondary education of some quality. Reform had taken place but of a kind little calculated to satisfy Liberal and Nonconformist critics.[24]

The mid-Victorian years were a time of considerable success for the school, thanks to Wright's eminent suitability to his task. A man of "polished, edifying and Christian conversation", he served the wider public as well as the school, acting as curate of Berechurch, chaplain to the Gaol and the tutor of Latin classes at the Literary Institute. He was at pains to see that the free places were filled by poor boys, though the fee-paying professional and business classes were more strongly represented among the pupils throughout the century. By raising the number of boys to sixty-five, including twenty boarders, he obtained the income to employ five assistants, including I. J. Cotman of Norwich as drawing master. He was himself among the pioneers of a more enlightened system of Classics teaching; Greek plays in translation, including *Antigone* and *Ion*, were performed by the boys, and the Inspectors of the Schools Inquiry Commission found Classics being taught with appropriate scholarship but also as a broad humanist subject. At the same time he encouraged Modern Language teaching — forty-one out of the fifty-three pupils were studying German in 1864 — and introduced the school's first Commercial course, which included Modern History. Some boys went on to Oxford or Cambridge. Football, introduced by 1854, athletics and cricket were played on the enlarged two-and-a-half-acre playground behind the school.[25] When Wright died at his work in 1870, his successor, the Rev. C. L. Acland, put even more emphasis on Modern Languages and did what he could to acquaint his pupils with the latest developments in Science, though his appeal for funds to build a laboratory where "modern science could effectively be studied" was unsuccessful.[26]

The school had long been a progressive and thriving establishment by contemporary standards when, in 1871, the School Inquiry Commission recommended that it should cease to be a First Grade School, that pupils should leave at sixteen years of age and attend a First Grade School elsewhere, that, in order to ensure the school's demotion, Greek should be excluded from the curriculum and that Economics and Science should be made compulsory; finally, there were to be no more free places for poor boys, unless they passed an examination. Local indignation at what was seen as doctrinaire arrogance on the Commission's part was immediate and powerful, erupting into protest-meetings and petitions to Parliament. Letters to the press demanded to know why poor boys should be denied the advantage of learning Greek, why there should be a break in a boy's education at sixteen and why free places should go only to boys whose parents could afford to have them coached.[27] However, the re-organisation scheme was soon forgotten and the school continued its vigorous progress, attracting even more pupils than in Wright's time and regularly achieving successes in the Cambridge Local Examinations. Greek and Latin retained their prominence in the curriculum; one of the trustees, commenting on the school's indifferent cricket record in 1875, advocated that next year the team should fight every inch of the way like Xenophon or Aeneas. The out-of-class activity included cycling, paper chases, a library, the first school magazine and 'scientific football'. The boarding house was, however, discontinued. The school's function in this predominantly middle-class town is illustrated by the careers of some of its former pupils; one Head Boy, an outstanding classicist, read Law, built himself a successful practice and later became a school governor; other old boys included a managing-director of Paxman's, a borough accountant, an outstanding mathematician who became a senior lecturer at University College, London, and editors of both the Conservative *Essex Standard* and the Liberal *Essex Telegraph*.[28]

The religious issue remained unsettled, despite Acland's strictly unsectarian approach and his popularity with children of all denominations. The Nonconformists pressed at two official enquiries for an end to the Anglican connection, and the prominent Quaker, Wilson Marriage, said in a speech that "there is no doubt that the school is carrying out the view of the Church of England section entirely to their satisfaction, but not to the satisfaction of the Nonconformist section, and in Colchester they are a large body". The Liberals' growing municipal influence made inevitable a final attack upon the school's sectarian bias. In 1891 the Town Council formally declared that the school should be made completely undenominational, with no free places and with a commercially biased curriculum. The trustees accepted that Governors should be chosen without regard to their denominational affiliations, that the headmaster should be an Anglican but not necessarily a clergyman, and that the Town Council should be well represented on the Board of Governors. The Charity Commission at first put a damper on local enthusiasm by emphasising that the school

had to be regarded as an Anglican foundation, and all through the 1890s
the controversy dragged on. The diarist of the *Essex Standard* wrote:

> "From time to time visitors, who have not been in the old
> town for many years, ask me whether 'that Grammar
> School matter' is settled yet. They recall it almost as if it
> were one of our antiquities and they question about it
> much as they might as to whether Middle Row or St. Run-
> wald's Church are still standing in the High Street."[29]

Meanwhile, Acland having retired, the temporary headmaster was the
Rev. John Thomas, who, ahead of his time, deplored examinations as
educationally harmful, declared the object of teaching to be the training
of boys to work out their own answers to life's problems, taught History
as the record of changing societies and, knowing that some half of his
pupils were Nonconformist, saw it as "a sacred charge that he should in no
way interfere with their religious scruples".[30] Thomas withdrew in favour
of the new headmaster, Shaw Jeffery, in 1900, when at last a new scheme
for the school's administration came into force. The fifteen governors
now included six from the Town Council and two from Essex County
Council, the free places were replaced by entrance scholarships and, with
grants from public funds and the Old Boys' Association, the buildings
were completely modernised and enlarged. In 1900 the school had sixty
pupils, in 1907 it had 140 and, on the eve of the War, 194. "A revolution
has been worked", wrote the educationalist, Michael Sadler, in a report
on Colchester's secondary education in 1906. It was, a local Liberal was
pleased to note, again becoming the town school, to which rich and poor
of all denominations could send their children to learn to face "the commercial and professional battle of life". When Lord Rosebery opened a
large range of new buildings in 1910, he claimed that the school "had been
transformed from a close borough to a great constituency".[31]

The Girls' High School

Throughout the century middle-class girls had been able to obtain secondary education only in private academies. Around 1900 about 360 of them
were attending a dozen such establishments, of which two were of quite a
high standard. Endsleigh House, then in Wellesley Road, had about a hundred pupils, thirty-eight of them boarders, with a staff of about ten, and it
regularly entered candidates for the Cambridge Local Examinations. The
'High School', a private school, had started in about 1880 and in 1894 was
situated at Minden House in Wellesley Road, with Mr. and Mrs. Gröne
as its proprietors. They improved the premises, enlarged the staff and,
though enjoying a reputation for Art, Music and Modern Languages,
tried also to develop the scientific side. Both these establishments
charged fees that debarred working-class girls but when, in 1906,
Michael Sadler reported on Colchester's secondary education, he found
their standard so promising that he advocated their amalgamation into a
new school at which the ablest girls of the district could be taught the full
secondary curriculum.[32] As this was unacceptable to the proprietor of
Endsleigh House, a different plan was adopted by which a grant was
made to the Pupil Teachers' Centre in the Albert Hall to enable it to

develop into a Girls' High School. A start was made in Autumn 1909 and in 1912, with the title of the County School for Girls, it took up its quarters in the new Technical College on North Hill, where the girls had their own purpose-built Sixth Form common room, a novel feature in a day school. An enlightened headmistress and a staff of four succeeded in those few pre-War years in creating a progressive school of some quality just at the time when, with women's emancipation developing fast, a service of this kind was much needed. The original enrolment of 1909 had been about fifty, this number had doubled by 1912 and on the eve of the war the school was growing fast.[33]

The Technical College

Technical and art education had begun in the Mechanics' Institute, the Literary Institute, the Y.M.C.A. and the thrice-weekly Elementary District School of Art, directed from the late 1860s by Charles Baskett, but this rather desultory activity served only to show the existence of some popular demand. The industrial development of the 1880s brought a new urgency to the issue and it was significantly the town's leading industrialist, James Paxman, who in 1885 brought together interested representatives of local industry and commerce at a Town Hall meeting. The Mayor expressed the general feeling of the meeting when he said that "we live nowadays in an age of great competition". A committee was elected, which proceeded to rent the Corn Exchange at the north-west end of the High Street and to raise £400 to adapt it. Six months later it was opened as the Albert School of Science and Art, with Charles Baskett as Art teacher, but only about a hundred students enrolled and its future looked doubtful. Again it was James Paxman who rescued the venture. Having become Mayor in 1887, he led a campaign, which raised £1,300 in subscriptions and £600 in loans with which to buy the building. There followed an unspectacular but steady rise in enrolment, from 125 students in 1888 to 288 in 1896. In the mornings people of leisure attended art classes and in the evenings workers and clerks from industry and commerce studied Physics, Chemistry, Mathematics, Architectural Drawing and Machine Construction. In 1894 the committee, after nine years of unpaid management of the School, handed it over to the Town Council which, having gained an annual grant from Essex County Council, set about the creation of a proper technical and arts centre.

The venture was next swept up in the wider movement for educational advance then under way in the town. This was a time of progress, with the setting up of the School Board and the Public Library, the improvement of the Museum, the success of the University Extension Movement and new stirrings in the working-class and women's movements. "In this ancient borough there was a remarkable intellectual movement going on" was the view of an eminent educationalist.[34] There was a need for a secondary school, other than the Grammar School, to provide, in the words of Wilson Marriage, "a continuous ladder from the least and smallest elementary school to the great university of Cambridge".[35] At the same time the promoters of the University Extension lectures had been enjoying great success with their courses and were thinking in terms of the establishment of a permanent Liberal Arts college. It was they who in 1896 called a conference of interested societies and individuals to start a 'Technical and University College' similar to the one recently founded at Exeter. The outcome was that, with a government grant, a College was started in the Albert Hall, consisting of two departments, a Technical and Arts School and a University Extension centre, to which were attached Pupil-Teacher classes. Although lack of teachers curtailed the Science programme, 500 students were in attendance within three years.[36]

In 1902 came yet another change, when Essex County Council assumed responsibility for Secondary and Further Education in Colchester, including the new College. It declared its policy as follows: "The object aimed at is to improve and co-ordinate the educational system of this important district, to bring the whole machinery into harmonious working and on a par with the general advance taking place all over the country, and to enable the rising generation to hold their own in the severe competition with the keen and well-equipped people of Germany, America and other nations". The new authority decided to retain the Albert Hall as an Art School, but to build a new college for technical training. For the time being the Albert Hall continued to be used for both purposes, until in 1908 the Board of Education threatened to withhold its grant until the proposed new college was built. So in 1912 the new building, now the Gilberd School, was opened on the west side of North Hill, having cost £18,500. It housed not only the Technical College, but also the Art School and the recently established Girls' Secondary School and was seen as "the centre of all the higher educational work of the district".[37]

Adult education

The first organisation in Colchester in any way connected with adult education was a very genteel one, the Castle Book Society, founded by Charles Gray in 1752. It met in the Library-room of the Castle and its membership was confined to thirty gentlemen paying a two-guinea entrance fee and an annual subscription of the same amount. Only slightly less exclusive was the Colchester Subscription Library of 1803, with its reading-room and library open all day in its High Street premises, to which the entrance fee and subscription were each one guinea. The same annual subscription was paid by those admitted to the Philosophical Society, formed in 1820 "for the promotion of scientific and literary pursuits". The sixty or so doctors, lawyers, clergymen and other well-to-do men belonging to it, together with a single workingman, James Carter, each delivered one of the monthly lectures at its Queen Street premises, the subjects including Heat, Taste, Wit and Electricity. It kept a Museum of Roman and other antiquities, which, on its dissolution in 1843, it presented to the Corporation. Poorer people must also have found themselves unable to afford membership of the Observatory which a Mr. Scott kept behind the site of the present General Post Office in Head Street until it was destroyed by a fire originating in the adjacent Marsden's Bazaar. The lending libraries of the time also had only middle-class customers, being commercial ventures charging fees for borrowing.[38]

The Mechanics' Institute, founded soon after the passage of the 1832 Reform Bill, was hailed as an amenity suitable to a new democratic era. "It is to the mechanics of Colchester that the Institution looks principally", its founders stated; half the places on the committee were reserved for workingmen and the membership fee kept down to 2s. a quarter.[39] By 1839 some fifty workingmen did belong, chiefly sober, Nonconformist artisans owning their own businesses — one of them was William Wire — but the Chartists, then the chief spokesmen for thoughtful workingmen, with a few exceptions preferred to seek enlightenment from discussions at their own meetings and stayed aloof from the Institute because, as one of its supporters admitted, it was "mainly supported by the employers". "Highly respectable ladies" were several times reported as attending Institute lectures and, after twenty years of its existence, the *Essex Standard* commented that it "has failed to reach the masses of the working class".[40] To the hundreds of thoughtful people who did belong at different times during its twenty-six years of existence, the Colchester Institute gave good service, with its usually well-informed lectures on such diverse subjects as Steam, Magnetism, Pneumatics and the History of Watchmaking, its Geography, English and Arithmetic classes, its Reading-room supplied with daily and weekly papers and improving magazines, but, above all, its library of 1,200 volumes, open nightly. The Institute acted as a club for thinking Liberals, though there were a few Chartists and Conservatives among its members, and it had its own social programme, with soirées, summer galas, outings and cricket matches.[41] Its decline began in 1849 when a Literary Institute was started which, according to William Wire, was "a rival society, got up purposely to injure the Mechanics' ". At first this competition spurred the Mechanics' Institute to improve its own facilities and seek new members, but its leaders became disheartened as membership fell in 1859 to 185 and its classes and lectures were discontinued because of poor attendance. Facing a debt of £59, the Institute was dissolved in 1860, the deficit being cleared by the sale of its assets.[42]

The Literary Institute was founded in 1849 by Conservatives and Anglicans who suspected that the Mechanics' Institute, despite its official ban on politics and religious controversies, was in fact in the hands of Liberals and Nonconformists. To guard against such influences in its own ranks, the new body gave the Anglican clergy special status on its committee. The rules also included the statement that "the object of this Institution is to afford the opportunity of acquiring scientific and other useful information under the sanction of, and in subservience to, Religion in accordance with the principles of the Church of England". There was little need for such precautions, because the 400 people who had joined by 1852 were hardly radical in outlook; the Liberals called them "ultra-Tory".[43] So successful was the Literary Institute that within two years it had bought and enlarged premises in St. John's Street, which included the valuable asset of a large assembly hall for its lectures. In a typical season twenty lectures, two public readings and three musical evenings were held, with attendances often reaching 200 and dropping to sixty only on one bitterly cold night. There were also full-scale concerts and on one occasion an art exhibition, attended by 7,000 visitors. The Institute maintained a bowling-green, a tennis court, a croquet lawn, a cricket club and a billiards table. As in the Mechanics' Institute, women were welcomed as members, provided that they left the Reading-room by 5.00 p.m.[44] Throughout its existence the Institute's most valued facilities were its Reading-room and Library. Six daily papers were provided, along with some of the best magazines then available. The library grew to 3,000 or so volumes, the sober quality of which is clear from a surviving catalogue; much of the annual income went to improve the library even further, and special appeals were made from time to time on its behalf.[45] From the 1870s some decline was observable. Book issues came to include more fiction than serious works, lecture attendances fell, and membership dropped to 314 in 1879 and to 168 in 1899, though support for weekly classes was well maintained. One cause was the opening of the Borough Library in 1893; when the Institute was closed in 1901, the local press attributed its closure to that event. Nevertheless, in the fifty-two years of its existence the Institute had held 600 lectures and made over 100,000 issues from its library, and it was, in a sense, perpetuated in the still flourishing Essex Archaeological Society which had originated in one of the Institute's sub-groups soon after its foundation.[46]

As the Literary Society entered its last years of existence, much of its educational work was passing to the University Extension centre, which, actually though not formally, was its successor. Founded in 1889 to hold Cambridge University Extension courses in the town, the new movement started slowly, but by 1895 was holding three courses, on Physical Geography, the Reformation and Ancient Greece. Its growing band of supporters started a members' society in 1898 to gain even wider support for its work, in which prominent Liberal as well as Conservative ladies were very active. The centre, besides its own large individual membership, had local organisations, including the Co-operative Society, affiliated to it and it commanded an annual income of about £200, including grants from the Town Council and Essex County Council. Its members could enjoy a full programme of interesting activities throughout the season, in addition to the courses; there were single lectures, a debating society, a play-reading group and a Students' Association, in which every week members heard a paper read by one of their own number. At the turn of the century, therefore, University Extension was a strong force and it exercised no little influence in helping to shape the town's technical education. However, towards 1914 its support fell away, partly because it lost its grants from the local authorities and partly through the attractions of other organisations, so that on the eve of the War its programme of courses and activities had been much curtailed.[47]

In 1913 a branch of the Workers' Educational Association was formed at a meeting in the Town Hall, presided over by the Mayor and attended by representatives of organisations ranging from the Conservative Association and the Junior Imperial League to the Boilermakers' Society and the local Labour Representation Committee. The founder of the W.E.A., Albert Mansbridge, told the meeting that, as the Association wished nobody to be denied its facilities through poverty, for a twenty-four-week class the student's fee would be no more than half a crown and that such a class would normally be taught by a tutor from a Cambridge College. To secure support for the classes which it was planning to hold, the Colchester W.E.A. began with a series of single talks by some of the town's leading lecturers on topics which included John Bright, the Lake Poets, Elizabethan Worthies, Keats, and Railway Nationalisation, but, just as it was about to commence its more serious work, the War began and its activity seems to have lapsed.[48]

Two other movements made a major contribution to adult education. For workingmen, the chief agency of self-improvement was the Co-operative Society, which established an education centre at its Culver Street Assembly Room soon after its foundation in 1861. An early step was the opening of a Reading-room where, in the evenings, members could read four daily papers and seventeen weekly and monthly magazines. Another was the establishment of a library of books "which tend to stimulate and strengthen the mind of Man and fit him better to take his stand in life". The expense was met partly from the Society's educational fund and partly by income from Penny Readings and tea-meetings, both of them being the kind of wholesome entertainment approved of by the Society. In 1875 the Society ran the first class ever to be held in Colchester under the auspices of the Science and Arts Department of South Kensington, in which, on the subject of Magnetism and Electricity, all twelve students gained passes, nine of them in the first class. Similar courses followed, some on the sciences or the arts, others on practical subjects like Ambulance work, Book-keeping and Shorthand. The formation of the Women's Guild in 1890 provided another channel for self-education, as did the opening of additional Reading-rooms at New Town, North Street and Rowhedge, which could also be used as educational centres. At this time there was a very active debating society and also regular lectures. The latter continued to enjoy large, sometimes very large, audiences up to, and beyond, the War. Altogether, the Society's contribution to Colchester's adult education was equal to that of any of the major bodies in that field, but among working men and women it was, at first, unique and, later, unrivalled.[49]

The least obtrusive of the town's adult education movements was that of the Friends' Adult Schools. Started by Wilson Marriage in 1867 at a Nonconformist chapel in East Stockwell Street and served by him as its secretary for many years, the movement sought to give people of eighteen years and over the elementary education which they had failed to receive when young. The earliest classes were held on Sundays, which attracted much criticism, and were taught by four volunteers, including Henry Fry of the famous Quaker family. From 1872 the new Friends' Meeting House in Sir Isaac's Walk was used for the classes. A Women's School was opened in 1876, followed by special classes for those under eighteen years, but the most impressive development was the expansion of the work among the growing population of the suburbs including Copford, Stanway, Fordham Heath, Lexden, Parson's Heath, West Bergholt, the Hythe, Old Heath, Shrub End, and Mile End where a new adult-school building was erected on the east side of the Nayland Road. Annual enrolment grew from seventy-two in 1870 to 145 in 1874 and to 355 in 1885; altogether, from 1867 to 1894 a total of 3,076 adults attended classes. The fellowship thereby engendered was reflected in a wide range of other activities, including a string band, a brass band, a library with 800 books, a Friendly Society, a savings bank, a Band of Hope and numerous socials and outings, at which attendances sometimes reached a thousand. Only around 1900, with the improvements in public education, did class-enrolments begin to decline, but on the eve of the War the movement remained a powerful force in the town.[50]

The organisations so far described were the most stable and influential in Colchester's adult education, but they also inspired scores of other societies and undertakings which extended opportunities for study and self-improvement to even wider circles. Mutual Improvement Societies were set up by a number of different bodies such as the Y.M.C.A., the Temperance movement, Headgate Chapel, St. James' Church and Culver Street Methodists. Most churches and chapels arranged lectures on secular as well as religious topics and often kept their own lending libraries. There were debating societies, most of them ephemeral; there was a Literary Institute at Lexden; the Cups Hotel, the Conservative Club and the Liberal Club each had its Reading-room, open daily; in the 1880s a vigorous Students' Association provided lectures on topics as varied as Stenography, Lucretius, Alcohol, Teeth, Bees and Civilisation; and a workingmen's club was set up by some Conservatives, Liberals and former Chartists in rare co-operation, which, despite a ban on tobacco and alcohol, enrolled 300 workingmen and held debates on such controversial topics as universal suffrage, strikes, secular control of education, capital punishment and Disestablishment.

Altogether, Colchester's record in adult education is an impressive one. Those affected were in the main middle-class people or artisans of Liberal convictions, but there were exceptions to this trend. Women gained much from the facilities offered and in the University Extension movement played quite an active part. The arduous work of organisation was performed entirely by unpaid amateurs in accordance with that principle which the Victorians called Voluntaryism. The total of the social benefits arising from adult education cannot be defined, but certainly the energy and effort evoked from the organisers and the students alike constituted a valuable access of strength to the public spirit of the town.

CHAPTER IV

Politics

The Parliamentary Reform Movement, 1815–32

Between Waterloo and the 1832 Reform Act Colchester's politics, though fully participating in the electoral corruption of the times, did to some extent represent, or reflect, the movement of opinion among quite wide and diverse sections of the public. The franchise belonged to those who had served an apprenticeship to an existing freeman or who had been given freeman status or been allowed to buy it; those thus enfranchised passed their privileges to their sons and grandsons. The freemen, who always resented sharing the dividends of their privileges with newcomers, had long put a stop to the gift or sale of freedoms, but because so many young men could qualify by inheritance or apprenticeship, Colchester had an electorate larger than that of most of the country's Parliamentary boroughs and, partly for this reason, experienced hardly any uncontested elections in this period. The voters were spread over large areas of south-east England and came from quite diverse social classes. Of the 1,382 men voting at the 1820 election, 331 lived in London whither a number of artisans had migrated because of the collapse of Colchester's cloth industry or in search of higher wage rates in the capital, and for similar reasons 608 were living in other parts of England, while only 443, not quite a third of the electorate, still lived in the borough of Colchester. Provided that they qualified by one of the entitlements to the franchise, freemen could retain their vote wherever they lived. Most of these 'out-voters' lived in London or in the small towns and villages of Essex and south Suffolk, but a few were found in Norfolk, Cambridgeshire, Kent, Middlesex, Bedfordshire, Hampshire, Huntingdonshire, Gloucester, Wiltshire, Devon and Lancashire. As was to be expected, many of them were artisans, but, especially in London, some were in commerce and the professions. Maritime interests were well represented, as also was farming if artisans, who were dependent upon it, are included. Thirty voters, resident in London, claimed the title of 'gentleman', while there was even a sprinkling of labourers and servants.[1] Consequently, the Colchester electorate could be said to be representative, however inadequately, of the main urban and rural handicrafts, farming, commerce and the sea, with only the new factory-based industries omitted. The poor of Colchester, as a class, exercised no influence at all on elections or on political policy.

There was much corruption. The poll had to last a week or more to allow outvoters to reach Colchester and record their votes, for doing which they expected lavish entertainment throughout the long absence from home, as well as other inducements. Much electioneering, with appropriate refreshment, had to be done among London voters by the candidates before they journeyed to Colchester for the Nomination. Thus the Reform candidate spent the first part of the 1818 contest rallying and regaling his supporters in the East End of London, after which he drove to Colchester borough boundary in a chariot and four, there to be met by a well-organised "immense concourse", who unharnessed his horses and themselves dragged his vehicle into the town. Lavish bribery would then follow. At the same election J. B. Wildman, the Tory candidate, was accused of spending some £12,000, "to say nothing of the little *etceteras* which no man could keep account of". It was alleged that, when he had thus exhausted his available funds, he was not readopted.[2] Both parties were guilty. D. W. Harvey, the leading Essex Reformer and proclaimed enemy of electoral corruption, was reputed to have spent between £12,000 and £14,000, given to him for that purpose by a doting relative. He, too, had to provide the same "little *etceteras*" as his rival did. "The way to the hearts of the burgesses, Mr. Harvey finds, is their throats", wrote the *Colchester Gazette* in 1825. "Suppers, dinners, etc., are very acceptable." Such inducements were commonplace and openly discussed in the Press. Readers of the *Colchester Gazette* cannot have been surprised to read that "Yesterday D. W. Harvey, Esq., M.P. for this Borough, distributed 500 bushels of coals among the free burgesses" and, a fortnight later, that "J. B. Wildman, Esq., M.P. for this Borough, has given upwards of 700 bushels of coals to the free burgesses".[3]

In 1815 the Tories held both the borough seats, as they had done for several decades past. The cloth industry's collapse and Colchester's transformation into a large market town, combined with the fears engendered among the well-to-do by the French Revolution, had greatly weakened the Whig cause. A majority of the freemen resident locally were strongly pro-Tory; if they were not, they might find themselves subject to economic boycott. However, such intimidation was not needed in most cases. Many resident freemen, being artisans and shopkeepers, were dependent upon the custom of the surrounding rural area and so of their own accord supported the political supremacy of the landed interests and measures designed to assist agriculture; one draper told a Parliamentary enquiry in 1821 that in his own interests he favoured the continuation of the Corn Laws. Protection for agriculture was a main point of Tory policy throughout the period. At the Loyal Association's dinner in 1825, for instance, one Tory M.P. said, "The English farmer could not compete with the foreign grower; the latter produced his corn at one-tenth of the expense of raising it in England and could therefore, if admitted to our market, as proposed, undersell us and ruin our agriculture".[4] Equally favourable to the agricultural cause were many of the 'country freemen', as they were called, men living in the small market towns and villages of Essex and Suffolk. Only the London voters constituted a group generally removed from farming influences and, significantly, it was from them that the Liberal, D. W. Harvey, from the start of his attempt to win a Colchester seat, sought the support needed to tip the balance in his favour. He was successful in winning about two-thirds of them. In Colchester itself he had the enthusiastic support of the Liberal minority, which could trace its Reform convictions back to the time of John Wilkes and which had never completely disintegrated, even in the bitterly unfavourable atmosphere following the French Revolution. This group included leading Hythe businessmen, like Charles Heath and James Thorn, both of them coal merchants with other maritime interests, and John Ward; two of the last clothiers in the town, Richard Patmore, who had been indicted for selling Tom Paine's works in 1793, and Peter Devall, who kept the cloth industry alive long after the closure of all the other firms; George Savill, a distiller; Samuel Tabor, a brewer; Bartholomew Brown, a miller; professional men like W. W. Francis, an attorney, and George Firmin, a chemist and the originator of a gas supply in the town; J. F. Mills, banker, and Thomas Wilmhurst, a Crouch Street grocer; and Nonconformist ministers John Savill and G. Francis. Less prominent but even more active were some artisans and shopkeepers, working in the public house clubs, such as Chignell Wire, confectioner and innkeeper; G. D. Dennis, S. S. Dennis and John Ward, all shoemakers; William Wiles, journeyman carpenter, and Thomas Watson, whitesmith. Generally the Colchester Whigs and Liberals were too weak to win a majority among their fellow-townsmen, but they enjoyed one very important success when, in alliance with fellow-Liberals among the London voters, they won a seat for Harvey in 1818 and again in 1826 and at all subsequent elections till 1835.[5]

There were no formal party organisations, but, to secure support from such a dispersed and comparatively large electorate, both parties ran clubs at public houses. The Ship in Head Street and the Waggon and Horses at the top of North Hill housed Tory Clubs, while the Sun, the Fencers and the Cross Keys favoured the Whigs. D. W. Harvey, when Liberal candidate, was assiduous in cultivating this form of support. In 1825, it was reported:

> "Mr. Harvey, accompanied by the principal inhabitants attached to Liberal principles, visited all the local clubs. These are six in number and have been established for some years . . . The number who sat down to supper on the evenings of Tuesday and Wednesday exceeded all former example . . . The morning of Wednesday presented a rare and pleasing object, that of upwards of 200 well-dressed, well-behaved women, the wives of the industrious burgesses, who were assembled, many of them with infants in their arms bearing the name of the favourite candidate, to receive a present of half-a-pound of souchong tea. This was presented by Mr. Harvey in person and each receiver was refreshed with a piece of excellent cake and a glass of good wine."

On these occasions, it was said, Harvey used to kiss not only the babies but their mothers as well.[6] What occurred at the public-house clubs was nothing very uplifting, as far as can be seen from the surviving minutes kept by the organiser of one such club, the Colchester Loyal and Independent Whig Club. When not being dined at the candidate's expense, the members paid 1s. 6d. for their monthly dinner. Their attendance varied between nine and thirty, averaging eighteen. They comprised seventeen artisans, of whom six were shoemakers and three clothworkers, and five retail tradesmen, three men from industry and ten from miscellaneous callings.[7] Politics seem to have played hardly any part in their proceedings. Such humble clubs received little publicity, but the more respectable associations, when they held dinners at some leading inn to bring together their party's influential supporters, advertised the function in the Press and often had the event reported there. The most reputable Tory organisation had a succession of titles, being called the Constitutional Club in 1790, the Pitt Club or the True Blue Club from 1806 and the Loyal Association from 1821; it used for its dinners either the Three Cups or the White Hart. The Angel was the favourite resort of the Whig association, called at various times the Hand-in-Hand Club, the Friends to Freedom of Elections, the Friends of Retrenchment and Reform, and the Independent Club. As only a minority of freemen lived in Colchester, many club meetings were organised in London and elsewhere. D. W. Harvey used the Fountain Tavern in the Minories and the Kent and Essex Tavern in Whitechapel. Nor did he neglect the Essex towns where there were large concentrations of voters. He had strong support in Kelvedon where he had once lived himself and where he won the votes of twenty of the twenty-one resident freemen. On one occasion he made a well-publicised visit to Harwich; his supporters met him at the borough boundary, unharnessed his horses and dragged his carriage into town amid the strains of a band and the ringing of church bells, after which he held a meeting and gave them entertainment at the White Hart.[8]

The town's politics were profoundly affected in those years by Harvey's candidature. Daniel Whittle Harvey was born in Witham in 1786, he was articled as a young man to a Colchester solicitor and then took Feering House, Kelvedon, from which he conducted his own legal practice. Though he moved on to London, his Essex connections caused him to conduct his Reform activities in the county with the result that the Colchester Whigs, seeking a protagonist against the long-established Tory control of the borough, in 1811 invited him to become their candidate. He exacted from them, as a condition, their agreement to Parliamentary Reform being made a prominent point of his programme and, with enthusiastic support from both Colchester and London Whigs, he went to the poll in 1812 and narrowly missed winning the second seat. Undismayed, he viewed "our poll of 704 burgesses as a complete victory, opposed as we have been by a host of contractors, aided by the united purses of the Treasury and the East India Company", but, though there was some substance in this analysis of his opponents' strength, he had himself spent so much money on the contest that he was unsure of his ability to maintain a struggle that gave every sign of continuing to be too expensive for him. So he boldly threw part of the financial burden on to his party, and such was his popularity that large sums were raised in his support throughout his successive candidatures. His Colchester friends themselves provided gigs and horses to convey voters to the polls and gave hospitality in their own homes to outvoters coming to the town to vote. He made history by inspiring fifty wives of London voters to form a group to raise funds for him and to assist in other ways, the earliest known case of women participating in Colchester politics. To what extent he was thus able to avoid using his own money in either legitimate or dubious electoral expenditure is unclear — he certainly continued to 'treat' his supporters throughout his years as candidate and as M.P. — but it required courage and conviction for him to break, even partially, with the corrupt practices of the past.[9]

He proved an outstandingly successful champion in the prolonged, uphill, struggle for Reform in the unfavourable setting of Colchester elections. His assets included his energy, acute intelligence, tactical skill, and easy but forceful oratory. When he died in 1862, one obituary saw this last quality as his chief advantage — "he could thrill you in his best days by reading the alphabet". An old supporter, James Hurnard, saw his superb oratory as the product of his intelligence and knowledge:

> "Tall and proportioned finely, with a face
> Beaming with lofty intellectual power,
> He was a very king in personal appearance,
> Casting all common men into the shade;
> In mien and port he seemed a demigod;
> His was the highest polish of his art;
> His dignity surpassed all other men's.
> Clear and melodious was his ringing voice,
> His action and his utterance full of beauty,
> Most ready was his ever playful wit;
> His memory was something wonderful;
> He could call every voter by his name.
> How admirable he was in argument,
> How keen in satire, terrible in invective!
> The matter and manner of his oratory
> Were not the dull results of memory,
> But the spontaneous efforts of his mind." [10]

Harvey was a Whig with radical sympathies, ready to declare that "the revolution of 1688 was the brightest page in our Country's history" and his programme, seen in retrospect, was little, if at all, different from that of the main Reform movement of the time. [11] To his middle-class supporters he offered an alternative to the Tory policy of agricultural protection as the only policy for country-town interests. He advocated lower taxation, an end to the financial corruption practised by governments, and the repeal of the Corn Laws and of all such obstacles to free trade. "Every branch of our agriculture and commerce groans under the weight of profligate taxation", he complained in 1818. The second group, on whose support he relied, were the Nonconformists; though they included many of his supporters from business, they had their own distinct and deeply felt grievances, such as their exclusion from certain public offices and their obligation to pay Church Rates for the upkeep of another denomination's places of worship. They were somewhat uncongenial associates for Harvey. One observer wrote, "I know few things more singular than his relations with the Dissenters of Essex. It was they who got him into the House and it was in their interests that he first became known. But he had no sympathy with their strict notions and antiquated ways, and never pretended that he had . . . They were proud of him in their secret hearts." [12] He never wavered in demanding for them complete religious equality with the Anglicans. Another strongly emphasised point in his programme was Poor Law 'reform'. The bigger ratepayers in his party, especially the businessmen who favoured financial economy and the free movement of labour, supported him fully in this, but the 'reform' was never defined in detail to his third set of followers, the enfranchised and unenfranchised workingmen, many of whom lived to detest the Whig Poor Law measures of 1834 more bitterly than they did any Tory legislation. Indeed, Harvey was rarely precise in defining the wrongs of the workers, despite his supporters' banners proclaiming him "Harvey, the friend of the poor", and, though in a speech he referred with sympathy to those who "have long been condemned to parish workhouses", he was in 1834–5 ready to defend the far more oppressive Union workhouses that were central to Poor Law 'reform'. He always implied that the grievances of the poor would be ended when free trade, lower taxes and economic expansion were made possible by Parliamentary Reform. Who, precisely, were to be enfranchised through Reform was not usually stated. When at one election Harvey said "I am prepared to sacrifice my life for the just rights of the people", the poor people in the audience cheered him, as they did at every election, because they thought that he meant he would never desist until every single man was given the vote. So his public appearances often evoked huge popular demonstrations. As he arrived for each election at the borough boundary, he was met by large crowds who unyoked his horses and themselves pulled his carriage into town, and at the ensuing nomination at the hustings he always won an overwhelming majority from the crowd. Indeed, he never made his appearance in Colchester but troops of children followed his footsteps from street to street, shouting his name; "nor did he appear to be either inconvenienced or displeased at this noisy and persistent demonstration of popularity among the incipient politicians of the borough". Whatever inconsistencies were revealed by his political conduct after the Reform Act, in one matter he was beyond criticism. He never ceased to protest at the Government's suppression of free speech and civil rights in the years after Waterloo, when such bravery seemed not unlikely to involve him in serious personal danger.[13]

After losing a by-election in 1818 to J. B. Wildman, son of a West Indies plantation-owner, Harvey captured the second seat in the General Election of the same year. In 1820 he moved to the top of the poll, but was disqualified on a technicality, whereupon he gave way to the Whig banker, Henry Baring, who was elected unopposed on a policy of "Baring and Commerce". The latter proved not to be an active Member, and Harvey remained at the head of the strengthened Reform movement in the town. His supporters were delighted at the discomfiture suffered by the King and the Government when in 1820 Queen Caroline seemed to have got the better of her husband in his attempt to divorce her for misconduct, and they defied Colchester Corporation's attempt to forbid their celebratory illumination, which was particularly well supported in the poorer streets. When in 1821, after the Queen's death, her body was brought through Essex on its way to embarkation at Harwich, Colchester Reformers joined their fellows along the route in demonstrating sympathy with "the wronged Queen of England", whom they regarded as a victim of the whole corrupt political system.[14] They also kept up a strong challenge to the Tory control of the Corporation, though with only occasional success. Their sustained efforts built the stronger basis which Harvey needed in Colchester itself, and in 1826, apparently through a temporary truce with Sir G. H. Smyth, Tory candidate for the other seat, he secured election again. From 1822 his cause had been much assisted by the pro-Liberal weekly, the *Kent and Essex Mercury*, which, by its Colchester reports, did something to counteract the influence of the somewhat older, pro-Tory, *Colchester Gazette*. By 1828 Colchester Reformers were confident enough to launch a new local paper, the *Sickle*, which, though at first very cautious in its comments, clearly supported D. W. Harvey and Catholic Emancipation, the issue that was then dominating national politics. Four months later, in January 1829, the paper was moved from Manningtree, its first place of publication, to Colchester. Renamed the *Colchester Courier*, it now firmly proclaimed its support for reform of the present 'aristocratic' political system, for an end to political corruption, for press freedom, religious equality and lower taxation. It showed much resolution in opposing the powerful campaign then being waged against the Catholic Emancipation Bill by Sir G. H. Smyth and the Tories and it backed the counter-petition of the local Liberals in favour of the Bill. When Harvey spoke for Emancipation, it wrote, "We congratulate Colchester and the country in having a Representative so honest and independent". Sir G. H. Smyth resigned in protest at the passage of the Bill, and at the ensuing by-election the paper gave publicity to an attempt by the Liberal burgesses living in London to put up a Liberal. This attempt failed, and so did the *Colchester Courier* after four months of publication in the town. It had attracted very few advertisements and was being run at too great a loss to continue. However, its proprietors succeeded in arranging a merger of the paper with the *Colchester Gazette*, by which the new paper would cease to be pro-Tory and would pursue an independent policy. This was a fortunate move for the Liberals, because, when the Reform Bill struggle began in 1830, the *Colchester Gazette* was well placed to give the Bill its firm support.[15]

Colchester was deeply affected by the Reform struggle of 1830–32. Under the old system many well-to-do and influential people did not possess the franchise, including a leading banker, five lawyers and the Headmaster of the Grammar School, and, since the Grey Government's Bill promised the vote to virtually all middle-class men in the borough, it was assured of strong and articulate support. A middle-class victory was in prospect but such was the mounting enthusiasm that workingmen, in this time of economic depression, were also swept along in the movement for the Bill. It was a measure of the current optimism that the 'outvoters' in London, who were to be disenfranchised by the Bill, "came to the poll to vote for the extinction of their own political franchise", as one surprised observer noted during the election of Spring 1831.[16] When the Tory candidate, Sanderson, arrived to open his campaign, the crowd threw his carriage into a pond, while the Magistrates read the Riot Act. The opponents of Reform, led by the Corporation itself, were active and influential. They founded the *Essex Standard* specifically to oppose Reform and they tried to widen the division between the two Reform candidates, D. W. Harvey and William Mayhew, a London wine-merchant and former Tory, whom some London outvoters had brought forward to offset Harvey's radicalism. Yet such was the popular support for the Bill that Mayhew, very much against his will, was forced to cooperate with Harvey and unity was maintained within the Reform

movement. It was in vain that the *Essex Standard* warned against "Mayhew and Harvey, the rabble candidates", for it had to report shortly afterwards that "anarchy and intimidation have triumphed over loyalty. Mr.
Sanderson has resigned. Mr. Harvey and Mr. Mayhew are the sitting
members and Colchester is indeed disgraced." [17] The paper continued to
harp upon the dangerously plebeian composition of the Reform
movement, noting that, when the Lords rejected the Bill in November
1831, "an inflammatory handbill tending to degrade the higher classes of
society in the opinion of those in the lower stations of life, has been circulated". It returned to the same theme in its account of the rejoicing in
the town when news arrived of the Bill's successful passage through the
House of Lords. A procession was quickly formed, it reported, which
marched through the streets with flags flying and a band playing, but it
consisted only of "a pretty collection of boys and girls and unwashed
artisans, but not one respectable person". It was pleased to note that,
when an illumination was announced in celebration of the Bill's final
passage into law, some respectable Reformers were reluctant to participate and that, even among the lower orders, relatively few responded. It
wrote "One rascal in an obscure part of the town had an effigy of the Duke
of Wellington suspended by his heels; and three or four other wretched
hovels in that neighbourhood had rushlights in their casements. We
forgot to add that, fearful that the lighting-up would not have its desired
effect, a band was engaged to parade the streets with a banner; but the
hundred-odd factory girls and a parcel of idle boys silently accompanied
the music, and no riot occurred." [18] D. W. Harvey and his associates, fearful of the effect upon his middle-class supporters of this pro-Reform
enthusiasm of the artisans and silk factory girls, affected not to notice how
this middle-class triumph had been forced upon the reluctant House of
Lords by the pressure of poor men, who were to gain worse than nothing
from the Reform Act and the legislation that was to follow it. He rose to
heights of triumphant rhetoric when he addressed his supporters:

> "The grand-children of your far-distant descendants will
> delight to trace back their pedigree to the men, who stood
> by their KING in the hour of their country's fate, rose as
> one man, and with one voice shouted 'COLCHESTER
> SHALL BE FREE'". [19]

Anti-climax, 1833–67

When Reform enthusiasm subsided, Colchester Liberals remained
exuberant about their prospects, none more so than D. W. Harvey who
assured his supporters that "many of your sturdiest opponents will, at no
distant period, become valuable converts to our opinions, and by their
respectability and character shed lustre on our cause". [20] The Tories at
first were downcast. Even if the *Essex Standard* had been correct in seeing
respectable Colchester's view of Reform as one of "the most dignified
neutrality", was there not in the country as a whole a creeping subversion
of age-old traditions and sentiments? The same paper noting the town's
unprecedented apathy in the celebration of the King's Birthday and Royal
Oak Day and comparing this to the jolly celebrations of days gone by,
attributed the malaise to the effect of Reform on the British nation:

"Reform, like a monstrous nightmare, presses down the energies of the country — and man goeth about for a vain shadow, disquieting himself in vain. Agriculture neglected, commerce decaying, a general seeking after that which satisfieth not, to the neglect of the private duties of life, have made England a desolation. It cannot then be a matter of wonder that we rejoice not now as we did when the country was prosperous and the people contented."[21]

There was anxiety too that the populace would proceed to greater lengths of innovation. Sir G. H. Smyth of Berechurch Hall thought the Reformers to be eager to surpass themselves: "Why, the Reform Bill was nothing after all — nothing would now content them but Universal Suffrage and Annual Parliaments". Even more alarming to the Tories was the apparent triumph of Industry and Commerce over Agriculture. This was an issue that the *Essex Standard* had kept to the front during the recent struggle and, when the first election took place after the Bill's passage, it wrote, "If ever there was a time when the Conservative party should exhibit themselves in their full strength, *now is that time*. The Reform Bill has made fearful inroads upon the agricultural influence; and the Free Trade system is hanging over them, ready to complete their ruin." It also published a letter full of eloquence about the impending world-wide triumph of industrialism:

"THE MANUFACTURERS MAD

Sir — The Manufacturers are now looking for a great change; that is, a free trade in all the productions of the British Empire, which will ruin every producer and all their dependants (that is those with whom they trade and employ), by forcing the sale of double the quantity of any commodity to raise any given sum; thereby doubling again in effect the present amount of taxation . . . The avarice of the Manufacturers knows no bounds; as they are not satisfied with their home trade, and that of our colonies, but they want the custom of the whole world, which they propose to supply with goods made up by their powerful machinery, not by hand. This machinery, Sir, is the curse of any whole or even half-populated country; as its excessive use has carried distress into every corner of this Empire, into France, and even into the heart of our East Indies, by superseding the labour of the poor natives . . ."[22]

The Tories quickly recovered their self-possession. Indeed, the *Essex Standard* had hardly lost it and continued to treat both Essex and Colchester Reformers as a temporary and rather silly combination of tradesmen and factory hands, whose main strength lay in the irresponsible enthusiasm of a few boys and girls. The paper was careful from the start not to make its cause seem irrelevant in the new age by turning its back on all current changes. It differentiated "between reform which, prudently and considerately undertaken, we do not object to, and those violent changes which are best described by the name of Revolution". The losing Tory candidate had also said during the 1831 election that "I hesitate not to repeat my honest conviction that the representation of the country in

Parliament requires amendment" and he therefore endorsed "rational and temperate Reform". Even Sir G. H. Smyth, who had gone so far as to resign from Parliament in 1829 over Catholic Emancipation, could bring himself to accept "such wholesome and discreet amendments as may ensure real improvement". He was sure that at the next election "a Tory administration will be formed, not an ultra-Tory one — that will not satisfy the people — but a Liberal Tory one, which will be the consequence of that Bill which I opposed — the Reform Bill".[23] Colchester Tories were, therefore, predisposed to accept Robert Peel's new definition of Conservative principles, designed to open to his party better prospects in post-Reform Britain, though, unlike the *Essex Standard*, they long found it hard to call themselves Conservatives instead of Tories. What was more important, they at once undertook the painstaking task of rebuilding supporters' clubs in the pro-Conservative inns; two of these bodies were already functioning before Reform was a few months old.[24]

Electorally the Reform Act from the start worked in the Conservatives' favour. The London and other outvoters, among whom Harvey had gained most of his following, had lost their franchise, except for those living within seven miles of Colchester town centre who, in the main, shared the now predominantly Conservative views of the north Essex farming community. Within the town the existing freemen retained their votes. A majority of them had been Tory before 1832 and, even when Reform enthusiasm was at its highest in 1831, the Liberals had never effectively overturned this majority. In addition, the Act had enfranchised hundreds of the town's middle and lower-middle classes, the £10 householders, who occupied house, shop, workshop or other property of at least £10 a year annual value. It was from such men, that is merchants, shopkeepers, professional people and substantial master artisans, that the Reform movement had drawn most of its influential support, but even before 1832 many of this class had been Tory and, after it, some of those who had become Liberals seem quickly to have lost their enthusiasm, perhaps because they had now been accorded political rights commensurate with their ideas of their economic importance and social position. In the 1835 contest, when the surviving freemen numbered 413 and the £10 householders 616, the Conservatives did well in each group, and this continued to be the position for many years as the number of £10 householders slowly rose. This middle-class support for the Conservatives, the avowed champions of agricultural interests, was often attributed by the Liberals to Conservative intimidation. For instance, the defeated Whig candidate in the 1852 election, Wingrove Cooke, wrote:

> "After the contest had closed, when men's passions ought to have subsided, when those who had been opposed to each other should have shaken hands at the end of the strife, as they had done before it began, and let bygones be bygones, it was told to him — and he could never repeat the fact without emotion — that the morning after the poll-book was published, the farmers of the neighbourhood came into the town and, going round among the small tradesmen of the borough with that poll-book in their hands, said to one and another — 'No, you voted for

Wingrove Cooke; we shall never darken your doors again'."[25]

Another Liberal, James Hurnard, wrote of similar "threats of loss of trade", which men of his party had to face, and he also pointed to the absence of the secret ballot as the main deficiency in the system:

"A few days afterwards the poll is published,
When all the world can see how each man voted,
And act against him as they find occasion.
All these abuses might be remedied,
And men might live in harmony and peace
by a well-ordered plan of secret voting."[26]

Consequently, the Secret Ballot for long remained the chief political reform sought by Liberals after 1832, but they may have been deceiving themselves, in Colchester at least, in thinking that this change would bring them victory; certainly in the two decades after the introduction of the Secret Ballot their electoral record was not a successful one. Probably many Colchester millers, maltsters, corn merchants, shipowners, shopkeepers and even master artisans saw their own economic prospects as closely linked with those of the surrounding rural area. It was claimed in 1843 that this class was strongly hostile to Cobden at the time when the latter was about to hold his great Free Trade meeting in Colchester, and it is clear that a number of the town's Liberals quietly disassociated themselves from the local campaign of the Anti-Corn Law League. Certainly the Conservatives assumed that the Colchester electorate largely supported their defence of agricultural interests, for in 1852 one of their posters asked "Would you like to see your rights transferred to Lancashire?" and went on "It is the wish and policy of the radical party to destroy the franchise in towns and boroughs which are dependent upon the prosperity of the agricultural interest, and they will give that franchise to some place in a manufacturing district".[27] Altogether, the two enfranchised groups, the surviving freemen and the £10 householders, showed by their rarely wavering political preferences between 1835 and 1867 that they were predominantly pro-Conservative. The town's poor, who had borne the heat of the Reform campaigns, showed at the mass meetings around the hustings that they opposed the Conservatives and wanted radical change, but in 1832 they had been left voteless. Another circumstance worked in the Conservatives' favour. In 1835 the old Corporation gave place to an elected Town Council, to the Conservatives' great alarm. Having dominated municipal life before 1835 and having used this power in Parliamentary elections, they expected to suffer serious political disadvantage from the change, especially when the Liberals won the first elections to the new Council. However, they quickly recovered local control and held it for forty years, gaining much prestige and influence in the process without suffering the sort of discredit they had once incurred from the corruption of the old system.

Among the first to realise the damage done to Liberal fortunes by Reform was the very man who had been Reform's chief advocate. D. W. Harvey, even amid the enthusiasm of late 1832, could win only the second place in the poll of that year. Two years later, when public disenchantment deepened, he was worried enough to issue a dramatic call to old

friends to rally behind himself and the cause of Reform. Aided only by a
Liberal movement in disarray and disunity, he was facing a revived Conservative party. Sir G. H. Smyth, of Berechurch Hall, one of Colchester's
several squires, who had resigned his seat a few years before in protest
against Catholic Emancipation, set aside his resentment and his differences with Richard Sanderson, the sitting Conservative, in order to help
present a united challenge for the two seats. They made a formidable pair,
as a Liberal journalist admitted in a review of Colchester's politics in the
1840s:

> "The influence of Sir George Smyth in Colchester is that of
> association and connection. He is a resident landlord and
> a popular one. He is regarded as a good practical agricul-
> turalist, and in all that pertains to farming Colchester
> delights. Personally he is respected and esteemed. Polit-
> ically he has done all his supporters have wished of him by
> voting True Blue of the deepest possible Tory shade on
> every available occasion. This is just the man for a thor-
> ough-going Tory agricultural town. Such a constituency
> does not desire genius or talent. On the contrary, they are
> rather suspicious of those qualifications. 'They were so
> deceived in Peel.' They regard even Mr. Benjamin Dis-
> raeli as doubtful, and would rather be excused having him
> than otherwise. Your old top-boot and pigtail member,
> without a word to say except at the agricultural show, is
> the sort of man for the Tories of such a town as Colchester.
> Mr. Sanderson's popularity in Colchester was maintained
> in a different way and at a higher price. He was the 'mon-
> eyed member'. Colchester boasts of numerous charities,
> great and small, and to all of these, miscellaneous though
> they were, Mr. Sanderson was a most liberal contributor.
> His extensive bounty was dispensed without reference to
> details. He knew neither High Church nor Low Church,
> nor any other class distinction — he only knew 'the town'.
> Hundred pound donations and ten guinea annual sub-
> scriptions were forthcoming from his purse whenever they
> were required. At the last election there was published by
> an ardent admirer a list of some of Mr. Sanderson's good
> deeds."[28]

Faced with such opponents, D. W. Harvey, after declaring "I will be at
my post, intent upon one sole purpose, the unflinching advancement of
effectual reform", withdrew almost at once and was not seen in the
constituency again until the next Liberal revival of 1847. His successor,
Henry Tufnell, "a stout gentleman from India" according to the *Essex
Standard*, and one of the small surviving band of Essex Whig country
gentlemen, took Harvey's place for the 1835 election. Fighting on a programme of full rights for Nonconformists and municipal reform, he canvassed "with about twenty gentlemen, all the respectability of the party"
and won a large majority of the mainly unenfranchised spectators at the
hustings, but came bottom of the poll with 505 votes to 639 for Sanderson
and 537 for Smyth. In 1837 the Conservative victory was even more deci-

sive with Sanderson gaining 472, Smyth 435 and Todd, a Whig, 306; on this occasion, too, the crowd at the Nomination voted for the Whig, who had during the campaign proclaimed himself a radical reformer. In 1841 the Liberals did not even advance a candidate, but the relative strength of the two parties was shown by the total Conservative vote of 759 against a Liberal vote of 493 at the municipal elections of that year, from which moreover the largely Conservative Parliamentary voters of the rural district were excluded.[29] The Town Council was also firmly in Conservative hands, having become, said one Liberal, "a closer confederation than that which existed in by-gone days". The Conservative supremacy was upheld by a well-organised network of public-house clubs which vanquished the similar clubs maintained by the Liberals. A conservative described the system as follows:

"Public house meetings became a systematised plan of operation; the municipal constituency was divided into First, Second and Third ward clubs; members were formally enrolled — officers appointed — and amid the fumes of tobacco and the reeking of pewter pots, the Conservatism and Liberalism of the day were enunciated by aspirants for municipal honours to ears none too critical . . . The evil was unquestionable, but it answered for the time the intended purpose — the wished-for results ensued: by steady perseverance for three years in drinking, talking and smoking, the Conservatives not only obtained a majority, but, with the exception of three Whig Aldermen chosen for six years, they were unanimous on the Council."[30]

The Liberals in their discomfiture were at first rent by deep disunity, when the more radical of them became critical of the Whig Government's failure to press on with further reforms. A prominent critic was John Bawtree Harvey, editor and proprietor of the *Essex & Suffolk Times*, the *Essex Mercury* and the *Ipswich Express*, who sensed the poorer Reformers' disillusion with the 1832 Act, the Nonconformists' disappointment with the continuation of Church Rates, the unpopularity of the Corn Laws among non-agriculturalists and the universal hatred of the New Poor Law by working people. J. B. Harvey approved of the New Poor Law and at first restricted himself to the advocacy of the Secret Ballot, but, as the Essex and Suffolk urban workers took up Chartism, he published Chartist speeches in his papers and ventured to declare support for some extension of the franchise. However, when Chartism ran into trouble in 1839, he ceased to report its activities and chided its leaders in his editorials. Yet even such very cautious radicalism had caused some orthodox Liberals to cease to purchase his papers and thus to compel their closure. He had some supporters, including the able minister of Lion Walk Congregationalists, the Rev. T. W. Davids, and during 1840–43 a distinct radical group came slowly into being. In 1843 it tried to start a local branch of the Complete Suffrage Union, a Liberal body formed to head off Chartism, and, though this attempt failed, it met regularly to plan a Liberal revival. According to its opponents, it turned the nominally neutral Mechanics' Institute into its own partisan discussion society, building up there "an enthusiastic band of younger men, whose better-regulated tastes had brought them to seek their pleasures at the fountain of literature and science rather than the beershops, the Garde Mobile of the anti-Conservative alliance". They ventured to criticise D. W. Harvey's refusal to come down and help the Colchester Liberals. "You are an old electioneer," one of them wrote, "retaining the same notions of securing a seat which prevailed during the borough-mongering days." The writer also criticised Harvey's "Plague-diffusing bribery" and his "indecent, unmanly and disgusting practice of canvassing for votes by kissing the wives and daughters of electors".[31]

The radicals' chief impact on politics in the 1840s was made through the local campaign of the Anti-Corn Law League. Repeal of the Corn Laws had been prominent in the programme of Colchester Liberalism ever since their first enactment in 1815, when D. W. Harvey had risked his future by attacking them in this distressed market town. When Reform triumphed, local Conservatives were convinced that the Liberals would make Repeal one of their most urgent objectives. In 1841, when Chartism was entering its second phase of popularity, Colchester Liberals advanced Repeal as an alternative to the Charter, gathering 900 signatures to a petition in 1841 and over 2,000 in 1842. In 1843 they intensified their campaign, holding lectures, distributing pamphlets and then moving on to their greatest success of all, the debate between their own champion, Cobden, and the two Essex Protectionist M.P.s, who had issued the challenge. The Essex Protection Society, the precursor of many similar bodies in the counties of England, put up posters in almost every village, urging farmers to attend the debate and vote against the intended ruin of English agriculture, and they arranged special trains to bring supporters to confront the "moneyed demagogues". The Repealers summoned their sympathisers from the north Essex towns, including the Chartists who, though suspicious of the Anti-Corn Law League's disregard of Universal Suffrage, did themselves dislike the Corn Laws. The debate, held in a meadow on the south side of East Street, was orderly, lengthy and serious. With the President of East Essex Agricultural Society in the chair, some 7,000 people "of highly respectable appearance" listened to long and reasoned speeches. When the vote was taken at 9.00 p.m. all but twenty-seven of the 2,000 people remaining voted for Repeal. It was in vain that Protectionists accused their opponents of prolonging the debate until the special trains had departed, taking the farmers with them. For, as an Ipswich Liberal paper pronounced, "The meeting at Colchester, fairly convened and fairly held, unquestionably decided against protection; and doomed protection is, for it is vicious and indefensible". This victory for the Repeal cause in a leading Protectionist county made a deep impression in the nation at large, but the struggle was far from over. Colchester Repealers had to keep up a sustained campaign, calling further meetings and on one occasion posting the Anti-Corn Law League's journal to over half the houses in the town.[32] Meanwhile the Conservatives, according to one of their own supporters, had become complacent about their continuing election successes, both Parliamentary and municipal, and even allowed their public-house clubs to decline into inactivity just when the young radicals were reinvigorating the

Liberal party. The latter, already encouraged by Corn Law Repeal, now received an accession of strength from some of the local Chartists, who, disappointed by their movement's decline in 1843–7 and weary of the political wilderness, seem to have begun at this time the process of reconciliation with the Liberals which was eventually to make them a recognised ally of that party. They proved indefatigable organisers for the Whig candidate at the 1847 election and were specially thanked at the huge tea-party held to celebrate his success in capturing one of the two seats for his party, the loser being Richard Sanderson. The Whig candidate was Joseph Hardcastle, a barrister who had married the daughter of the proprietor of the large Writtle Brewery, near Chelmsford. He was "a smart young fellow, thin and tall, but well proportioned", so youthful in appearance that when the veteran Whig organiser, Chignell Wire, went to interview him, he exclaimed "Why, he's only a boy". But he had energy and ambition, and he proceeded to confront the Conservative establishment in a campaign so vigorous and enthusiastic that hard-bitten Chartists and radical Liberals did not let themselves notice that he was equivocal about suffrage extension and even about the Ballot. When D. W. Harvey spoke for him from the first floor of the George Hotel, some 5,000 people, mostly non-electors, gave Harvey an ovation reminiscent of earlier times. The contest was remembered in Liberal circles for half a century, and Hardcastle's obituary in 1899 recalled the occasion:

> "During that eventful day there was the usual excitement;
> bands were playing about the streets and in the afternoon
> the excitement became intense. In those times of open
> ballots, the trend of things could be pretty well gauged and
> the scene that took place when Mr. Hardcastle, Mr.
> Stephen Brown then a big man at the silk factory where
> hundreds of hands were employed, Mr. Bawtree Harvey,
> Mr. Fenton and others joined arm-in-arm in a string which
> reached across the road and bounced up High Street, was
> most exhilarating."

Sanderson, on hearing the result of the poll, drove to the station, never to be seen again in the town. "The Conservative cause of Colchester is falling", said a Liberal after the election, "and will soon be numbered with the things that were."[33]

The Liberals did do well in the 1847 municipal elections, but that was the limit of their recovery and within a few years they were as far from political dominance in the town as before. Corn Law Repeal had done surprisingly little damage to the supremacy of the Essex agricultural establishment which almost at once entered a quarter of a century of prosperity and stability. Consequently, the economic situation within Colchester itself, which had helped the Conservatives to recover control after the 1832 Reform Act, remained quite unchanged, while the Continental upheavals of 1848 and the Chartist revival of that year reinforced middle-class fear of radicalism. From 1850 to 1867 Colchester politics followed the same Conservative path as they had done since 1835. Hardcastle was beaten in 1852, leaving both seats securely in Conservative hands except when, in 1857, Gurdon Rebow of Wivenhoe Park captured one of them, an exception that proved the rule because, though nominally a Whig, he was anything but a Liberal. There was even a municipal truce for a time, with the Liberals firmly dissuading a few radical members who wanted to break it. Politics became dreary and conventional, now that Chartism had dwindled into insignificance; its remaining sympathisers joined the Liberals or busied themselves with the new Co-operative Society. The radical wing of Liberalism was quiescent except for a few meetings in 1859–60 in support of cautious proposals for suffrage extension and a demonstration of support for the North in the American Civil War. The sole radical to stand for Parliament, the unpredictable W. R. Havens of East Donyland, received seven votes. The radicals' only solid gain at this time was the successful publication of a new Liberal weekly, the *Essex Telegraph*, partly through J. B. Harvey's initiative. Otherwise the Liberal-Conservative conflict had largely subsided. The Conservatives even spoke of the Whig, Gurdon Rebow, with respect, and the *Essex Standard* surprisingly declared that "we are by no means disposed to support men simply because they call themselves Conservatives". The only departure from the ordinary occurred when one of the Conservative candidates at the 1852 election, Lord John Manners, was strongly attacked by some of his own party, notably the proprietor of the *Essex Standard*, for having supported in Parliament an official grant to Maynooth College, a seminary for Roman Catholic priests in Ireland. Manners, one of Disraeli's colleagues in the 'Young England' group, was a friend of the Tractarians who, through the Oxford Movement, were seeking to revive catholicism within the Anglican church, but was not himself a Roman Catholic. The feeling over his candidature was strong enough to provoke the output of numerous posters, leaflets and speeches alleging or denying his 'Popish' sympathies; one leaflet reproduced Morant's account of the burning of Colchester's Protestant martyrs and concluded with "NO POPERY". Manners retained the support of a majority of his party and won the seat. Yet though bitter feelings divided the Conservatives for some years, the Liberals were too feeble to reap any benefit from their opponents' disunity.[34]

Despite the unimportance of orthodox politics in these years, elections remained one of the town's most popular entertainments. In about 1860 James Hurnard described them as follows:

"At length arrives the day of nomination,
A wasted day of jangling noise and riot:
A motley crowd of men surround the hustings,
Where stand the candidates amidst their friends,
Bowing, grimacing, bandying badinage,
And making speeches, or attempting to,
Amid the plaudits of their partisans,
And the fierce hootings of their adversaries.
Sometimes a shower of rotten eggs is thrown,
And sometimes something even harder still,
Or something softer, a dead cat, or rat:
Disorder is the order of the day.
At length the uproarious show of hands is taken,
The Mayor proclaims the candidates elected,
The losing candidates demand a poll,

And then the tumult closes till the morning;
But all night long the tug of war goes on.
Watchers of either party prowl the streets,
For foulest influences are brought to bear
To win the election of the coming day.
What eagerness possesses everybody
To ascertain the progress of the poll;
What cheers are raised as every vote is given
By one or other of the opposing parties;
And as the closing hour of four draws on,
What frantic efforts either party makes
To turn the quivering scale of the election!
St. Peter's clock strikes four. The struggle ceases.
All has been done that mortal man could do;
The Wires and Aylets have achieved their best,
And nothing now can alter the result.
Men breathe again, confer upon the contest,
The victors triumph, and the vanquished sulk;
Vengeance is vowed against the renegades,
And harsh reproaches lavished on the false;
Family feuds afresh are fed with fuel,
And jealousies and rivalries revive.
Meanwhile the Mayor comes forth upon the hustings,
The golden chain of corporation glory,
Glittering afar, suspended from his neck,
And having counted up the numbers polled
Reads the result and tells the multitude,
Who crowd beneath him thick as swarming bees,
On whom the election of the day has fallen.
    Then each successful candidate steps forth
With hat in hand, amidst uproarious cheers,
With cat-calls, groans and hootings intermixed,
Smiling and bowing to return his thanks,
Making the usual speech on such occasions
About the proudest day of all his life,
And duty to his new constituents.
The beaten candidates make parting speeches;
Thanks to the Mayor are then proposed and carried;
The crowds retire to talk and drink and feed,
While bands of music march with colours flying
Throughout the town followed by ragamuffins." [35]

Politics and the poor, 1815–67

Parliamentary representation, electoral contests, municipal affairs, political clubs, newspaper controversies, all the ingredients of Colchester's politics so far discussed, were the concern of the middle and upper classes of the town and its neighbourhood; the few poor men, who possessed the franchise as freemen of the pre-1832 borough, never acted as an independent force and were the appendages of one or other of the two parties of the political establishment. Yet many Colcestrians were poor, voteless and, for the early part of this period, alienated from respectable society and orthodox politics. The tension thereby created could not fail to affect powerfully, if indirectly, the attitudes and policies of those who ruled the town. Sometimes an impression was received that many thousands of the poor of Colchester and rural north Essex were deeply disaffected, when, for instance, 3,000 people attended the 1838 Chartist rally in the High Street, when the Tendring Hundred farm workers set up a trade union within a couple of years of the transportation of the Tolpuddle labourers or when Colcestrians could see from North Hill the incendiary fires on farms at West Bergholt or Great Horkesley. To people who were comfortably off, such manifestations seemed to call for the stern régime which the Conservatives were more willing to offer and did indeed urge at the time of the so-called Newport Chartist Rising of 1839. The Liberals claimed to be the more effective defenders of order and property because their reasoning approach to thoughtful working-men and their readiness to make some political concessions would in the end prove more persuasive than political repression. However, since they could be shown to have been the instigators of the earlier Reform movement, from which Chartism was thought to have originated, and since they still professed attachment to minor political reforms, it was plausible for Sanderson, the Conservative candidate, to state at the 1847 election that he was going to Parliament to "defend the citadel of the con-stitution against Whigs, Radicals, Repealers, Chartists and Socialists". In face of such attempts to blame them for Chartism, the Liberals disasso-ciated themselves from the Chartists; J. B. Harvey's newspapers in 1839–41 contained frequent reproaches against the Chartists and proposals for weakening their influence.[36]

These effects upon the policies and prospects of the two parties were the superficial aspects of Colchester's divided society. There were also undercurrents deeper and more powerful than the study of official politics can reveal. Even in this market town of Colchester the social crisis was acute, its solution as urgent as it was difficult. Both Conservatives and Liberals, indeed all people of property and position, could not fail to be concerned, sometimes preoccupied, with the problems of controlling the poor in those years of economic stagnation, deprivation and unrest, when the cloth trade had ceased, the barracks had been dismantled and the sur-viving market-town trade was in deep depression through the post-War agricultural slump. In addition, rapid population growth was making control still more difficult, the geographical segregation of the classes was beginning — the Lexden Road area was now being developed — and the whole working population saw in the New Poor Law a heartless, calcu-lated decision by the well-to-do to discipline and subject them. The con-sequent resentment of the poor became a source of continuing concern, especially when the newspapers carried alarming accounts of social revolt from places all over Britain. In Colchester dozens of speeches in these years at charitable societies, school anniversaries, church and chapel gatherings, showed in various ways the prevailing anxiety of the well-to-do about the disaffection of the poor, the indifference of many of them to religion, the prevalence of crime, their drunkenness and supposed self-indulgence, the street-corner loitering, prostitution and numerous other indications that the values and approved way of life of Victorian England were being widely disregarded among the classes constituting the majority of its population.

The basic method of controlling the poor remained that of punishment under the law. Those appearing at Colchester Quarter Sessions were mostly poor and the charges were mostly concerned with theft. Until the strengthening of the borough police in the late 1830s, punishments were very harsh. The following sentences were passed at the January and April Quarter Sessions in the tense year of 1832, when the old Corporation, from whose Select Body the magistrates had been drawn, seemed likely to be abolished as soon as the Reform Bill should become law:

Conviction	*Punishment*
Two men, stealing calico sheet	21 days in Borough Gaol
One man, stealing beaver hat	14 days in Borough Gaol
Two men, stealing 2 tea trays	one month in Borough Gaol two months in Borough Gaol
One man, stealing 9 lb of mutton fat	2 months in Borough Gaol
Two men, stealing 3 leather shoes	14 days in Borough Gaol
One man, not assisting constable, when asked	21 days in Borough Gaol
Boy, 12 years old, stealing 6d.	7 days in Borough Gaol
One man, assaulting constable	2 months in Springfield Gaol (including 1 month's hard labour)
One man, stealing pieces of iron	1 month in Springfield Gaol
Three men, stealing iron from a foundry	2 months in Springfield Gaol (1 month's hard labour, 1 month's solitary confinement)
Two men, stealing 29 pairs of second-hand stockings and a pair of boots	7 years' transportation
One man, stealing 3 pairs of shoes	7 years' transportation
One man, stealing tea and tobacco and obtaining groceries by false pretences	14 years' transportation
One man, stealing groceries, cloth, money	14 years' transportation

In every case of imprisonment in the Borough Gaol, the convict was also whipped, but this punishment was no longer inflicted in public as had often happened a few years earlier.[37] At the April Quarter Sessions in 1836, seven years' transportation was imposed upon a woman for stealing clothes from her master, a man for the same crime, a man for stealing a saddle, a man for stealing a tame rabbit, two men for stealing some tilting attached to a cart and a man for stealing a 5s. leg of mutton. Fourteen years' transportation was a girl's punishment for stealing two gold rings and a pair of earrings. There were also sentences of imprisonment and of hard labour, but only one of whipping. On another occasion a girl who had left the silk factory for a life of prostitution was condemned to fourteen years' transportation for stealing 12s., the severity probably being due to her "effrontery" throughout the trial.[38] Comments made by the Bench and the calculations on which sentences were apparently based make it clear that the courts were being used not only to punish individual offences but also to inculcate obedience and respect towards authority and the values of respectable society; the harsher sentences were often imposed, it would seem, because the accused had offended before and had not been deterred by punishment from offending again. It is hard to deny that in the process people suffering from want and neglect were sometimes being punished for offences against property, in which they themselves had no share, under laws which they were deliberately prevented from having the right to make or to change. Those convicted seldom voiced their feelings, were inarticulate when they did so and were rarely quoted in the Press, but, from what little evidence there is, they certainly seem to have felt that the society against which they had offended did not in any way belong to them or their kind.

Punishment by the law was not the only instrument of control available to deter insubordination. The power of employers to dismiss, in the age of the New Poor Law and of economic insecurity, was just as potent and it affected the whole employed population, causing the most independent-minded to think hard before risking notoriety. Yet lasting security could not be founded upon such crude deterrents alone. The most effective way to counteract discontent would have been to pay better wages, provide employment and give adequate unemployment relief, but policies directly opposite to these were often adopted. So, in the absence of proper remedies, the well-to-do increased their charitable work. Individual acts of charity were increasingly forthcoming and were deliberately reported in the Press so as to encourage emulation. At Christmas-time readers would not infrequently come across reports like these:

> "Last week Sir G. H. Smyth, Bart., with that regard for the comforts of the poor which peculiarly distinguishes him, distributed four sheep among the most necessitous at Berechurch."
> "W. Hawkins, Esq., with his accustomed liberality, distributed 750 lb of meat to the poor of St. Giles and St. Botolph's parishes."[39]

Subscriptions would be raised at times of special hardship, such as for a coal fund in the depth of winter in 1838, the announcement of which expressed the hope that "the call will be generously responded to by those who have the ability and disposition to diffuse comfort around them, so that the hearts of the poor at this inclement season may be cheered, and they be encouraged to submit to the portion assigned them by Providence with resignation . . . With kindness much may be done, even with the ungrateful." Thoughtful advocates of charity, however, wanted its distribution to be less casual and more carefully planned, so as to have the greatest possible social results. So they pressed successfully for greater support to be given by the well-to-do to the organised network of permanent charitable organisations which had come into being in the town from the time of the French Revolution. Their arguments were generally accepted; for instance in the harsh winter of early 1845 the Mayor deliberately delayed the launching of a special coal fund so as not to damage the parallel work of the Provident Labourers' Society. Horatio Cock, a surgeon who had married into the prosperous banking family of the Rounds, after an early life of comfort and affluence became a most generous, self-sacrificing dispenser of personal charity, but in the end was distributing his wealth largely through the organised evangelical, educational and charitable societies, to which he left legacies amounting to £35,000.[40]

The second point stressed by the theorists of charity was the insufficiency of a mere financial subscription. They saw it as essential for more and more individuals from the middle and upper classes to become directly and personally involved in administering the grants made by the main organisations, if the poor were to see with their own eyes that the more fortunate were really concerned about the less fortunate. When at the height of the Chartist revival of 1842 the Colchester Provident Labourers' Society was formed at a gathering of the most eminent local Conservatives, the *Essex Standard* noted with approval that the clergy, instead of acting as the main collectors of the labourers' subscriptions, were going to draw upon the help of "a sufficient number of persons, in their respective parishes, either to collect or to receive the weekly payment. By this means a communication will at once be opened between the higher and lower classes of a parish, and a medium of kind and confiding intercourse be established." The same paper also referred with approval to a recent book which maintained that "if the rich give their time to the poor instead of their money, they part with a commodity which the poor will see is valuable to the giver and consequently esteem the more, as it implies an interest in their prosperity".[41] One successful method of involving the well-to-do personally in charitable work was the Colchester Lying-in Charity's practice of helping only applicants recommended by one of its subscribers, who were allowed to claim such help for a number of applicants proportionate to the amount of their subscription. A similar practice was adopted by the Colchester and Essex Hospital which normally accepted only patients recommended by its private subscribers. Thus quite a few middle-class ladies and gentlemen were brought into a personal relationship with one or more poor families and a patron-client system came into being which must greatly have strengthened the dependence of the poor.

Many of the charitably minded did become active social workers, setting aside any reluctance to work with people of opposite politics or denominational attachments. For instance, in the work of the Ragged Schools, set up in 1854 in a building in Osborne Street to which young people were brought in from the streets to learn or relearn elementary literacy in a religious atmosphere, Mrs. Round, an Anglican and a Conservative, readily co-operated with J. A. Tabor, a Liberal and a Nonconformist, no small achievement at this time. Each of them took their turn with other prominent citizens at the gruelling work of teaching one of the classes. There were other cases of inter-party and inter-denominational collaboration. J. B. Harvey was for many years secretary of the Labourers' Provident Society, which had been mainly founded by Conservatives. In the supervision of the Hospital the Liberal leader, James Wicks, worked alongside the Tory John Lay, long secretary to the Hospital Governors. Similar bi-partisan co-operation, together with a high degree of personal involvement, was in evidence at an immense gathering of the young workers of the town, at which Tory and Liberal ladies in apparent accord presided over the supper tables and kept good behaviour among their guests.[42]

The girls in the St. Peter's Street factory became the special concern of Mrs. C. G. Round, who entertained them annually at her house, Birch Hall, with homilies and tea-drinking, and also visited them at the factory, where on one occasion they presented her with a Bible. The practice of employers giving their workers an annual treat also grew steadily. The proprietor of the small silk firm, in Military Road, sent his employees to the Great Exhibition in 1851 and on later occasions to Ipswich and to Walton. Moses' clothing factory was among the earliest firms to provide a summer outing. Others chose Christmas-time. Joseph Grimes, one of the largest-scale builders in the town, regularly gave a breakfast at this season. In 1866, for instance, the *Essex Standard* reported that "between 60 and 70 of the workmen sat down to a substantial breakfast provided by their much-respected employer, who presided, supported by several friends. The customary loyal toasts were heartily responded to, after which Mr. Grimes forcibly set before his men the benefits arising from unity between employer and employed, and the evils consequent upon the union of employed against the employer."[43]

A third principle, to which the town's leaders attached much importance, was that of persuading the recipients of charity, wherever possible, themselves to contribute towards the cost, in the hope that they would thereby learn financial self-reliance, commit themselves to promoting the country's economic prosperity and political stability, and identify themselves with the aims of their patrons. Thus the purpose of the Provident Labourers' Society, started in 1842, was to help labourers to buy themselves coal and clothes by means of a weekly contribution of one penny, augmented by a bonus derived from the subscriptions of well-to-do supporters; in its first three years of existence, according to the Mayor, 1,300 families received benefit from it. Similarly, certain old people with an annual income of £25 or less, by having paid a guinea a year, became eligible for a vacancy in the pleasant Providence Place, built east of the Balkerne Gate in 1837 by the Provident Asylum Society, where they also received a chaldron of coal annually and a small money allowance. This building was intended to provide artisans or small shopkeepers and their wives who had fallen on bad times with a refuge in their old age and, significantly, it stood about a hundred yards away from an almost contemporary institution, the Union workhouse, which offered an altogether bleaker lodging to those who had not been so prudent in their working lives. Perhaps the most popular self-help organisations were the Friendly Societies, the aims of which were entirely acceptable to those engaged in charitable work, provided that the societies could be made part of the approved network. The difficulty was that many workingmen preferred to join the numerous public-house benefit clubs, the financial shakiness of which seemed to be compensated for by their good-fellowship and freedom. The town's leaders lost no opportunity to publicise any failures or sharp practices that came to light in these clubs and strongly endorsed, as an alternative, the carefully supervised Essex Provident Society — "there was no public house business about it", said one of its Colchester advocates.[44]

Charitable aid was eagerly sought after in those years when acute poverty and insecurity of employment beset the great majority of Colchester households, especially after 1834 when the able bodied could only be given public assistance if they and the whole of their families entered the Union workhouse. Some impression of the influence exerted by the charities may be obtained from the record of two of the several societies which touched directly, if inexpensively, the intimate lives of many working-class families. In 1839 the Lying-in Charity was administered by a committee of ladies, the wives of leading men from both political parties. In that single year it gave help to 260 poor women in childbirth, a figure reached in almost every year in the preceding and succeeding decades. In twenty years, therefore, some 5,000 applications were granted, the cost averaging £1 per case, so that several thousand poor families must have received skilled help and other assistance on one or more occasions of anxiety and danger. It was calculated by one supporter that the gratitude of the husband would be secured by this service as well as that of the wife:

> "I don't know any occasion in which a man is or ought to be, more grateful for assistance than when the partner of his life lies under Nature's sharpest trial, exposed to sufferings increased by the privations of poverty, often miserably deficient in the comforts and even the necessities of her situation — it is then that the Lying-in Charity, like a ministering angel, steps in and supplies what is more valuable than gold".

Another influential body was the Female Friendly Society, which was maintained entirely by well-to-do subscribers "for the relief of the industrious, afflicted and aged poor, particularly in those cases that relate to female affliction and distress". From 1815 to 1842 it gave assistance, mainly gifts of clothing, in 22,965 cases.[45] There were a number of other charities which added to the lines of dependence of the poor upon the affluent; for, as Cromwell's *History of Colchester* claimed in 1825, "perhaps no town in England, in proportion to its size and population, has originated, and at present supports, so many benevolent and charitable institutions as Colchester".[46]

Victorian society's defenders were too far-sighted to rely solely on palliatives. In the longer prospect, social stability required a new generation of working people, ready not merely to accept but to uphold the approved way of life. The children of the poor comprised so large a part of the population that they needed close and sustained regulation; in 1851 nearly a half of the town's inhabitants were under twenty-one and over a third were under fifteen years of age. The under-fifteens were not yet subject to the economic discipline which controlled those in employment,

and special measures were called for to bring them within control. With
this object in mind, the organisers of charity undertook that expansion of
elementary education which by 1870 had drawn in some three-quarters of
the town's children. For the youths, and for any adults willing to be enrolled, there was established the network of adult education so frequently
noticed in the contemporary press. In this field there was disagreement
about methods between Liberals and Conservatives. J. B. Harvey in his
Liberal weekly advocated "wholesome" adult education as the best
means of defeating militant Chartism:

> "These are not times in which it is safe for nations to repose
> on the lap of ignorance. Tranquillity may have been form-
> erly insured by the absence of enlightenment; but that
> season is past. Everything in the social condition an-
> nounces the approach of a great crisis, for which nothing
> can prepare us but the diffusion of wholesome and sub-
> stantial knowledge among the people."[47]

So Colchester Liberals promoted the Mechanics' Institute, not only
because it would assist workingmen "in finding out by their intellectual
importance the means of forgetting their worldly inferiority", but also
because, by hearing the right lectures and reading the right periodicals,
they would see that their interests lay in supporting the new economic
system rather than in rebelling against it. Conservatives and Anglicans,
however, mostly felt it inadvisable to rely upon the teaching of political
economy and similar subjects in order to promote sound knowledge and
virtuous behaviour. A sermon in St. Peter's on the anniversary of Colchester National Schools put this forcibly:

> "I cannot but think that the support of good government
> and good order on the part of the people, to whom it is
> now in good measure confided, is not so likely to come of a
> rational investigation of the theory of government and of
> the advantages of order, as of a *religious* conviction that
> government 'is ordained of God' and that 'He is the God
> of order'. I cannot but think that . . . a severe, however
> wholesome law, for instance, would be more likely to be
> received with forbearance because the Bible, they know,
> encourages submission and promises a blessing to the
> 'meek' than because the principles of the economist may
> be found to recommend it to their good sense. I should
> have more hope of teaching the poor man contentment
> with his condition, by reminding him of the text that 'the
> poor shall never cease out of the land', that the 'poor we
> are to have *always* with us', as though such were God's
> decree; or again of that other text, that the 'poor are
> chosen of God, to be rich in faith and heirs of the kingdom
> which he has promised to them that love him', as though
> God had precious things in store for them, than by dwell-
> ing ever so long and so learnedly upon a common benefit
> of a diversity of ranks. I should have greater confidence in
> a poor man's honesty, who founded it on God's command,
> 'Thou shalt not steal', than upon the reasonableness of the

rights of property. I should have more trust in his chastity and sobriety when springing from his remembrance of the exhortation, 'I beseech you as strangers and pilgrims, abstain from fleshly lusts which war against the soul', than from his acquaintance with the physical ill-effects of ardent spirits or the social convenience of the marriage bond." [48]

The *Essex Standard*, however, without dissenting from this view, did recognise that such simple doctrine was not enough, that some working-men had "acquired an appetite for reading that must be satisfied". So it recommended the more thoughtful publications of the Colchester Tract Society for distribution to "those who would otherwise be led away by the pernicious pamphlets, political and irreligious, which are put into their hands by the evil-minded". [49]

There was a further form of defence against social disintegration. The great Victorian movement to enlarge churches and chapels, to build new ones and to bring about universal religious attendance was in part re-inforced by the belief that society would thereby be made so much the more secure. The *Essex Standard* believed that "by sending the Bible to every poor man's cottage, the further dissemination of the pernicious and infidel doctrines of those deluded persons called Chartists would be pre-vented". Both church and chapel increasingly emphasised the need for as many people as possible to participate in their evangelical work. This was partly due to the same considerations as the attempt to persuade the patrons of charities to help directly in the distribution of their bounty, but it also arose from sheer necessity, from the magnitude of the task of re-claiming for Christianity the growing mass of the town's poor. The Rector of St. James's said in his farewell sermon in 1850:

"I believe that there are at this moment nearly a THOU-SAND immortal beings in this parish, who are morally and practically, if not intellectually, as utterly heath-enish as those in heathen lands. It may appear incredible, but I hesitate not to affirm that there exists a dense mass of population in your midst, to which the zeal and intell-igence, the sympathies and courtesies, the energies and resources, of any individual Minister, have been, and must still be, found altogether inadequate, without the helping-hand of those around. I say this . . . with a view to . . . provoke the pious laity to 'come to the help of the Lord'." [50]

How effective was charity in creating gratitude, dependence and loy-alty? If the denominational schools are included, as they should be, with the directly charitable societies and the subsidised Provident Societies, there can have been only a minority of working-class families in the town not receiving some benefit at some time. The qualifications for assistance were thought by the poor to include attendance at a place of worship and regular despatch of children to school, just as their presence at a dis-reputable public meeting or as a defendant in the Courts was calculated to be a disqualification. The Blanket Society made its grants to "applicants who should be judged worthy". Grants of £3 were given to approved female ex-pupils of the Blue-Coats School who entered domestic service, "their best employment", provided that they remained in one house for a year and brought testimony of good conduct from their employer. Applicants for help from the Female Friendly Society underwent two tests, one by a subscriber who alone could issue a ticket of application, and a second by the member of the Society's executive committee who was responsible for the part of the town where the applicant lived.[51] The great network of charitable provision, linked to an establishment strongly entrenched in the Town Council, the law courts, the religious denominations and the places of employment, made up between them a massive concentration of power, against which radical workingmen had almost no chance of making an independent stand for any length of time. Colchester by the 1860s gave the appearance of an orderly, respectable, loyal and devout town. By that time the New Poor Law had been so successfully imposed that the poor regarded it as irreversible, Chartist rallies had become a memory, school attendance was rising, new places of worship were being opened. There could be rowdy scenes at the hustings, drunken crowds roaming the streets on Guy Fawkes night, fights between the soldiery and civilians in the public houses near the new barracks, and, in 1870, a really ugly business, the mobilisation of the mob against Josephine Butler by the drink and brothel trade, but, with the disappearance from Colchester of radical working-class politics and their subsidence nationally, these incidents were judged, and rightly, not to be manifestations of social disintegration, as they would have been in 1840, but to be regrettable survivals from the disorderly past and certain to be swept away by the onward march of morality, piety and respectability. While poverty, insecurity and other social evils still surrounded working-class life, the middle and upper classes of Victorian Colchester had, by a sustained effort of tireless and devoted service, gone a long way to create the kind of society which they wanted in their own interests and thought to be best for the whole of that society.

Party politics, women's rights, 1867–1914

The 1867 Reform Act, though its provisions would have been triumphantly welcomed by the Chartists twenty years earlier, evoked only moderate enthusiasm and produced only limited electoral change. The controversy accompanying the passage of the Act had had its origin in 1859, when an abortive movement had arisen in the town in support of a proposal to enfranchise £6 householders. The argument then turned on whether the Chartist challenge had sufficiently subsided and whether the country was prosperous enough for some of the town's poorer householders to be enfranchised. A Conservative speaker forecast that political reform would be followed by the redistribution of landed estates. A Liberal also questioned the wisdom of greater democracy in an increasingly industrialised Britain:

> "May we not all learn a lesson from the Builders' strike? The men engaged in these combinations, which have brought one important branch of business to a standstill in the metropolis, are soon to be invested with electoral

> power. The inevitable tendency of public opinion is in the
> direction of strengthening Democracy. What *sort* of de-
> mocracy is it to be? That country whose *proletaire* order —
> the class that has no property but is solely dependent upon
> masters and wages — outnumbers all the rest, cannot fail
> to be in constant danger of disorder if the issues of govern-
> ment are placed in their hands."[52]

The controversy subsided with the dropping of the 1859 proposals, but
was at once resumed in 1866 when a fresh Reform Bill was put forward by a
Liberal Government. An editorial in the *Essex Standard* criticised the Bill
on the grounds that it would, by enfranchising most workingmen, "enable
them at every election to swamp all other classes and return workingmen
to Parliament"; in that event Britain would probably take the same revolutionary path as France had done. In reply, J. B. Harvey reassured such
critics:

> "In those boroughs where the working classes were already
> in a majority, they were not found combining together to
> elect men of their own class, but rather to send those men
> who were best qualified to represent them in the House of
> Commons; and with an extended franchise, he believed
> they would find the working classes acting in harmony
> with men of intelligence and right principles".[53]

Colchester's participation in this Reform movement was not very widespread; all that the Bill's supporters claimed was that there was "deep
interest". Some leading Liberals abstained from their party's public campaign, but meetings were well attended and a pro-Reform petition num-
erously signed. When a Conservative government replaced the Liberals
and proceeded itself to take over the Reform Bill, Conservative
opposition in Colchester was reluctantly abandoned, so that the final outcome in the town was a subdued satisfaction.

The electoral results were not dramatic. After the 1832 Reform Act
some 1,100 men, 7 per cent of the town's population, had possessed the
franchise and, as more people had become £10 householders, the number
of voters had slowly risen to about 1,400, of whom only a quarter were
thought to be workingmen. As a result of the 1867 Act the electorate was
increased to 2,970, about 12 per cent of the population, and a larger proportion of these were workingmen than had previously been the case.
The Liberals expected to benefit from this change and they did win both
seats in 1868, though they lost one of these in a by-election in 1870. They
also saw advantage for their party in the introduction of the Secret Ballot
in 1871 — "when we have got that, we will carry all before us", said one of
their candidates — but they lost both seats in the election that followed.
Colchester was still a market town in which the presence of army officers
now reinforced the still dominant Conservative agricultural interests,
while industrialisation was far too limited yet to alter the balance.
Colchester remained a Conservative constituency in which many of the
new working-class electors, themselves dependent on the prosperity of
agriculture, were by no means Liberal. After the 1870 by-election, a Conservative paper wrote, "After all, we have only won back a seat
legitimately ours, one that we never should have lost".[54] Nor did they lose

it, except on one occasion, during the next quarter of a century. As their older electoral advantage diminished with the deepening of the agricultural depression, they were gaining as much as they had lost, by drawing upon the support of the military; the Liberals always contested the registration of soldiers and attributed their 1892 defeat to solid military support for the Conservatives.[55] In addition, the participation by soldiers in town life and the economic advantages accruing to the tradesmen from the presence of the Camp reinforced the current Jingoism to make the Colchester electorate more imperialist and more enthusiastically patriotic than most. In 1879 the Conservatives were laying much emphasis on their party's patriotism and the Liberals' lack of it. In 1886, too, the same feelings helped to make Liberal abstentions over Irish Home Rule more numerous than elsewhere. Among those supporting the Unionist cause at that time were Aldermen Kent and Goody, James Paxman, W. Daniell, Gurdon Rebow, Joseph Blomfield, Hugh Stannard and J. B. Harvey himself, all leading Liberals most of whom afterwards returned to their party. The wife of the defeated Liberal candidate described how "the question of Home Rule in a place like Colchester made ours a perfectly hopeless battle. If we had the Church against us before, we now had added to that a large and powerful body of Liberal Unionists." The Conservative majority was nearly doubled, compared to the election of the previous year after a contest so tense that one man died from excitement; it was all the more exciting because Colchester polled one day earlier than other boroughs and its result was consequently awaited by the national press as an indication of the general trend. Their defeat at this election and the desertion by some of their leaders left Colchester Liberals so weakened that they accepted the Conservative offer of a municipal truce which lasted three years. Meanwhile, the imperial cult became so widespread that even W. G. Blatch, once a Chartist Republican, could tell women Liberals how proud he was of the way in which the British Empire was bringing its blessings to such distant parts of the earth. A reporter wrote in 1900 that "Colchester's celebration of Mafeking will never be forgotten in the borough". That was an occasion when Colchester was doing no more than participating in the nation's joy, but military events, which elsewhere in Britain received only moderate attention, in Colchester often evoked the warmest enthusiasm.[56]

In spite of these difficulties, Liberalism, without making the quick gains expected from the 1867 Reform Act and the Secret Ballot, was growing into a much stronger force than it had ever looked like being between 1832 and 1865. The Secret Ballot caused few voters to switch their support from the Conservatives, but, by making bribery and intimidation ineffective, it encouraged a development towards a more enlightened form of politics from which the Liberals thought they derived most advantage. Political behaviour improved generally, party organisation largely replaced the old-style drinking-clubs, the standard of newspaper debate rose and as early as 1874 one editor could write that "the late election has been conducted in a spirit of fairness and mutual good feeling highly creditable to the borough".[57] As agriculture entered a depression, Colchester's industry grew rapidly. Most industrialists had not yet joined the Conservatives and were still supplying Liberalism with its leaders. The proprietors of the expanding engineering works, especially those who had ceased to depend upon supplying Conservative agriculturalists with machinery and had begun to produce new types of goods for a wider market, openly avowed their Liberal sympathies, including Thomas Catchpool, James Paxman, W. C. Stannard and Joseph Blomfield. Others to support the party at different times were the shoe manufacturers, J. Warmington, John Kavanagh and Samuel Knopp; S. S. Brown, proprietor of the silk-milk; the clothing manufacturer S. Hyams; W. W. Daniell, of the brewing family; Wilson Marriage, the Quaker miller; Thomas Moore, largest wholesale grocer of North Essex; William Butcher, wool stapler; T. S. Barrett, oil and colour man; James Wicks, wine merchant; and professional men like the lawyers H. S. Goody and J. S. Barnes and the auctioneers, C. M. Stanford and E. J. Craske. At an election rally in 1880 there was such a massive presence of industrialists on the platform that one speaker could say "Who were the great employers of labour in Colchester? ('Liberals.') They certainly would not find them to be Conservatives. Indeed, there was not a large Conservative employer of labour in the borough."[58] Until the 1880s such men had little opportunity of serving on the Town Council because of Conservative predominance there and they tended to enter public life by taking office on other authorities or in voluntary societies. Thomas Moore was an Improvement Commissioner and a Director of the Essex and Suffolk Insurance Society. H. S. Goody was clerk both to the Improvement Commission and to the Colne Oyster Company, a Hospital Governor and a Gas Company Director. The outstanding worker for public causes was the newspaper proprietor and printer, J. B. Harvey, who became chairman of the Improvement Commission, the Gas Company, Colchester Building Society and the Trustee Savings Bank, a Director of the Idiot Asylum and Auditor of the Hospital.[59] When he and other leading Liberals did gain membership of the Town Council, they at once constituted an able and experienced group. With modern industry temporarily on their side, the Liberals felt that theirs was the party most in tune with the spirit of this enterprising age. Their paper, the *Essex Telegraph*, sought to present an appearance consistent with this role. In answer to the Conservative *Essex Standard*'s claim that it "circulates among the very best classes in Essex", the *Telegraph* was proud that it had "by enterprise and pushfulness made its way amongst all classes".[60]

The nonconformists remained, in the words of a Liberal candidate's wife, "a powerful body and the very backbone of our party". In 1851 they were found to be almost equal in numbers to the Anglicans. Lion Walk Chapel, described by a Conservative as "that Colchester Radical House of Commons", supplied no less than forty Town Councillors up to 1900, all or almost all of them Liberals. When at the end of the century the Liberals won a majority on the Council, it was alleged that the behind-the-scenes director of their policies was, of all things, a book club, called the Milton, which, though including nonconformists of several denominations, was particularly associated with Lion Walk.[61]

Finally, from 1884 the Liberals were much strengthened by the increasing number of working-class voters. These men were far less dependent for their employment on market-town occupations than the artisans of 1867 had been. The leaders of the Co-operative Society and the trade unions mostly took the Liberal side, and some of them were active canvassers and propagandists among fellow-workingmen. They also constituted a pressure group within the party, working for the establishment of a Liberal Club open to all the party's supporters, and, despite opposition from the Liberal right wing, they won their point in 1884. The Club was first housed in the Public Hall at the north-west end of the High Street and subsequently found accommodation in a succession of buildings until it opened at the Headgate the purpose-built premises which it still occupies. The party held its large working-class vote by fighting elections on the new radical Newcastle Programme. When the industrialist, Weetman Pearson, later to become Lord Cowdray, first contested the seat in 1892, he proclaimed himself "a radical, in full accord with the Newcastle Programme, supporting Irish Home Rule, abolition of plural voting, payment of M.P.s, shorter Parliaments and the institution of Parish Councils". His answers to the Trades' Council's questionnaire secured him that body's official endorsement, causing the *Essex Telegraph* to call the contest "a workingmen's battle".[62] Most, but not all, Liberals now acquiesced in their party's new radical direction, though John Kavanagh, the boot manufacturer, transferred his support to the Conservatives at the 1895 election because, as he said, when faced by a strike of his skilled workers in 1892, he had received no support from his fellow Liberal Councillors.[63] In 1895 the Liberals were at last victorious. They held the seat until 1910 — after the 1884 Reform Act the borough had had only one seat instead of the previous two — and were generally in control of the Town Council as well, so that in 1902 a Conservative said sarcastically that "membership of the Liberal Club is the only essential qualification for a seat in the Council Chamber". Against the national trend the Liberals held the Parliamentary seat in 1902 and they did so again in 1906, for which in part they had to thank their able and wealthy champion, Weetman Pearson. Yet he was also partly responsible for the loss of the seat in 1910. He had then evidently lost interest in Parliament, which by 1907 he rarely attended; "it does seem a pity that Sir William should have persisted in claiming to represent Colchester, the only thing he is so obviously not good at", wrote the *Essex Standard*. Even so the party fought a spirited campaign, during which the largest indoor meeting in the town's electoral history was addressed in the Corn Exchange by one of the leading Liberals of the day, Winston Churchill. However, by that time Colchester Conservatives were on the way to recovering their former political supremacy. The town's industrialists were moving towards their side or at least away from the Liberals, the military vote was growing in strength to their great advantage and, according to the *Essex Telegraph*, they now commanded "the vast influence which the three breweries and 160 licensed houses in the borough were able to exercise".[64]

Up to 1914 the established parties still dominated politics, but two radical issues were at the same time forcing their way into public attention. One was the campaign of the Independent Labour Party to create a working-class party independent of Liberalism, the other was Women's Suffrage. The latter was not a recent issue in the town. It had even been considered in 1838 when the *Essex Standard* reported a northern Chartist's advice to women to participate in politics and to girls not to marry any man who was not a Chartist. The editor gave his comments in verse:

> "Women may influence great possess
>   But on certain conditions;
> One of them is — they must ne'er
>   Set up for politicians.
>
> Mothers, for Radicals who train
>   Their babes — not for the Lord —
> May live to reap in rebel sons
>   Their bitter just reward.
>
> Those maids, too, must expect to meet
>   The fate they well deserve
> Who all their smiles for Radicals,
>   And them alone, reserve.
>
> Not but you're welcome, luckless girls —
>   Quite welcome those to pet;
> For who a *Radical* would wed
>   That could another get."[65]

By 1867, when the second Reform Act inspired a national movement for limited extension of the suffrage to women, 132 Colcestrians signed a petition for presentation to Parliament by one of the town's M.P.s. The Colchester committee of this movement included the wife of a local gentleman and the proprietress of a dressmaking business.[66] From this time the idea of women's suffrage began to gain ground. In 1870 Josephine Butler, during her Colchester electoral campaign, heard a woman say at the close of a meeting she had addressed, "Ah, she's right . . . I'm sure I'll vote for her, whenever I have a vote". In 1874, when Mrs. Henry Kingsley, a relative of Charles Kingsley, spoke in favour of the Parliamentary vote for women ratepayers, who had already been conceded the municipal vote in 1869, the Mayor took the chair and endorsed the proposal. Conservatives and Liberals supported him, while stressing that married women and non-ratepayers must remain voteless. One of the few opponents was a Conservative who thought that public men should be able to return home to the soothing attentions of a non-political wife, though he also felt that self-interest would have inclined him to desire the enfranchisement of a sex which would vote predominantly Conservative. The meeting, which included many women, voted in favour of a petition to Parliament in support of the proposal.[67] Enlightened middle-class opinion now favoured some reform; James Hurnard wrote at this time:

> "The growing tendency of Christianity
> Is to raise women to the level of men.
> Why should not women sit in Parliament
> If men should think fit and proper to elect them?
> Their presence would at least promote decorum,
> And might conduce to wise deliberations.
> A dozen women such as I could name

I think would prove a blessing to the country,
I am for equal laws for men and women,
Fair play for all and favour for the weakest
But whether women have a vote or not,
Or whether working men enjoy the franchise,
May England ever be ruled by gentlemen."[68]

There was enough interest for the issue to be utilised, however facetiously, by advertisers. The following appeared in the local paper, "Women's Rights — a Wheeler or Wilson Sewing Machine — Nearly 300,000 Ladies have already obtained them".[69]

In 1870 occurred the by-election at which Josephine Butler intervened to bring to the fore the matter of the Contagious Diseases Acts. Several issues were involved, including legal discrimination against women and, indirectly, women's right to engage in political controversy. However, this startling event, so disagreeable to respectable Colchester, was speedily forgotten and the more orthodox movement for women's suffrage, such as it was, continued its spasmodic course. In 1884 the enfranchisement of many poor men by the new Reform Act caused a renewal of feeling in favour of the extension of a similar concession to middle-class women. The *Essex Standard* expressed this feeling very clearly when it wrote "The late Liberal Government thought, in their wisdom, that the period of enfranchisement had arrived for two million new voters, principally uneducated and uncultured, but that it had not come for one million of women householders, principally well educated and highly cultured". The paper noted that in Colchester 600 women were already municipal voters. Meanwhile, the modern suffragist movement had reached the town, for in 1886 "an immense gathering" in the new Corn Exchange, mainly female, heard its leader, Millicent Fawcett, advocate the claims of "duly qualified women". Such was the meeting's enthusiasm for a new Parliamentary petition that the *Essex Telegraph* would write "In Colchester, at all events, a very strong feeling has grown up in favour of Women's Suffrage".[70]

In the 1890s Colchester women began to be directly involved in public affairs and to throw aside some of the restrictions on their social life. They had by then their own branch of the Oddfellows; the University Extension centre at one time had a female chairman, a Conservative, and a female secretary, a Liberal; a Ladies' Golf Club was started and in 1895 there was even a ladies' football match on the Cambridge Road ground which, however, led the reporter to write "She ain't built for football".[71] The Primrose League had its Colchester 'Habitation' and, on its closure, a Conservative League of Women Workers was started. The Co-operative Women's Guild was founded in 1890 and the Women's Liberal Association in 1892. The latter was perhaps the most influential force in favour of women's rights. Liberal women had been busy at election time at least as early as 1847, when they were thought to have contributed considerably to their candidate's victory, and they had been praised for their zeal at a number of contests since then. Their new organisation enrolled over 200 members in its first year and a decade later had grown so large that it had branches in every ward. It met regularly to discuss women's rights and general political questions, sometimes reaching very radical

The west end of the High Street in early Victorian times, dominated by the 'Fire Office' of 1819 and with St. Runwald's in the distance. (see p.39)

A less genteel view, showing cattle-pens outside the 1845 Corn Exchange, just before their removal in 1863 to the new Cattle Market. (see p.45)

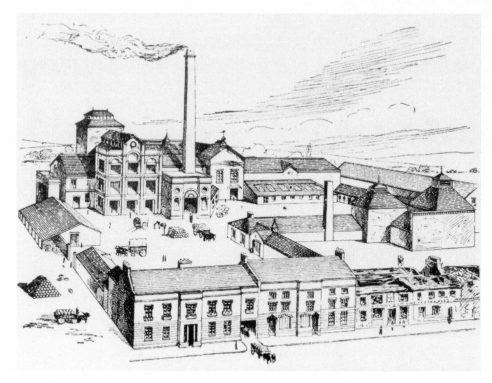

One of the town's few industrial plants in mid-Victorian times, Charrington Nicholl's Brewery on East Hill, expanded late in the century from what had once been a 'bays factory'. (see p.22)

Knopp's 'Time Will Tell' boot factory in Portland Road, a pioneer of Colchester's belated industrialisation. (see pp.25, 27)

*James Paxman, Colchester's leading indus-
trialist and at one time the most influential
man in the town's government, seen here,
in 1897, during his second term as Mayor.*
(see p.67)

*Paxman's arms, combining a Liberal's
internationalism with a clever pun.*

*An artist's impression (1897) of the Davey Paxman foundry at Hythe Hill, during
the early years of expansion.* (see pp.31–32)

The old Moot Hall in the High Street, demolished 1843. (see pp. 45, 157)

The new Town Hall of 1844. (see p.45)

St. Runwald's church and Middle Row, standing in the middle of the High Street in 1857. The corner of the 1844 Town Hall can be seen on the left. (see p.160)

St. Runwald's in course of demolition in 1878, the last phase of the clearance of Middle Row. (see p.160)

Pages from the Poll Book for the Parliamentary election of 1830, indicating, as was normal in the open voting system of the time, how votes were cast for the three candidates, Harvey, Spottiswoode and Mayhew. (see p.73)

The Rev. T. W. Davids, youthful Minister of Lion Walk Congregational Chapel, 1841–74, evangelist and political Reformer. (see pp.85, 120–122)

The Rev. J. T. Round, at different times Rector of St. Runwald's, St. Nicholas's and All Saints', Rural Dean, and the man chiefly responsible for the building of St. Botolph's church. (see pp.153–4)

The Congregationalists' 'Round Meeting' in Lion Walk, which was replaced in 1863 by the present building. (see p.170)

St. John's church, built in Ipswich Road in 1863, one of the achievements of Anglican evangelicalism. (see p.170)

The grandiose scale of the Victoria Hotel and the heavy traffic depicted in this lithograph reflect early hopes of a new-found prosperity to be derived from the coming of the railway. (see p.14)

The Theatre Royal in Queen Street, photographed in 1915, just over a century after its opening and three years before its destruction by fire. (see pp.152, 171–2, 175)

conclusions; in 1893 one meeting was reported with these headlines, "Colchester Liberal Women's Association. Crusade against the House of Lords. Trenchant Speeches. Reform of a very Radical Character or Revolution." With trade union support, the Association won four seats on the Board of Guardians in 1893 and 1894. Some of its members were already trying to organise tailoresses and other women workers into trade unions. It was very active in support of the Central Council for Women's Suffrage, to which it affiliated soon after that body's foundation.[72] The Conservatives included some determined suffragists, too, and, when the Colchester branch of the National Union of Women's Suffrage Societies was formed, it included among its members Mrs. W. G. Benham and Mrs. Hunt, both Conservatives, as well as the radicals, Mrs. Alderton and Mrs. Patricia Green; the Socialists were represented by Dr. Ruth Bensusan-Butt. The branch sent a deputation to the Town Council and persuaded it to vote, by twenty to three, in favour of a measure of women's suffrage. It was strong enough to hold off the challenge of the militant suffragettes when they attempted to gain a foothold in Colchester from their base in nearby Clacton. "The Suffragette Invasion. Remarkable scenes at Colchester. Street Meeting Rushed" were the headlines, when four good-looking middle-class ladies trundled a barrow, labelled "Votes for Women", along the High Street and attempted to hold an open-air meeting. There was an attempt to upset the barrow and the women speakers on it, but the press agreed that the opposition was jocular and the crowd not unsympathetic; at meetings on the same day in St. Mary's schoolroom and the Co-operative Hall the support was quite strong. However, this event occurred in 1908 before the militant campaign was at its height. There seems to have been no breakaway from the existing suffragist body which continued a steady campaign up to the outbreak of war, holding large propaganda meetings, running a Suffrage Shop and maintaining pressure on the Conservative M.P., Worthington Evans, to support the various pro-Suffrage moves in Parliament. Despite lack of any firm success, the movement had a long-run importance, precisely because its supporters were obliged to take up positions of prominence in public life in pursuit of their cause. It was quite an impressive sight when in July 1913, leading ladies from the Liberal and Conservative parties, the I.L.P. and the Co-operative Guild, after giving overnight hospitality to the East Anglian Suffragist Pilgrimage, escorted the marchers in a solemn procession up Lexden Road on their way to London.[73]

Between 1900 and 1914 Colchester's politics were never more varied nor more vigorous. Both the main parties ran active ward associations, special women's branches and youth organisations. The I.L.P. was smaller, but even more energetic in its day-to-day activities. No party could ignore the mounting determination of the suffragists. Elections were less violent and less corrupt than before but quite as enthusiastic and noisy. At the 1906 election the crowds were so boisterous that some shopkeepers put up their shutters on polling day. This was the "Hardest Fight on Record. A Battle of Posters and Motor Cars", according to the *Essex Standard*. The Conservatives used forty-one motor vehicles, the Liberals nearly as many, and the 92 per cent poll was attributed to the unprecedented efficiency of the parties' electoral machinery.[74] At different times National Insurance, Irish Home Rule, Free Trade and other great issues brought thousands of people to mass meetings to hear speeches, often of a high standard. The deep interest and the partisan fervour were showing no signs of weakening when in 1914 the outbreak of war caused a temporary intermission.

CHAPTER V

Working-class Movements

Early years

Colchester's working-class movement probably had its origins in the clothworkers' struggles to protect themselves from the consequences of the decline that brought their industry to an end in the eighteenth century. In several respects they were well placed to take concerted action. Though working at home, weavers had identical wage rates and working conditions; two-thirds of the 1,600 weavers of 1707 lived close to one another in certain parts of the town, such as St. Martin's parish, Stanwell Street and Magdalen Street; as firms became larger and fewer, hardly any small masters survived and journeymen had no prospect of setting up on their own. Woolcombers, though less numerous than the weavers, were just as spirited, and their ability to organise themselves was shown every year in their colourful processions in honour of their patron, the mythical Bishop Blaize. The inn of that name was their resort, while the Weavers' Arms was one of several serving the weavers; even the minor trades of Beaters and Roughers had their own favourite inn bearing their joint name. The full extent of organisation by clothworkers cannot be known, because it was inadvisable for them to confess to forming combinations. One permanent weavers' body known to us for certain is their Sick and Unemployment Friendly Society, which in 1700 charged a weekly contribution of 6d., but in 1715 they showed how effectively they could act by improvised methods when by very vigorous demonstrations they defeated what they saw as a concerted attempt on their employers' part to solve the industry's decline at the workers' expense. As this decline became deeper and their prospects bleaker, they continued to protect themselves by various methods, such as petitioning in 1749, a threatening letter in 1762 and a strike in 1791. Their struggles came to an end only with the complete collapse of the industry at the onset of the Napoleonic Wars, when the clothworkers themselves disappeared from Colchester's history.

What is of interest here is whether the clothworkers' solidarity inspired parallel feelings among the town's other skilled trades. It seems likely that the particular activity which clothworkers handed down to the craftsmen of the next generation was the maintenance of Friendly Societies. In addition to the Sick Society already referred to, there were at least two other weavers' 'clubs', each meeting at an inn. At the end of the century twenty Friendly Societies were registered in the town and there is reason to believe that these included large numbers of artisans among their members.[1] Some societies may have had trade union functions as well as offering social benefits. In 1785, for instance, the town's shoemakers sought to exclude from their trade any lads who had not served their apprenticeship, and the method they chose was to declare their intention of taking legal action through the agency of their "Friendly Society". In 1812 Essex Quarter Sessions, the licensing body for Friendly Societies, refused recognition to the Colchester Subscription Society of Carpenters and Joiners, probably because its rules were more appropriate to a trade union; during that period of the Combination Acts such subterfuge was advisable.[2] In spite of these Acts, however, some combination occurred when the situation was favourable, as it was briefly in tailoring. The officers stationed in the neighbourhood during the War often ordered expensive uniforms from local tradesmen, and the journeymen tailors used their improved bargaining position to gain an increase in wages. Their leader, James Carter, claimed that this success came from his having persuaded his fellows to discard the methods of militancy for those of polite negotiation. He also refers in his autobiography to his comrades' growing interest in Reform politics, which in post-war years were to implant strong democratic sympathies among local artisans.[3] There was little scope for independent working-class political activity within the main Reform movement, which in Colchester, as in most other towns, was firmly under middle-class leadership, but the aspirations then aroused and the intermittent attempts at trade union organisation combined to create among thoughtful workingmen in Colchester the attitudes and expectations which gave a ready welcome to the youthful Chartist movement of 1838.

The Reform Act of 1832 was a disappointment to many Colchester workingmen who had expected to be given the vote when Reform triumphed, and they were not reassured when, after municipal reform in 1835, the new Liberal majority proved to be as self-seeking as their predecessors. The Whig Government's enactment of the New Poor Law filled Colchester's working-class leaders with disgust and bitter hostility. The first outcome was a temporary revulsion from politics and a brief outburst of militant trade unionism. In 1834 Robert Owen's Grand National Consolidated Trades Union, the most famous members of which were the Tolpuddle Martyrs, inspired the formation of a number of branches in the town. The alarm caused among the town's rulers is evident in the following report which appeared in the *Essex Standard*:

> "We are sorry to learn that the emissaries of these unconstitutional associations have been at work among the mechanics of the town, who have established provincial branches here, to co-operate with the parent Societies in London, the sole object of which is to organise an odious tyranny by the workmen over their masters, the public. We rejoice, however, that it is in contemplation very shortly to call a meeting to counteract these illegal combinations, when it will be proposed to pass a determined resolution not to employ any tradesman who allows a Unionist to work for him."[4]

The Liberal paper, the *Colchester Gazette*, was no more tolerant; it denounced "this fallacious conspiracy" and declared its confidence that "the good sense of the mechanics" would defeat it.[5] The strength of the unions in the town must have been considerable because the press continued to vilify them. The *Essex Standard* declared:

> "The Trades Unions have for their avowed object the universal combination of the working classes against their employers and, in short, to invert the natural order of

things, by making the master obedient to the servant, and the Legislature and the Government the passive tools to register and enforce the enactments of the mob".

The same paper deplored the passing of the terms 'Masters and Servants' and derided the solemnity of the organised "operatives (as, in the mincing phraseology of the day, the latter are called)".[6]

This brief acquaintance with trade unionism — for it was little else — was not without influence on the formation of working-class opinion, but it left behind it no new permanent organisation among those trades not already associated with trade unionism. In any case, by 1835 Colchester workingmen were facing a threat to their social security which demanded a political reaction. The New Poor Law was implemented in Colchester, as elsewhere, in such a way as to impose stricter economic discipline upon the whole of the employed population by frightening them with the prospect that, if they became unemployed, they and their families could receive relief only under the most humiliating and forbidding conditions in the bleakest of institutions. There was no attempt at Colchester to prevent the building of the new workhouse in Balkerne Lane by the kind of direct action used at Ipswich, but the 1837 Parliamentary election was dominated by the issue of the New Poor Law, to a remarkable extent when it is remembered that, since the Reform Act, the Colchester electorate was predominantly composed of men who were unlikely to be subjected to the New Poor Law's rigours. At the hustings the crowd, which interrupted the speeches with shouts of "The New Poor Law", certainly included thousands of poor non-electors, but the election addresses and placards, which were specifically directed towards the chiefly middle-class electorate, also made the New Poor Law a central issue, presumably because the intense bitterness of the working-class population of Colchester was exciting both sympathy and alarm among the town's middle class. Even the tough veteran politician, Sir Henry Smyth, who was regarded by many workingmen as their enemy because of his harshness in dealing with agricultural workers on strike at Mile End in 1830 and his acceptance of the chairmanship of one of the new Boards of Poor Law Guardians, volunteered the promise, "I pledge myself that, if I am returned to Parliament, I will vote for every amendment that makes that Act less harsh to the poor". Being Tories, Smyth and his party found little difficulty in criticising this Whig measure, but such was the feeling among the electorate that the Liberal candidate, Todd, and the Colchester Liberal leaders, who had never hitherto raised their voice against the Act, suddenly began to deplore its "objectionable clauses" and, rather vaguely, to promise support for "every amelioration that is required to adapt it to that particular class for whom it was intended".[7]

Another indication of popular disillusion with Reform was the direct action taken against the Church Rate, when the Whig Government, contrary to expectations, failed to repeal it. A nonconformist ironmonger, having refused to pay this rate, had some of his goods seized for auction. The result was described as follows:

"The lots, consisting of copper-teakettles, a fender, etc., having been knocked down at very low prices, the

people, who had assembled in number about 400 or 500,
made a sudden rush towards the auctioneer, knocked him
down and, uttering loud cries against the Church and its
exactions, trampled upon and completely destroyed the
goods which had been seized and sold; after which they
quietly dispersed".[8]

Such militancy by so many people over so seemingly minor an issue
suggests a deep disenchantment. In addition, the methods of protest used
were of a kind much deplored by many Dissenting leaders, and their
employment was another indication of cleavage within the once united
Nonconformist-Liberal movement. However, it seems characteristic of
popular radicalism in Colchester that its deepest feelings were aroused by
a religious issue, while the New Poor Law, resented and feared though it
was in the town, failed to excite the violent opposition reported from elsewhere in the region.

Some of the artisans who had supported the Reform movement, disappointed though they were both with the provisions of the 1832 Act and
the departure from Colchester of their former champion, D. W. Harvey,
did not share this disillusion with politics and remained members of the
Reform clubs. One of these was William Wire, watchmaker and self-
taught archaeologist. In 1835 he took the lead in establishing an Independent Club to speak for "the humbler class of voters", which, by at
once enrolling forty-six electors and holding a series of critical discussions
on current issues, so alarmed the official Reform Club that it offered its
new rival joint control of the selection of municipal candidates and of the
formulation of policy. At the same time leading members of the Reform
Club sought membership of the Independent Club, allegedly in order to
disarm its challenge, and were accepted only on condition that they
should not be eligible for office. The degree to which the Independents
were ready to cut adrift from official Liberalism should not be overrated,
but it was probably they who arranged in Colchester a series of lectures by
an emissary of the Birmingham Political Union, the body which was soon
to launch the petition for the People's Charter.[9]

Chartism, 1838–50

In January 1838, the London Working Men's Association wrote to some
"old friends" in Colchester, inviting them to start a local society to work
for the radical measures of reform which were afterwards given the name
of the People's Charter.[10] The response from Colchester, as from other
towns in Essex and Suffolk, was enthusiastic. Within a few weeks of the
call the Colchester Working Men's Association was enrolling members,
holding regular discussion meetings and preparing to publicise its programme. By comparison with the Chartists of the industrial North, even
with those of Ipswich, Colchester Chartists were a moderate group,
partly because so many of them had had their political apprenticeship in
earlier Liberal movements, parting company with the latter when the
Independent Reform Club was started and when the Church Rate was
left unrepealed by the reformed Parliament. William Wire, G. F. Dennis
and John Verlander came from families long associated with D. W.

Harvey's campaigns, while John Coveney and Charles Francis, the W.M.A.'s secretary, seem to have been active in the Independent Club. A number were strong Nonconformists. Several were new voters under the provisions of the Reform Act, as occupying workshops or other premises with a rateable value of at least £10, such as Samuel Westoby who kept a shoemaker's shop and William Cranfield who was building up his cooper's business, while others like W. G. Blatch, a master shoemaker, already held the franchise as free burgesses. Artisans and small tradesmen predominated in the leadership. The Chartists, whose occupations are known, comprised six tailors, four shoemakers, two bakers, two cabinetmakers, and one each of the following trades: carpenter, cooper, brushmaker, harnessmaker, blacksmith, millwright, silversmith, ironworker, innkeeper, fruiterer, toy-dealer and flock-manufacturer. Colchester Chartism, though much less militant than that of Ipswich, resembled it closely in its social composition, except that the building trades, so prominent at Ipswich, were hardly represented at Colchester.

So moderate were the Colchester Chartists that their Association at first hesitated to commit itself to the full Chartist programme and confined its demands to an "extension of the suffrage", triennial Parliaments and the secret ballot. At the opening meeting William Cranfield, a self-made master-cooper, claimed the vote, not for everyone, but for those who, like the members of the Working Men's Association, had acquired "general knowledge and political intelligence". He thought Whigs to be little different from Tories, but had confidence in a government of Liberals. When in the same discussion an unnamed young man, probably W. G. Blatch, advocated a Republic, he was rebuked by other members and assured that the Queen, being an educated person, would prove an ally, not an enemy, to the advance of democracy. It was characteristic that the strongest criticism was reserved for local masters who obliged their apprentices to worship in ways that conflicted with their consciences. On a subsequent occasion three members were actually expelled because their employers had complained that they had left their work in an unfinished state in order to attend the Association's meeting. Self-education was from the start proclaimed as one of the Association's chief aims. Lectures were regularly given on such unexceptionable topics as the History of Commerce and National Education. Little was said that would have seemed out of place at the Liberal Reform Club. These cautious proceedings seemed to be justified by the steady rise of membership from the original hundred or so to a figure of 220. Attendances were high, often approaching a hundred.[11]

The non-Chartist public was obliged by the success of the Association to take sides. The editor of the *Essex Standard* issued a warning:

> "We seriously advise these people to attend to their respective occupations; they will by this course serve themselves much better than by troubling themselves with imaginary grievances, and interfering in questions of which they know rather worse than nothing. It was out of such an Association as this that the Glasgow cotton-spinning assassins formed their secret committees and made a scale

of rewards for the murder or mutilation of people who
were unfortunate enough to be proscribed by the club. We
again warn every uncorrupted working man to shun this
association as he would a path which might lead him to
crime and irretrievable ruin." [12]

The writer singled out for special criticism G. F. Dennis for allegedly
wanting to "top and tail the Queen and the Nobility", and William Cranfield for attacking "his betters" when he himself had been taken from the
workhouse, apprenticed at a £20 premium, clothed and set up in
business, all at the expense of a benevolent gentleman. Cranfield at the
next W.M.A. meeting replied that his only connection with workhouses
was to be born the son of the Copford workhouse master; a gentleman
had paid his apprenticeship premium, but this was in return for rescuing
his son from drowning; the gentleman had given him a pair of second-
hand trousers and lent him £2 for his business, since repaid; subsequently
his benefactor had demanded that he should vote Tory and they had
parted. The Liberal paper, the *Essex Times*, now firmly took the
W.M.A.'s side. It applauded Cranfield's struggle against poverty and his
manly independence. It was glad to note Colchester Chartists' denial
"that they had any intention of molesting property" and it commended
the Working Men's Association as worthy of support. [13] However, it
endorsed no specific reform other than the Secret Ballot. The paper's
editor was the energetic radical, J. B. Harvey, who had recently moved
from Ipswich where he had previously been apprenticed to the editor of
the *Suffolk Chronicle*, a Liberal paper also favourable to Chartism in its
early stages. Harvey's chief reporter was a personal friend of leading
Colchester Chartists and he conceived it his duty to report scrupulously
the words of the humblest workingman who lifted his voice at Association
meetings. The paper's sympathy with Chartism, according to Harvey,
antagonised a number of its moderate Liberal readers and led to the
paper's subsequent closure. [14]

At this time of Liberal-Chartist concord the Association's proceedings
remained unexceptionable. After a discussion of Education it resolved
"that this meeting considers the education given to the working-classes of
this Empire of a kind by no means sufficient for their instruction, being
for the most part confined to reading, writing and a little arithmetic,
whereas, at no great expense and at the same time, the children might be
instructed in the elements of a more useful branch of knowledge and
thereby trained to more industrious, prudent and virtuous habits, and
that, when the subject comes before Parliament, a petition be presented
from this Association". At another meeting William Wire recommended
adult education as a counterpart of children's education. The impression-
able age was a very young one, he maintained, and the parents' example
was therefore all-important. At a later age, too, the child must not return
from school to find the standards of conduct at home inconsistent with
those taught in the classroom. What was the point of parents teaching
Christian morality to their children, when they accepted bribes at elections? Parents should prefer the Mechanics' Institute to the pot-house.
"Let it be seen that the working classes, who meet for mutual instruction,
are no longer influenced by intoxication (cheers). Let me entreat all of

you to abstain from drunkenness. It may be asked, what are we to do with our time? I will tell you. There is a Mechanics' Institute in the town, open every night; the subscription is only 2s. a quarter and every member can go and read the newspapers and periodicals and have the privilege of taking home a book to read to his family. That would be a much better way of spending your time — in pursuit of knowledge. 'Knowledge is power' and you can command it; you would also be instructing your children and making yourselves better men for society, and doing everything to render you worthy of your franchise."[15]

Wire was at this time very much the Association's main source of counsel and inspiration. He it was who presided at a dinner at the radicals' favourite inn, the Angel, held to celebrate the Coronation, and gave out the toasts in the following order:

The People

The Queen and may she govern with equity

The Five Points of the Charter

National Education

D. W. Harvey and the Radicals of the House of Commons

Wakley and the Dorchester Labourers

Civil and Religious Liberty all the world over

Villiers, Molesworth and the Repeal of the Corn Laws

The Working Men's Associations of the United Kingdom.[16]

Wire and his friends seem to have ignored D. W. Harvey's coolness towards Chartism and to have entertained no suspicion of the anti-Chartist purpose that underlay the launching of the Anti-Corn Law League. They differed from their Liberal friends on no important issue other than the New Poor Law, which the *Essex Times* supported with minor reservations. The W.M.A. promised outright opposition to it. Young G. F. Dennis, now the secretary, and the moderate Cranfield joined in proposing thanks to the politicians leading the resistance to the hated measure, and W. G. Blatch delivered a well-researched attack upon conditions in the new workhouses.

By Summer 1838, the Association was campaigning for a massive rally at which to launch the petition in favour of the Charter. The *Essex Standard* at last gave generous space to Colchester Chartism:

"We observe that the fever of change is extending among the lower classes of this district. The Workies of Braintree and Ipswich have already adopted the Revolutionary Petition; and during the past week their brethren of Colchester have been evoked to a like demonstration by a placard, of which the following is a copy.

UNITED WE STAND   DIVIDED WE FALL

Working Men of Colchester

Arise and assert your Rights — Follow the Example of your Brethren of the North!

Come to the Meeting at the New Market Place, on Monday Evening next, September 10th, at Six O' Clock, to vote for the Birmingham Petition,

Demanding Universal Suffrage, Vote by Ballot, Annual
Parliaments, No Property Qualifications, Payment of
Members, and Equal Voting Districts.

GEORGE FREDERICK DENNIS, Secretary"

The *Standard* followed with its own version of some of the points of the
Charter:

"First, Universal Suffrage — That every houseless irresponsible vagabond shall have the same voice in the
councils of the country as the man of large possessions,
estimable character, and high standing in society.

Second, The Ballot — That every scoundrel shall have it
in his power secretly to blacken the fair name of the most
honourable of his fellow citizens.

Third, No Property Qualifications — That every violent
demagogue, who chooses to follow Lord Anglesey's directions, 'Agitate, Agitate, Agitate', may obtain a place in
the House of Commons, to the exclusion of those fitted by
education, and talent, and station, for its important duties.

And, fourth, Annual Parliaments — That every year shall
be branded with all the abominations of a contested election, rendered more vile, and more violent, in consequence
of their frequent recurrence."

The meeting was "the largest remembered in Colchester for many
years". The Mayor having refused the use of the Town Hall, it was held in
the New Market Place in the High Street, with the police held ready but
out of sight. Two hundred Chartists acted as stewards, successfully controlling a further 3,000 people, who stood around a platform bearing the
speakers and delegates from neighbouring Working Men's Associations.
The speeches, reported almost *verbatim* in the *Essex Times*, are valuable
evidence of the thinking of local working-class leaders at this time of
social crisis. The opinions expressed were representative of many of the
radical ideas that had enjoyed influence in Britain over the past fifty
years. Some of these were moderate enough. A brushmaker and a shoemaker repeated Liberal views on current politics and a Colchester freeman spoke from a Cobbett standpoint. W. G. Blatch again voiced
Republican sentiments and attacked the New Poor Law, Malthus and the
1832 Reform Act. The normally moderate Cranfield spoke with unusual
fire, stating firmly that, when the Charter was won, "every man should be
properly remunerated for his labour and should not be deprived of what
the Almighty had created him to enjoy. That Almighty Being did not
make one man rich and another man poor, one a tyrant and another a
slave. The wickedness of man had effected this . . . The rich man lived on
the produce of the poor man's labour." The most Socialist speech came
from the Ipswich delegate, who saw the Anglican Establishment and the
Corn Laws, which had been so strongly criticised by previous speakers, as
the inevitable consequences of class-domination; there was continued
conflict between economic classes; the landowners had once ruled but
had since been displaced by the merchants, who, having grown rich on the
National Debt and War contracts, were now wiping out the remnants of

the old regime; one day they would destroy the Church, the Corn Laws and the landowners, and in the final conflict the workers would have their chance to win power. At present, Whig and Tory were quarrelling about the spoils obtained from the exploitation of labour, which alone produced the nation's wealth. This injustice was upheld by the social influence of the rich and the armed force of the state, and only a General Strike could bring it to an end. "If we get our rights", he said, "we would establish the empire of reason over tyranny of fashion. We would make this world worth living in, because we are conscious that it can produce everything that is calculated to make us happy, free and social beings."

In so orderly and enthusiastic a meeting the few interruptions were quickly and peaceably silenced. The speeches had lasted four hours when the vote to adopt the Petition was passed with only one dissentient. The Liberal newspapers of Colchester and Ipswich expressed strong approval, while the *Essex Standard* argued that the tone of the meeting had been sinister and its principal participants ridiculous. The W.M.A. was elated. Many signatures to the Petition had been obtained at the rally and more were put on the copies subsequently left at public houses. New members joined at each meeting and the Association saw itself as dominating the political scene. A member wrote to the *Essex Times*, "The Tories are divided, the Whigs are quarrelling, the Sober Radicals are at a standstill; but the Workingmen, the Rational Radicals, the great unrepresented body, are united".[17]

A few weeks later the London Chartist leader, John Cleave, spoke at the Association's headquarters at the Angel, when "the room, and all the avenues leading to it from which a word could be heard, were filled to suffocation". He drew "rapturous cheering" for his attack on War and his plea of "no vote, no musket", he attacked upper-class education and urged, instead, a system of moral training and adult education suited to the circumstances of working-class life. "I say, good men and true, all you who are willing tonight to pledge yourselves solemnly to aid and assist the Workingmen's Associations in working out their regeneration, hold up your right hands. (Almost every hand was held up, and three times hearty cheers followed.) Now let us see who is on the contrary (Cries of 'not one' and tremendous applause)." An Ipswich Chartist maintained the revivalist atmosphere with an impassioned protest against War. "I have not the least doubts", he said, "that very shortly you will have the recruiting sergeants in Colchester to enlist you and send you to Canada to put down the Canadians; but let your reply be, 'No, we have to redress our own wrongs at home'. I entreat of you not to lift a murderous hand against the Canadians; they only ask for what we ask for, and because they ask for justice, they give them the dagger and the broadsword . . . No, do not take the shilling, there is murder, there is slavery in the offer."[18]

The excitement engendered by such large meetings and the expectations aroused by the forthcoming National Chartist Convention in London to some extent counteracted the Liberal orthodoxy of the Colchester leaders, by strengthening the small militant group around G. F. Dennis who, at a Chelmsford Chartist rally, warned against following the wealthy manufacturers and their Anti-Corn Law League. "I look upon wealth with a suspicious eye, because I cannot see that men of wealth can sympathise with the working millions . . . No longer put confidence in either faction; they are neither of them friends of yours. Combine together, lead yourselves (Cheers). You do not want leaders." As for the Corn Laws, "let us get Universal Suffrage and we will repeal them". Another member of the same group wrote to the press attacking the policy of Chartist-Liberal unity; "What do we care for these half and half reformers?" Though wishing to avoid insurrection, this writer declared he could see no alternative to revolution, if the authorities used the armed force of the state to suppress the democrats. At the same time a strenuous effort was made to collect money for the expenses of the National Convention.[19]

The pro-Liberal Chartists remained the stronger influence. One of them, Henry Downes, a blacksmith, gave a lecture to the Association advocating a straight Liberal programme, Disestablishment of the Church, an untaxed Press, lower taxation, the Secret Ballot, but, above all, Corn Law repeal which would bring "cheap bread, cheap government, plenty of employment and a gradual extension of civil privileges as education advances". Downes and his associates still admired D. W. Harvey, despite the latter's now obvious dislike of Chartism, and they persuaded the Association to send him a message of support when he resigned from government office. When Stephens and Oastler, national leaders of Chartism's militant wing, were given hostile treatment in the Press, Wire persuaded the Association to disassociate itself from them in a resolution that stated:

"This Society views with fear and alarm the means adopted by Messrs. Stephens and Oastler to draw the working classes from the duty they owe to themselves and their country, and take this method of expressing their repugnance at such proceedings, and couple with it their determination to use no other means but such as are more legitimate for the attainment of the object they have in view".

Reinforced by the approval given to this resolution in the *Essex Times*, Wire persuaded Halstead W.M.A. to declare for Moral Force, as the moderates termed their policy, and the Colchester Association also wrote to the newly formed Romford Chartists, urging them to shun violence and to open study groups as the quickest way to real democratic progress.[20]

This caution gained the moderates no credit. For, when the National Chartist Convention assembled and Chartist militancy erupted in other parts of the country, Colchester Liberals drew away from Chartism in some alarm. One of them wrote that "the determination to preserve security will unite Whig, Radical and Tory, who, merging their political distinctions, will unite in mutual defence against lawless ruffians and their deluded tools. Working Men's Associations must henceforth be regarded with suspicion, and their supporters must expect to be reproached as abettors in procuring anarchy and strife." Under pressure from many readers the Liberal Press withdrew its support and almost ceased to report Chartist meetings, so that much less is known about the weekly proceedings of the W.M.A. after the Spring of 1839. Much has therefore to be conjectured, but it would seem as if the pro-Liberal group withdrew from the Association, leaving the initiative to the more radical group.

The latter was not militant, but it was more willing to remain in unity with national Chartism despite the aggressiveness of the latter's so-called Physical Force wing. They worked hard to raise their share of the financial support needed by the National Convention and, in particular, rejected any idea of compromising over Universal Suffrage just to appease the Liberals. The issue arose in the Summer of 1839, when the Liberals held a public meeting to celebrate Peel's dismissal from office and the Chartists attended in some strength. Their former chairman, Cranfield, not only urged the Chartists present to support the Liberals and to join in congratulating the Queen on her recall of the Whigs, but urged them to agree to a policy of limited electoral reform. Uproar greeted these remarks, with a large part of the audience shouting "We will have the whole", "It is our right", and "It is injustice to withhold a fraction of it". The crowd were with the Chartists and the chairman reluctantly allowed two of their leaders to speak. One of them attacked the new Whig Ministry, while the other, G. F. Dennis, classed Whigs, Liberals and Tories together as equally hostile to the people's democratic rights. "Three Cheers for the Charter" were given as the chairman swiftly closed the meeting.[21]

For all its loyalty to the full Chartist programme, Colchester W.M.A., even after the secession of its pro-Liberal members, felt no sympathy for the revolutionary developments in Northern and Welsh Chartism. Nor was it in any position to carry out the National Convention's plan for a General Strike to force Parliament to accept the Charter; the economic composition of Colchester's Chartist membership made such a plan irrelevant. It decided not to act upon the proposal and, by a majority, even turned down the Convention's recommendation of a boycott of excisable articles. The *Essex Standard* made merry at the prospect of Lord Melbourne and Daniel O'Connell coming, cap in hand, to the Chartists to beg them, after all, to light their pipes — "The Town of Colchester and the Whig Ministry have each had a most fortunate escape", it declared. The Chartists were more at home in the petty controversies of Colchester's municipal politics, as when the new Hythe Bridge collapsed on 1 April. The Mayor, told about this as he sat in Court, was unlucky enough to think of the answer, "It is the First of April. It won't do." But the news was true, and all the more galling because Sir Henry Smyth M.P. had recently called the bridge "elegant, substantial, and in every way commodious" and because the Council had omitted to include any protective clauses in the contract. The Chartists passed a resolution "that as the possession of wealth has invariably been considered a proof of the possession of wisdom by those in authority, and the Town Council of this borough having already expended the enormous sum of Eleven Hundred Pounds in an attempt to erect a bridge over the River Colne at the HYTHE, and that attempt having failed, and there appearing no prospect of a new and better plan, this Association do volunteer to appoint a Committee from their own body, to draw up a plan for the erection of a substantial Bridge, which the FIRST DAY OF APRIL NEXT shall pass over without finding it in the river".[22]

Such parochial politicians had not the stomach to face the storm of condemnation that overwhelmed Chartism in November 1839 when the

Chartist miners and ironworkers of Monmouthshire marched upon New-port and were dispersed by a company of soldiers. The local Tories blamed the Whigs for their earlier leniency to Chartism. At a True Blue Dinner at the Three Cups the North Essex M.P., G. C. Round, pictured the crestfallen Attorney-General, who had earlier expressed confidence in the peaceful intentions of the Chartists, now travelling down to Newport and lecturing the Welsh Chartist leader, John Frost, with the words, "You naughty boy, I told them your conduct was good, but I must flog you, I must". The Liberals, on the other hand, professed to find the cause of the Newport 'Rising' in "High Church neglect and anti-Poor Law Malice, non-Education, dear bread, the want of food for mind and body".[23] Both sides agreed in discounting Chartism as possessing any further importance, and Colchester W.M.A., unlike its counterpart in Ipswich, succumbed to the overwhelming disapproval of Whig, Liberal and Tory and quietly disbanded.

After a year or so of recuperation Chartism revived in Colchester, having completely shed its pro-Liberal wing. William Wire returned to his old Liberal attachments and increasingly devoted himself to his archaeological work. William Cranfield also went over to Liberalism, to the busy life of Lion Walk Congregational Church and to furthering his own business. Others to secede were Henry Downes and John Verlander, who now gave much time to the Mechanics' Institute, itself a Liberal organisation. Even G. F. Dennis ceased to give active service to Chartism, though he remained a supporter of Universal Suffrage, a friend of leading Chartists and an adviser of the shoemakers' union. The seceders seem mainly to have been small tradesmen and artisans with their own bus-inesses and, though this class continued to supply Chartism with some of its leaders, in the 1840s journeymen artisans probably played a more prominent part than in the movement's early years.

The Chartists nationally had regrouped themselves in the National Charter Association, Britain's first working-class party, with a closely knit, well-organised structure of local branches. The Colchester branch was formed in Spring 1841, and among its members were some of the leaders of 1838–9, W. G. Blatch, Thomas Rawlings, a baker whose loyalty to Chartism remained steadfast until its very end, and members of the Clubb family. These men were master tradesmen, but alongside them are to be found a number of journeymen artisans not previously prominent in the movement. Very little is known about Colchester Chartism in these years, which may have been its most influential phase, because both of the local Liberal papers had closed down, while the *Essex Standard* resolutely ignored it. However, reports in the national Chartist press suggest that Colchester N.C.A. branch was a flourishing one, and this was consistent with its success in gaining signatures for a new Parliamentary petition in favour of the Charter. An early count showed that it had been signed by 2,250, double the number who had done so in 1838–9; at a time when the open ballot at election-time and the prevalence of unemploy-ment made men wary of exposing themselves to economic victimisation, it was no light matter openly to subscribe to a cause so vilified by respect-able opinion and so obnoxious to a majority of employers.[24] The outlook of Colchester Chartists had changed noticeably since 1838–9, having come much closer to that of the militant national leadership. In response to yet another Liberal invitation to compromise on the full demands of the Charter and accept a limited extension of the suffrage, the branch sent a message to the national committee to state that "at a spirited meeting . . . a whole hog resolution in favour of the Charter and No Surrender was adopted". When Dr. M'Douall, leading advocate of closer relations between Chartism and trade unionism, visited the town, he was adopted by the branch as its representative at the next Convention. The branch contributed to his expenses and, at a further public meeting, heard a report from him on his missionary work for Chartism.[25]

Once again came disappointment. When Parliament completely disregarded the three million signatures attached to the new Petition, there were widespread strikes in the industrial areas, one purpose of which was to force the enactment of the Charter, but the Colchester branch, with economic depression and unemployment all around them, could not command enough support for sympathetic action. When the strike failed, they did collect money to help the dependants of their arrested national leaders and, at least during 1843, continued to hold public and private meetings and to send financial contributions to headquarters. By 1843–4 public attention had passed to the unprecedented campaign of incendiarism being pursued by Essex and Suffolk farm workers. West Bergholt, on Colchester borough's northern boundaries, was particularly affected, and on one occasion, when a fire was raging on a farm in that parish, Colchester Chartists allegedly impeded the despatch of a fire engine from Colchester. A hostile account in the *Essex Standard* described their action as follows:

> "We regret to learn that while the Engine was waiting on North Hill, a spirit highly discreditable to the parties, who attempted it, was manifested. A few of that violent body called 'Chartists', by whose perverted minds the most lamentable occurrences are seized upon with avidity, if they can in any way be dragged in as auxiliaries to forward their political views, endeavoured to excite a feeling against the Corn Laws, shouting and hurra-ing at the progress of the flames, intimating that it was an affair of national interest, and that it was by such means that they could get the Corn Laws abolished, with other such expressions of a similar nature. Some attempts were also made to get upon the engine and obstructions offered to the firemen."[26]

Such reports are almost the only source of information about Chartism at this time and they are unlikely to be accurate. It is much more probable that the Chartists saw the fires as a protest against the New Poor Law, because that was a particular object of Chartist dislike and because the incendiaries, by selecting for attention the farms of Poor Law Guardians, also made clear which law they most wished to see repealed. However, Colchester Chartists had always opposed the Corn Laws and, when in the Summer of 1843 Richard Cobden announced his intention to visit the town for a debate with the Essex M.P.s on the subject, the *Essex Standard* said that he would receive the support of "the Chartist Club".[27] At this time the Chartists were also giving much attention to helping the trade unions, as Dr. M'Douall had advised them to do. Thomas Plummer, one of the younger Chartists, organised both Colchester and Maldon tailors into a new national union, which the national Chartist movement had recently established, and G. F. Dennis assisted the local Shoemakers' Society, the secretary of which was another Chartist, called Chapman.[28]

The N.C.A. branch probably lapsed into inactivity towards the end of 1844, but Chartism was soon to be revived in a new form. Its national leaders in 1844–5 launched a Land Company to buy estates for subdivision into smallholdings; workingmen were invited to buy shares in the Company with the prospect of being allocated one of the smallholdings as soon as they were fortunate enough to be chosen for this privilege in a periodic draw; meanwhile shareholders in each place were encouraged to form Land Branches, in which they could study the technical problems involved in their future occupation of a holding and could continue to work for the enactment of the Charter. The first Land Branch in the region was at Sudbury, but this was soon joined by others, including one at Colchester, until there were enough to form an East Anglian federation of branches. This revival and the deepening of economic distress combined to encourage Colchester Chartists to join the national movement in a third attempt to carry the Charter. The occasion for the refoundation of an N.C.A. branch in the town seems to have been the exciting electoral contest of 1847 when the Whig owner of Writtle Brewery, Joseph Hardcastle, defeated one of the borough's two retiring Tory M.P.s, Richard Sanderson. Hardcastle, as his election address clearly showed, was so opposed even to limited extension of the suffrage that he failed to satisfy some of his own Liberal supporters in the Colchester Reform Club, but this deficiency was forgotten as the election campaign was given apparent significance by Sanderson declaring himself an enemy of "Whigs, Radicals, Repealers, Chartists and Socialists". The strength and enthusiasm of the Liberal revival caused by the contest were such as to submerge Chartist doubts about the Whig candidate's democratic sympathies. H. S. Clubb, G. F. Dennis and Thomas Plummer, the leader of the tailors' trade union, spoke for Hardcastle, and in the canvassing, according to the Tories, "the Dennises and the Wire-Work" were especially prominent; the Chartists were warmly thanked for their work.[29] The N.C.A. branch had now been revived and was meeting regularly at its room in St. John's Street, with at least four of its former leaders again in the lead, Thomas Plummer, Jonathan Beal, Thomas Rawlings, who gave a lecture on the Land Scheme, and Benjamin Parker, who gave one on the History of Chartism. The secretary was the youthful, but very able, H. S. Clubb. A number of members had by now become active pacifists and internationalists, but this did not prevent the branch from passing a firm vote of support for Feargus O'Connor, still the symbol of Chartist militancy.[30]

Just as in 1838 when Chartism was riding high on popular support, a number of the more radical Liberals offered support, including the Quaker Thomas Barrett, and the minister of Lion Walk, T. W. Davids. The latter was deeply moved by the revolutionary events in France and, to the indignation of the *Essex Standard*, preached a sermon which included the following words:

> "It cannot be denied that the horizon of the World is critical in the extreme. New movements are in progress to which history supplies not the appearance of a parallel. I admit that issues — for I cannot honestly say Means — are thus far illustrious with high encouragement and brilliant hope. But those very issues have developed the multiform responsibilities for which I plead. ENGLAND WILL NOT, CANNOT, LAG BEHIND. Leader of the world for generations past, England MUST be leader yet. Here, too, power is descending to the MASSES: and it is the MASSES the Church of our day particularly wants to reach. The little that has been done, God has eminently blessed. THE NATION IS IN OUR HANDS."[31]

The Chartists, too, were insistent that the English counterpart of the popular advance on the Continent must be the enactment of the Charter. Being internationalists and pacifists, they were concerned that the British government, as at the time of the French Revolution of 1789, would seek by force to crush the progress of democracy abroad. Thomas Plummer told an Ipswich audience that such reactionary policies must be resisted and that only Universal Suffrage could preserve peace.

Disappointment followed even more swiftly than on the two former occasions of Chartist upsurge. The efforts made were considerable. H. S. Clubb succeeded in uniting the region's Land Branches and N.C.A. Branches into an Essex and Suffolk Union, which held meetings in villages to advocate Chartism and found new centres. The Union also collected signatures to a new Petition and planned to elect an Essex delegate to the National Chartist Convention to join the Ipswich delegate, already adopted.[32] When the Colchester Magistrates banned the adoption meeting, recourse was had to Donyland Heath, a few miles away, where the local squire was persuaded by his pro-Chartist son to authorise the event. There was a large attendance, but the two National Convention delegates, who were expected to be the main speakers, were unable to arrive in time. In April a large party took the train to London to join the march which was to escort the Petition to Westminster, causing some surprise to the *Times* reporter who saw so many of them emerging from Fenchurch Street station. Despite the authorities' show of force and Parliament's determination not to make the smallest concession, there was no immediate collapse of morale; one local Chartist was quoted as saying "What does it signify? The Charter must become law before long, for if Parliament does not grant it, the people will take it", adding that in the North the movement was strong enough to defeat the Government.[33] The Chartists now found the town's ruling circles increasingly hostile to them, and even their Liberal sympathisers tried to persuade them to modify their demands for Universal Suffrage. W. R. Havens, the Rev. T. W. Davids, J. B. Harvey and other radicals formed a branch of a new body called the People League, the programme of which included the Secret Ballot, Triennial Parliaments, and a Household franchise in preference to Universal Suffrage, the so-called Little Charter. They admitted that, in the words of one of their number, this programme meant that only 15s. in the pound was being offered to workingmen, but claimed that it represented the maximum concession that Parliament might be persuaded to grant. At a public meeting to adopt the Little Charter the N.C.A. failed to carry an amendment in favour of the full Charter, but nevertheless had a large minority of the audience on its side. The new body proceeded to launch a petition for the Little Charter, but soon afterwards disbanded.[34]

Though it continued to collect money to help dependants of the imprisoned Chartist leaders, the N.C.A. gradually broke up in 1849–50, leaving behind two unofficial groups. One of these evidently set itself the task of energising the advanced Liberals. It met regularly at the Essex Arms and in 1851 felt strong enough to invite the two Whig candidates to dinner at the Cups Hotel at its own expense. After some hesitation both guests declined, but the dinner proceeded without them. H. S. Clubb and W. G. Blatch were among the diners, and the latter made a speech repudiating his former Republicanism but insisting that universal suffrage must remain their aim.[35] Another group was also meeting regularly, composed of still-loyal Chartists, who in 1852 decided to levy themselves 1s. each to help the launching of a new Chartist weekly, *The People's Paper*. When this was first published, a number of orders were placed for it and articles from it were read aloud and discussed by the group. Its editor, Ernest Jones, travelled through the Eastern Counties in 1853, but by then Colchester Chartism was too weak to organise a meeting for him. However, a group of former Chartists remained in being and received occasional notice in the press as the 'ultra-radicals'. They attended a rally called in 1859 by the Rev. T. W. Davids and Thomas Barrett, whose reference to the Charter evoked loud applause, as also did the mention of Feargus O'Connor. The official purpose of this rally was to gain support for a limited Reform Bill, then being prepared by the Liberals, but the ex-Chartists carried an amendment for Universal Suffrage by a large majority. The latter were still in touch with the last national Chartist leader, the Marxist Ernest Jones, for whose Parliamentary candidature at Nottingham they collected subscriptions, and they even contemplated sending a delegate to the last Chartist Convention of 1858. When in that year Chartism itself came to a formal end, the Colchester group did not dissolve but turned to new activities, which proved to be the origins of the town's modern labour movement.[36]

Colchester Chartism was, like its counterparts in other non-industrial towns, firmly on the side of what was called the Moral Force policy. It knew nothing of the outbursts of political excitement and militancy which briefly characterised the movement in Wales and parts of the Midlands and the North, and it was not even in a position to take part in the proposed general strikes of 1839 and 1842 because the town contained no large groups of industrial employees; a considerable proportion of active Chartists owned their own businesses. It was noticeably less radical in views and tactics than was its counterpart in Ipswich, a town that, except for the presence of Ransomes' foundry where the workers showed no strongly pro-Chartist sympathies, was very similar in economic structure and social composition to Colchester. Yet Colchester Chartists were entirely loyal to the movement's official leadership, which was predominantly militant in tactics and inclined to favour radical social legislation. When in 1840–1 a few former 'Moral Force' Chartists tried to win the movement away from its existing militant leadership, they received no support at all from Colchester.

It is hard to assess the importance of the Chartist experience in Colchester's history. Being deplored and sometimes feared by respectable circles, for most of the time Chartism was ignored by newspaper proprietors who could not afford to offend well-to-do readers and advertisers. Its week-by-week meetings and discussions, its patient organising and its advocacy of democratic principles were unlikely, in any case, to give occasion for comment in the Press, though it was mainly in this humdrum activity and its unspectacular effect on sections of the public that Chartism's importance lay. Its immediate political gains were nil, its social gains not easy to evaluate. For instance, what was the long-run advantage for the poor, when respectable local society displayed fresh zeal in increasing charitable provision, including educational facilities, in an attempt to minimise the influence of Chartism among them? For Chartism certainly provided new impetus to charitable endeavour in Colchester.

The real gain from Chartism lay in its effect upon the outlook and self-reliance of those who believed in it. Between 1838 and 1858 thousands of people, chiefly male, became convinced that it was an outrage for any man to be denied the right to help decide the policy of the country in which he lived and worked. This conviction remained a powerful force in Colchester politics and public life for decades to come; if the struggle for universal male suffrage flagged in post-Chartist years, that was not because the majority of the unenfranchised ceased to believe in their rights but because they had lost confidence in their ability to obtain them. More important than its influence on the general working-class public, however, was Chartism's effect within a more limited circle, that of the several hundred workingmen and tradesmen who, in one period or another of its existence, had worked actively for it. The training in working-class leadership which Chartism gave its more devoted followers, and the knowledge of political, social and economic affairs which they gained in the process, enabled some of them to give many years of useful service, especially within the working-class movement, long after organised Chartism had ceased to exist. Colchester Chartists were almost all young men and had much of their adult life still to live. G. F. Dennis was twenty-two years old when he became W.M.A. secretary in 1838, W. G. Blatch was twenty-three when he occupied the same office in 1841–2, and H. S. Clubb, N.C.A. Secretary in 1847–8, was only eighteen.

A score of Colchester Chartists are mentioned in the Press in later years as playing a leading part in some form of public service. John Howe's record is described elsewhere in this chapter. John Castle, who was associated as a young man with the last Chartist group of the 1850s, has left his own account of his defence of his fellow silk-weavers from redundancy and of his foundation of Colchester Co-operative Society. Two further examples must represent the others. W. G. Blatch, after years of devoted work for Chartism, in the 1850s moved towards the radical wing of the Liberal party, where he always upheld an advanced

position on political issues. He was chiefly responsible for the organisation of a meeting to support the North in the period of the American
Civil War.[37] He had been married during the second year of his Chartist
membership, but this did not cause him to abandon his political activity.
However, as his family increased to eight, he expanded his shoemaker's
business until, at the age of thirty-three, he was employing three men and
doing well; his wife helped him in the workshop and was also for a time a
postman. He later became an estate agent in a minor way. He lived all his
life in North Street, probably in the same house, and in this neighbourhood he became "well known as a friend and adviser of many of the
inhabitants, his rugged knowledge of law making him valued". His generosity to people in trouble often went "beyond his means". Like other
Chartists, he was a well-read man and he became chairman of the Ben
Jonson Club, a social and literary group that held its meetings near his
house on North Hill. His "quaint, homely speeches" made him a favourite speaker at all sorts of gatherings and because he had, by accident,
come to be the regular proposer of the toast to the Navy at Liberal
dinners, he was affectionately known as "Admiral Blatch". Though a
widower for the last twenty years of his life, he lived comfortably enough
until a few months before his death at the age of seventy-six. His close
friend and neighbour, John Howe, represented the Ben Jonson Club at
the funeral. The Liberal *Essex Telegraph* gave him an appreciative obituary and so did the *Essex Standard*, which, oblivious of its contemptuous
comments on his Republicanism nearly sixty years before, wrote "Exit
the Admiral. Regretted by all who knew him, W. G. Blatch passed to his
rest on Thursday, a man of sterling worth and integrity."[38] Very different
was the career of H. S. Clubb, who emigrated to America in 1853 and was
soon earning a living as a journalist on the *Chicago Tribune*. He supported
the North in the Civil War, serving in the ranks but, because of the pacifist
principles learnt from Colchester Chartism, not carrying arms; he was hit
by a bullet and was saved because it lodged in a wad of dollar bills which
he was carrying on his person. Entering politics as a radical, he was elected
senator for the state of Michigan. Retiring from politics, he became an
advocate of Vegetarianism, rising to become President of the American
Vegetarian Society. Finally, he served as pastor of the Bible-Christian
Church of Philadelphia until his death at the age of ninety.[39]

Mid-Victorian movements, 1850–90

The dissolution of Colchester Chartism released its remaining supporters'
energies for other activity, including the organising of trade unions.
Several of them had been active in this field while Chartism still existed in
the town. In 1844 Thomas Plummer founded branches of the Tailors'
Protection Society at Maldon and Colchester and was elected to the
Society's national executive. Though composed of skilled male workers,
the Colchester branch was very concerned about the female outworkers
and tried to persuade them to attend its meetings. Its aims were moderate,
being "to raise themselves from their fallen position by the support of the
principle that fair living wages for labour, and fair remuneration for
capital, are not merely beneficial to our class, but to every class in

society". Plummer's view was that only "unity, sobriety and perseverance could ameliorate their condition" and, as a Temperance advocate, he persuaded his fellow members to change their meeting-place from the Greyhound, St. Botolph's, where they had formed their branch, to the Mechanics' Institute.[40] The branch remained in existence for several years and, though it seems by 1850 to have been closed or to have cut its connections with the national society, the tailors retained some organisation and by 1867 were again connected with a national body, the new Amalgamated Society of Tailors.

The Chartists, J. Chapman and G. F. Dennis, were active in connection with the Colchester Shoemakers' Society; Chapman became its secretary, and Dennis, a master shoemaker, seems to have been its adviser. This trade, which was well represented among the town's Chartists, had long been organised — in 1840 the Society's secretary had taken up the case of a shoemaker from outside Colchester who had failed to obtain treatment in Colchester Hospital — but in 1846 a brief expansion of trade had enabled a 'closed shop' to be established. The Society's very existence might, however, have gone unrecorded but for a court case in which it was involved in that year. A tailor called Wisbey was accused before the Colchester Bench of assaulting a shoemaker, William Duggin, who had been sent down from London to breach the shoemakers' closed shop on two separate occasions. On the first occasion he and two others had been invited down by a Colchester employer called Mills, who told them that he wished to employ them in place of other men whom he had dismissed for being drunk and idle. Mills's real purpose, as he admitted in court, was to circumvent "the blocking" of the town, imposed by the Shoemakers' Society in order to keep non-Colchester workers out of the town until the closed shop had been completed and the employers had conceded certain improvements of pay and conditions. Duggin proved a poor instrument for Mr. Mills's purpose. He spent the money given him for his fare from London and had to be bought out of Colchester railway station by his intending employer. Next he was interviewed by the local committee of the Society and, being apprised of the dispute and, no doubt, of the possible consequences to himself if he stayed, he returned to London. Later he was again sent down by Mills's London agent, only to find on his arrival that Mills had been obliged not only to give in to the Society but also to pay it a fine for trying to breach the closed shop. Duggin remained in Colchester, however, and shortly afterwards was drinking in a public house when Wisbey saw and recognised him, called him a "scab" and threatened to strike him. For Wisbey, to the reporter's surprise, "though a tailor, had espoused the shoemakers' quarrel".

At Wisbey's trial the Mayor elicited the information that Shoemakers' Societies in a number of places had co-operated in the "blocking" of Colchester. He disagreed strongly with G. F. Dennis, who, on behalf of the shoemakers, contended that the object of the Society was a benevolent one. He and his colleagues, said the Mayor, "had been anxious to investigate the case as fully as possible . . . to show the public the sort of system which had existed in the town. Of all the exposés he had heard in Court, he had never met a case in which greater tyranny was exercised towards a hardworking man." After admonishing Wisbey at some length, he fined him 15s. in costs, but threatened Chapman, as the secretary, with stricter punishment; "they should take other means of dealing with him and of showing to the inhabitants and master tradesmen of the town that they should be protected in their occupations and left at liberty to employ what workmen they pleased". It was later decided not to prosecute the secretary, though allegedly the Mayor received several letters urging such a course. Chapman was probably ignorant of the law, it was explained, but any further instance of the Society's "tyranny" would be treated severely and members should resign from it forthwith. This anti-climax was possibly due to the realisation that to victimise a man for being a trade unionist or a Chartist was by then less easy than it once had been, and also that Duggin was not an impressive champion of anti-Chartism. It was subsequently reported that the Society had been dissolved but, if it was, it recovered very quickly, since, by 1853, a shoemakers' organisation was not only in existence but was strong enough to win an advance in wages from almost all the town's employers.[41]

The incident is an interesting one. The obvious strength and effectiveness of trade unionism in this important Colchester occupation would never have been known but for the casual quarrel between Wisbey and Duggin, nor would the evident sympathy of a member of one trade for a member of another. The Chartist involvement is interesting, too, since Chartism generally has been criticised for its preoccupation with politics when it should have championed the youthful trade union and co-operative organisations with which the labour movement's future lay. The support given Colchester shoemakers by societies in other towns was of some significance, too, as foreshadowing the imminent formation of national 'Amalgamated' unions among skilled workers. Finally, the town's working-class leaders could derive some confidence from the affair. Those who ruled the town had clearly believed that, through their control of the law courts, they could intimidate trade unionists, but such power, though by no means at an end, had been modified by recent political changes. So, even if Victorian Colchester was not the most favourable field for vigorous trade union growth, the prospects were not hopeless.

Another large group offering scope to trade unionism were the building workers, whose numbers and bargaining power grew steadily as new houses and commercial establishments were built in the town and in some neighbouring villages; the construction of a permanent army camp in place of the Crimean War tents also favoured the industry. By 1861 there were 554 adults in the various building trades, besides a number of younger workers. A few firms were growing fast. Joseph Grimes of Northgate Street, whose father had founded the business in 1822, had sixty regular workers by 1864 and seventy by 1871. In the latter year George Dobson employed thirty-four at his yard in Princess Street, Charles Shepherd twenty in Castle Street, while the largest employer, H. J. Everett in Magdalen Street, had forty-five 'artificers', forty-one labourers and two boys working for him. Alternative work at higher wages was usually available in London, to which young men could easily move, and this situation enabled the carpenters to carry through a successful strike in 1853. Fifty of them met at the Waggon and Horses, at the top of North Hill, and applied for an increase of 6d. a day to bring their rate a little nearer to that in London. Meeting with no response, they struck and, when some of them left for London, those remaining were quickly given an increase varying between 4d. and 6d.[42]

Shop assistants, though they were unlikely to be able to support a trade union, were becoming one of the largest occupations in the town. By 1848 there were at least 219 shops in Colchester, of which about a score, mainly situated in High Street and Head Street, were large and well-staffed concerns. In 1871 at 30 High Street the draper, William Sewell, employed two men and ten women, of whom the two men and six 'shopmaids' lived in. Frederick Jones, whose grocery was probably next to the Red Lion, employed twenty-six men and two boys, ten of whom lived in; three domestic servants were needed to look after this large household. On the other hand, of the sixteen employees of Robert Sanders, High Street woollen-draper, not one lived on the premises. Altogether, eighteen of the largest concerns between them employed over 250 assistants. The latter, however, were not well placed to combine, being young, often recruited from the villages, easily replaceable, working and sometimes living under their employers' eye and engaged in a trade very dependent upon well-to-do urban and rural patrons. Yet so long were their hours of work that, when some of them appealed for a shorter working day, they met with considerable sympathy, though there were those who, in the Chartist period, resisted such movements "as having very revolutionary designs". It was in 1838, the first year of Chartist activity, that an audacious assistant wrote to the Press complaining that the working day was one of at least fourteen hours, leaving no time for the cultivation of the mind. In 1844 a meeting held at the Mechanics' Institute decided to form Colchester United Assistants' Association. Its statement of aims stressed the difficulty of self-improvement for those whose hours of work were so long, just the argument to appeal to the early-Victorian middle class, and the response was enough to oblige most of the drapers to concede 8 p.m. closing in Summer and 7 p.m. in Winter, with an extension to 10 p.m. on Saturdays. The attempt of two employers to withdraw these concessions two years later met considerable criticism. A movement in 1857 to win 7 p.m. Winter closing in every type of shop proved to be premature, but this was soon made standard practice as a result of a campaign, initiated by forty young assistants and supported by no less than 230 employers, who "were desirous of giving the assistants in their establishments time for physical exercise and mental improvement". The next claim was for 4 p.m. closing once a week, a concession gained by the town's handful of bank clerks in 1861 and at once sought by the shop assistants for themselves. By 1868, and possibly earlier, this practice had become normal in summertime, at first on Wednesdays, but soon on Thursdays because Wednesday was a day when many rural carriers came to town to shop for their customers. By 1872 the better employers had granted 4 p.m. closing in Winter as well as in Summer. Finally, after the Bank Holidays Act of 1871, pressure had to be applied to persuade reluctant shopkeepers to grant all the new Bank Holidays instead of just Easter Monday and Boxing Day.[43]

This was a movement which had little in common with trade unionism and relied mostly on gaining the goodwill of the shops' richer patrons, whose professed support for self-education was taken at face value by the assistants. It was characteristic that the very first meeting had been held in the Mechanics' Institute and that the renewal of the movement in 1863 sprang from an evening class in the French language, attended by assistants who were failing to arrive punctually because they were often detained at work. The leaders were always at pains to emphasise their loyalty to their employers and they maintained so respectful a demeanour that they enjoyed the patronage of successive Mayors and of both the local papers. Such organisations as they established were short-lived, never developing any activities other than social and athletic ones. Their limited success in gaining one early-closing day each week was, however, of wider significance because it gave impetus to the general movement for a weekly half-holiday throughout industry and commerce. In 1866, for instance, some carpenters and bricklayers applied for 4 p.m. closing on Saturdays, using the evidently compelling argument that they would thus be enabled to improve their minds. Two of the larger firms did comply and Grimes, then perhaps the most important of the local employers, granted the reform in principle, but delayed final implementation because, he told the applicants, they already had "time for all needful mental improvement . . . the want of which appears to be the chief point in your application".[44]

Another group of workers who tried to protect themselves without the aid of formal trade unionism were the 400 or so girls in the St. Peter's Street silk-mill, who were virtually alone in representing the industrial revolution in Colchester. Their wages fluctuated around 5s. weekly for a seventy to eighty hour week which was, in real terms, much worse remuneration than the 3s. to 4s. received by their grandmothers at woollen-spinning in the previous century. Employment was insecure in this precarious industry and it was a slackening of trade in 1843 which caused the firm to dismiss a number of girls and to demand more work from the remainder, requiring them to operate four reels instead of three. Normally, when four reels were worked, 1s. per week was added to the 5s. weekly wage, but on this occasion no increase was given and 300 girls held a meeting, shouted down their employer and paraded the streets to the Town Hall where a deputation asked the Magistrates to require their employer to give the customary increase. The latter arrived in Court, rebuked the girls and told them that they could be sent to prison for three months for their conduct. He explained to the Magistrates that he had put on the extra reel to stop the girls from falling asleep, that he was continuing to employ many of them only out of kindness, but that he would reconsider the matter of the extra shilling, provided that the strike was at once called off. The girls, ignorant of their legal position, were frightened by the prospect of imprisonment which the Magistrates did nothing to dispel. They wavered and then prepared to leave, thanking the Bench for its attention. The Chairman warned them against repeating so foolish an action and dismissed them. The precise outcome was not reported.

In 1846 rising prices occasioned another strike, this time for a 6d.-a-week increase which had been promised the girls because of the recent rise in prices. When the 6d. was not forthcoming, 500 left the factory, only twelve remaining at work, and they again marched to the Town Hall to see the Magistrates. Again the owner appeared and pointed to a Susan Enos as ringleader. The Mayor read out a clause from the 1825 Act to the effect that conspiracy to prevent other employees from working was punishable by three months' imprisonment, whereupon Susan Enos fainted. The Mayor then promised that there would be no prosecutions if the girls returned to work. They hastily agreed and were assured by the owner that he would waive the 6d. fine usually levied for absence and that he would also reconsider the whole system of fines, about which he knew they felt aggrieved. He also promised to give the 6d. increase in a few weeks' time if prices continued to rise.

In 1853 there was again strong discontent because of a proposed reduction of 6d. a week. Anticipating trouble, the owner in September applied for police support, but it was not until April that a strike took place. When it did, the Mayor, supported by police, brought about a resumption of work, but, as the reduction was not cancelled, 150 girls struck next day at 6 a.m., the starting-time. This time, disregarding the police, the girls paraded the town and only returned when promised that wages would not be reduced. When the owner revoked this promise, 300 girls, probably the whole of the employees, left work and demonstrated through the streets. The outcome is unclear. Some girls obtained employment at the Coggeshall silk-mill, where wages were allegedly higher, but others returned to work. Probably the reduction was imposed, since trade was slack. It was slack again in 1861 when the firm reduced the working-week from six to five days with a corresponding reduction of wages, and the 250 girls then employed went on strike. The result was not recorded, but a few weeks later they were all given a summer party at Birch Hall, the first in what became an annual series. Indeed, at this time they became the object of considerable attention, possibly as a result of their industrial record and certainly because their sex, combined with low wages, was thought to make them vulnerable to the temptations of urban life. For instance, during their 1864 visit to Birch Hall, after singing "We won't give up the Bible, that precious word of God", they were advised by their hostess, Mrs. Round, to stay away from the forthcoming fair. The girls responded by giving Mrs. Round a Bible when she visited them at the factory, but this concord did not prevent the employer from reducing wages in 1867 and threatening a further reduction, nor the drawers and winders from going on strike, again unsuccessfully. In 1872 there was yet another strike, but by then, in an industry observably struggling through its exposure to free trade, militancy was pointless and no further strike was reported during the nine years before the silk industry came to an end.[45]

The silk-workers in St. Peter's Street seem not to have been in any alliance with those in the much smaller silk-factory, situated first in Military Road and later in Stanwell Street. Nor apparently did they receive help or guidance from the handloom weavers who, as John Castle described in his autobiography, were at this time quite active in fighting for their own survival. Finally, there is no evidence of any local working-class leader having any connection with the strikes, which seem to have been entirely spontaneous and in each case to have arisen quite suddenly.

The girls certainly needed all the help they could get; for, although their weak position in a precarious industry was a major cause of their invariable defeats, if they had been able to draw upon friendly legal advice, they might have gained some protection from the intimidation, to which they were subjected not merely with the Magistracy's connivance but with its active co-operation.

No other group of female workers showed such spirit as the silkworkers. Domestic servants would have been too easily dismissed, had they behaved in so insubordinate a way. Sewing-machinists numbered 350 by 1861 and their industry was expanding, but their bargaining position was weak, with the almost unlimited supply of domestic tailoresses in every north Essex village.

By 1860 trade unionism's immediate future lay with the skilled trades, where, because of the sporadic efforts of previous decades, there were men with some experience of organisation and enough confidence to give leadership when conditions became favourable. They had to take account of the limitations of a market town where farmers and landowners exercised a strong influence not modified by any significant industrialisation. Borough affairs were dominated by the Conservatives until quite late in the century and they were less sympathetic to trade unionism than the still struggling Liberal party. However, since the 1815–50 slump had passed, the political atmosphere was somewhat relaxed and trade unions began to operate in less oppressive conditions. The Conservative and Liberal Press had been equally hostile in reporting the 1834 trade union upsurge, but by the 1870s it approached such matters with some attempt at objectivity. There were other developments favouring trade unionism, such as the availability of suitable meeting-places, the Mechanics' Institute or the Culver Street Co-operative Rooms, for instance. Colchester trade unionists felt less isolated when the new national unions, with their experience, confidence and business-like methods, absorbed their local trade societies.

Quite the most important event in Colchester's early trade union history was the foundation in 1861 or 1863 at the Marquis of Granby, North Hill, of a tiny branch of the Amalgamated Society of Carpenters and Joiners. Its founder, secretary and leader was John Howe, who for the next thirty years or more devoted himself to furthering its interests and those of any other part of the working-class movement to which he could be of service. He regularly reported to his union's London headquarters current rates of pay, hours of work and the number of members in his branch. In 1866, when there were only nine members, Colchester wages were £1 .1 .0 for a fifty-eight-and-a-half-hour week. Steady work to improve these conditions gradually attracted recruits, so that by 1879 there were fifty members and by 1892 about a hundred. In the latter year a carpenter was paid 31s. 6d. for a fifty-three-and-a-half-hour week and, as John Howe proudly stated, wages were no longer handed over in a public house. The real value of the wage was double that of 1866 because of the falling cost of living, while hours of work were down by about a tenth. Furthermore, the branch had achieved public respectability, as Chartism had never done, which was made very clear by the speeches at its eighteenth anniversary. This took the form of a members' dinner to which the two Liberal Parliamentary candidates came as guests; the Conservative M.P.s had also been invited. Loyal toasts were the occasion for a eulogy of the Army's valour at Rorke's Drift. The secretary then described, presumably for the visitors' edification, the Friendly Society benefits available to members for their 1s. weekly contribution, the weekly 10s. unemployment and the 12s. sickness grants, the £100 paid to those totally disabled and the £50 to those partially disabled, the 7s.-a-week super-annuation pension after eighteen years' membership and the 8s. after twenty-five years when the member could work no longer, and the death grants to the nearest relative. One of the Liberal candidates commended the union for these provisions and added, "I think that these Societies encourage forethought and self-denial, and that the social, moral and intellectual advancement of the people is the result of such organis-ations". The other Liberal compared the Britain of 1839, the year of the Newport Chartist "Rising", with that of 1879, when workingmen under-stood the financial problems of their employers and kept the law of the land. The cause of this improvement, he thought, was "the formation of provident habits on the part of members of Societies such as this, the improved and increased intelligence of the working men and of those who toil, their clearer apprehension of the difficulties which attend manufac-turing operations".[46]

Equally characteristic of the period were the speeches at a meeting held in 1882 to found a Colchester branch of the National Union of Boot and Shoe Riveters, Finishers and Seatsmen. Sixty workers attended and heard two Union representatives explain the purpose and methods of the organisation. The chairman was a local man, who assured the meeting that the law was now much less hostile to trade unionism than previously. He assured employers that strikes occurred rarely and only under the strict control of the union's Executive. Membership conferred intellec-tual advantage as well as financial benefit. Employers should welcome unions because "they combined labour and capital to a mutual under-standing". The town's chief employer, John Kavanagh, who was in the audience, supported the chairman. He thought that "the Society was a means to the moral, social and educational advancement of the men . . . the Society would contribute quite as much to the welfare of the employer as the employee . . . It would be the means of securing a more industrious and steadier class of men." He went on to suggest that this deeper sense of responsibility would help to counteract the industrial indiscipline in his works. The two visiting officials also stressed that the union "protected the employer against the dishonest workmen" and they laid most emphasis upon the friendly society benefits which the weekly contribution of 6d. secured. Forty joined the new branch.[47]

The Amalgamated Society of Engineers, the A.S.E., was late in taking root, despite the rapid expansion of the three foundries here in the 1870s, with their 200 workers. There was one incident that illustrated the need for some self-protection among the trade, however. In 1872 the Nine Hours Movement, after sweeping through the engineering industry, met a response in Colchester. Forty mechanics at the Britannia Sewing Machine works, adjacent to St. Botolph Station, struck for a nine-hour day and an increase on their existing wage of 24s. a week to bring it closer to the 30s. to 36s. being paid in London. The Manager turned these demands down, adding that "until the Commune is established, we intend to manage our business without the assistance of any professional agitators", and he sacked a respected worker for being the ringleader. The latter was not worried, as "he thought a change would do him good"; presumably, at this time of industrial expansion, he was confident of finding work in London or elsewhere. Workers from the other foundries in the town held a sympathy meeting, at which the chairman, a tailors' leader and an ex-Chartist, praised the First International for organising support among Continental workers for the Nine Hours Movement; hence the manager's reference to the Commune. A committee of six was elected, two representatives from each foundry, which put an agreed programme of improvements to the three firms. Met with a complete refusal to negotiate, the workers set up a formal organisation with a weekly subscription of 3d. The conservative *Essex Standard* asked the employers not to resort to a lockout, as the workers faced rising prices, while employers grew rich; Colchester wages were only two-thirds of those in London, and, perhaps the most significant comment, "Labour is a commodity which the owner has an undoubted right to sell at the highest price he can obtain".[48]

The outcome is unclear, but the movement seems to have helped to stir militant activity among other groups in the town. The carpenters, through their new trade union branch, now sought 6d.-a-day increase and improved overtime rates to offset rising prices and apparently had both requests granted. The increased cost of coal caused several of the labour leaders to set up a co-operative organisation to buy directly from the collieries. The Hythe coal-porters struck for a penny-a-ton increase in handling-rates and there was yet another strike in the silk-factory. The year of 1872 was also the time when the National Agricultural Labourers' Union set up branches in scores of north Essex villages, causing deep anxiety among farmers about the stability of the whole rural social order. Colchester was indirectly involved in the ensuing struggle, partly because of its own agricultural connections and also because it was used as a centre by the neighbouring village branches. During a bitter clash between the union members in the area south of Colchester and the farmers in their new Defence Association, the labourers caused a great stir by marching into the town wearing their membership cards in their hats. Joseph Arch, their leader, twice spoke in Colchester, on one occasion to a full house in the Theatre made up of town workers and leading Liberals as well as farm workers.[49]

The engineering workers, meanwhile, despite their militancy in 1872, did not join the A.S.E. till 1882, by which time the number of workers in the trade was growing quite fast. Their reluctance was probably due in part to the strong paternalism of two of the chief employers, whose original employees had been with them from the start and had received promotion as activity expanded. When the A.S.E. branch was founded, it grew steadily, reaching a membership of 125 by 1894. Other branches of skilled workers were formed from time to time. The Amalgamated Society of Tailors had members in the town as early as 1869, their meeting-place being the Co-operative Hall in Culver Street. By 1891, when the

Trades Council was started, besides the unions already referred to, there were branches of the boilermakers, metal planers, steam-engine makers and bricklayers. It was from among the more active members of these older branches that men emerged to guide the new unions that were founded in the upsurge of 1891–5.[50]

A posthumous success of Chartism was the foundation in 1861 of the Colchester Co-operative Society.[51] The silk-weaver, John Castle, was too young to have been a Chartist from the start, but in the 1850s he was one of the band of ex-Chartists who remained attached to the Universal Suffrage cause, and it was with the help of some of these, Thomas Rawlings, Dand, G. F. Dennis and some of the Hayward family, that he took the steps which resulted in the Co-operative Society's foundation. We are fortunate in having his own account of the early years which, because of the modest success then achieved, must have been heartening times for men, most of whose earlier public activities had brought them only disappointment. The Society enrolled twenty-eight members at its start in May 1861, by August it had about fifty and by 1863 some 250. The *Essex Standard*, the proprietor of which was partly instrumental in ensuring the Society's foundation, noted that generally its members were "of the respectable artisan class" and commended them for giving two guincas for the relief of the Lancashire cotton-workers left unemployed through the American Civil War, a far better use for their money than "spending it at the beerhouse". The 800 per cent increase in membership and turnover that followed between 1863 and 1891 was accompanied by the expansion of services and enlargement of premises. As new suburban areas were developed around the town, for instance in the New Town vicinity, the Society was quick to start new branches in them. At the same time the Society's leaders vigorously pursued their aims of social regeneration and adult education, which for them remained the chief motive for founding and maintaining the Society. Reviewing the progress of the first year's operations, they wrote:

> "Would that many such generous hearts could be redeemed
> from the pestilential and degrading influences of the beer-
> house and gin-shop. What a standing protest is this Co-
> operative Society against those mantraps which lure the
> body and mind to degradation and the soul to destruction
> for the sake of unholy gain."

The early opening of an Assembly Room next to the central store in Culver Street not only facilitated the provision of adult education but gave the growing working-class movement a convenient meeting-place; the numerous Temperance advocates within its ranks were particularly appreciative. It also enabled the Society to open a free library, which was soon as well used as that in the Literary Institute, and to hold readings, lectures, classes and socials. At one of the annual Soirées there, the members heard "a poetical history of England and Colchester from the invasion of Julius Caesar to the formation of the Co-operative Society in the town, written and read by G. F. Dennis". Other ventures were the opening of three Reading-rooms in different parts of the town and in 1890 the foundation of the Women's Guild, the first self-governing women's organisation in Colchester, which proceeded to organise its own vigorous educational and social programme. All this was made possible by the annual grant of a small proportion of the profits for educational purposes in the tradition of the Rochdale Pioneers.

At this time political commitments seem to have been avoided, partly through a desire to obtain the widest support from influential townsmen. Both Conservatives and Liberals, in Colchester as in other Essex towns, regarded Co-operation as a safe and practical way in which workingmen could improve their lot without recourse to politics, while developing self-reliance and a respect for commercial principles. Leading townsmen from both parties helped in various ways. The *Essex Standard*'s proprietor provided accommodation for the Society's first shop at an almost nominal rent, while James Paxman, then a rising Liberal industrialist, acted as a trustee and allowed the use of a meadow near his new works for one of the annual galas; James Round also opened the grounds of Hollytrees for a similar gathering. The Mayor, P. O. Papillon, was the chief speaker at one of the annual meetings and he chose the occasion to urge Co-operators to shop at their own stores. Mrs. Round opened one of the annual bazaars which the Co-operative Women's Guild regularly held in order to provide treats for the elderly. Wilson Marriage served for a time on the Education Committee of the Society. Another indication of Colchester co-operators' acceptance of the social order was the foundation in 1869 by Castle, Rawlings and the A.S.C.J. Secretary, John Howe, of a Co-operative Building Society, which in its first decade of existence lent £26,000 for the purchase of 192 cottages. Its depositors consisted almost entirely of artisans, and the £2,300 deposited in the single year of 1879 was a measure of their capacity for prudent self-help.

Friendly Societies were more important in working-class life even than trade unionism or Co-operation, especially among those influential artisans who could afford to pay the dues. The protection the Societies gave against the misery and indignity of the New Poor Law was most acceptable to self-respecting Colchester artisans, while, like Co-operation, the movement was welcomed by middle-class opinion as likely to encourage self-reliance and distaste for revolution. Colchester's first Oddfellows' Lodge, founded in 1844 and named the Victoria after the Sovereign, was told by its chairman at an annual dinner that "poor men who invested their money in these clubs were not only raised in self-respect, but felt they had a stake in the well-being of the country and the continuance of public tranquillity". In the early nineteenth century there were already a number of societies, some originating in the previous century and the majority of them meeting in public houses. Unsound financial practices caused some closures among them, but a few were run with care and success. The Colchester Provident Benefit Society, founded in 1809 "for the support of its members in sickness, infirmity and old age", increased its membership from 220 to 270 in 1818–34 and its stock from £800 to £2,000. However, such local bodies were gradually superseded by the great national organisations which steadily increased their dominance through the century. A survey of Colchester politics in 1867 noted "a number of Odd Fellows, all of whom are Tories, and Foresters, who are all Liberals", though such a distinction, if it ever existed, had become blurred a decade or so later. By the 1890s when the great

majority of the town's workingmen belonged to one or more societies,
the Colchester District of Foresters reached a membership of 10,000 and
a fund of £125,000. The Oddfellows were no less successful and a number
of other leading societies had branches in the town, including the Hearts
of Oak with over a thousand members, the Royal Liver and the Sons of
Temperance. The societies' annual church parade had become an
important local occasion and the public was particularly impressed on the
first occasion on which full regalia were worn by a thousand members,
who, "amid huge crowds", marched from St. John's Green to the Town
Hall, where the Mayor awaited them, and then back to Eld Lane Baptist
Chapel for the service. The *Essex Telegraph* considered the Societies so
influential that it devoted a weekly column to their affairs. One of its
editorials commended them as follows:

> "Such a body of men and such an accumulation of money
> for provident purposes are a standing bulwark against
> extreme Socialism. Men who thus combine for such excel-
> lent purposes and who voluntarily surrender contributions
> from their hard-earned wages in order to provide for rainy
> days, constitute one of the most stable elements of our
> social life."[52]

The same newspaper wrote with approval of the progress of Colchester
Savings Bank, with which many local Friendly Societies deposited their
funds. Founded in 1817 for working-class savers, it increased its depositors from 282 in 1818 to 460 in 1819, to 1,887 in 1840 and to 2,633 in 1877.
It continued to serve the working-class public — half of its 2,205 depositors in 1846 had balances of less than £20 — and was often referred to as
"the poor man's bank".

The protection afforded by craft unions, Co-operation and Friendly
Societies was entirely suitable to prudent workingmen in the mid-Victorian period. They needed a union to help them cope with the changing
economic conditions in their trades. Building-workers were increasingly
employed by large firms; shoemakers were beginning to face the
consequences of the mechanisation then developing fast in the local footwear concerns; tailors, who had long been concerned about competition
from badly paid female outworkers, now saw these competitors brought
into their own employers' factories to work the new sewing machines; and
the handloom silk-weavers were soon to disappear altogether from the
town's economic life. The workhouse off Balkerne Lane was an ever-
present incentive to friendly society membership. Few workingmen were
so comfortably off as not to value the quite small savings in living-costs
which they could make by shopping in co-operative stores. Yet they were
not now looking for a new social order, as some of their fathers had done
in Chartist times. In certain trades there was still opportunity for men to
become their own masters, though the autobiography of the tailor, James
Carter, shows at what personal cost such elevation — it could hardly be
called independence — might be gained. Some who were unable
themselves to achieve such advancement might hope to see their sons
better themselves. With the economic advance in the last quarter of the
century there were prospects of rising living-standards for many, especially when alternative work in London was becoming more plentiful, the

cost of living was falling and trade unionism had grown into an effective instrument for those with the spirit and patience to use it. A Colchester trade unionist said in a speech in 1892 that "when he looked around and saw the condition of trade unionists today and compared it with 40 or 50 years ago, he saw a great difference. Trade Unionism was elevating the men. Before him he saw a well dressed crowd, and that used not to be so."[53]

Workingmen's social aspirations were therefore limited and in politics they were no more adventurous. The sensible policy seemed to be to attach themselves to the Liberals, some of whom seemed ready to extend the franchise, albeit slowly, to prudent workingmen. But to win Liberal patronage it was necessary to abandon Chartism completely; John Castle's autobiography makes no reference to it at all. In the 1860s the *Essex Telegraph*, the new Liberal weekly, gave its support to a very timid extension of the franchise, but made this conditional upon the willingness of workingmen to abdicate their Chartist ideals. The most radical of the local Liberals, J. B. Harvey, during the controversy over the 1867 Reform Bill guaranteed that the Bill's beneficiaries would not pursue an independent policy but would support the two established parties.[54] However, even though they acquiesced in the surrender of their right to universal suffrage, the working-class radicals had still to convince many of those who controlled the Liberal party that it would be advisable to make them some concessions. This proved to be a long-drawn-out process. No progress was made until in the struggle for the 1867 Reform Bill the Liberals felt the need for popular support and brought the ex-Chartists into the party. After the Bill's passage, with the working-class part of the electorate increased from barely one-fifth to about a half, additional canvassers were needed at election-time, who were able to talk convincingly to the new electors. So the Colchester Working Men's Association was formed by the Liberals, not to revive the town's first Chartist organisation of 1838, which had borne that name, but to campaign for the party in the 1868 election.[55] This Association was disbanded, but was later revived under the name of the Liberal League. It resumed its electoral activity at the 1880 election and, when the 1884 Reform Bill proposed universal male suffrage, it campaigned for it at open-air meetings in various parts of the town. After the Bill's passage it used its now reinforced influence to persuade the reluctant Liberal leaders to permit the founding of a Liberal club, a type of organisation which the latter feared, and the League hoped, would become a power-house of radicalism. The Club helped to retain for the Liberal Party the support of many politically minded workers until the trade union upsurge of 1892 heralded the first revival of independent working-class politics since Chartist times.

The rise of the modern movement, 1890–1914

The trade union upsurge at Colchester in 1892–5 was partly a response to the national trade union expansion that had been taking place since the 1889 London dock strike. The town was readier to respond than ever before. The skilled workers in the footwear trade, whose strike of 1892 set the process in motion, were reacting against an overwhelming onset of mechanisation. Engineering and tailoring were being centralised in larger factories and, even in less industrialised trades, the total number of employees and the size of individual firms were growing steadily. This was very much the case in the building industry, but railwaymen, printing workers, brewery workers and municipal employees were also affected in one way or another. The town's population, up from 19,000 to 35,000 between 1851 and 1891, was becoming more divided in its place of residence, with many middle-class families living in or near Lexden Road and workers concentrated in the vicinities of Stanwell Street or Hythe Hill. The prospects for trade unionism had been made brighter by other developments. Both the 1867 and the 1884 Reform Acts increased the working-class electorate and caused both parties to seek its support. The Conservatives started their own Workingmen's Club in 1872, and in 1877 a new Conservative paper, the *Colchester Gazette*, declared in its prospectus that it would "appeal especially to the masses for support . . . uphold the rights and interests of the working population";[56] nor was this approach unsuccessful, for a strong minority of trade unionists, even of trade union leaders, in Colchester at the turn of the century were thought to be Conservatives. Finally, waiting for just such favourable conditions as this, there was a sturdy group of able and confident men from the existing craft unions, led by the experienced John Howe.

Howe's connection with the labour movement had been an early one, and the whole of his youthful and adult life was devoted to it, mirroring in its phases the developments which that movement underwent in the nineteenth century.[57] At Thetford in Norfolk, where he had been born, when twelve years of age he attended his first Chartist meeting and was given the task of snuffing out the candles when it was over. After serving his apprenticeship he obtained work in Colchester, where he married Harriet, four years his junior. He soon moved to London, possibly in 1853 when a number of younger carpenters left Colchester for the capital during a trade dispute, and he settled in Camden Town where his first three children were born. In about 1860 he returned to Colchester, taking a house in North Station Road, only two doors away from another one-time Chartist, W. G. Blatch. Possibly through the latter's influence, though more probably because he had joined a union in London, he set about forming a local branch of the Amalgamated Society of Carpenters and Joiners. At some time between 1861 and 1863 he was successful in forming a very small organisation, after which he began the painstaking work that was to increase its membership and make it the strongest force in Victorian Colchester's trade union movement. Meanwhile, on little more than 21s. a week, he succeeded in apprenticing his eldest boy to his own trade and keeping his four other children at school, including a daughter who remained there until the then unusually late age of seventeen. In these years he gave his support to any group or movement needing it. In Ipswich he organised a branch of his own union, in Colchester he helped start the Co-operative Building Society, which, in his opinion, had to be kept as an entirely workingmen's organisation. This desire to obtain for his class the best that the existing economic order could offer was also the main reason for the vigorous support which he gave to the Liberal Party's radical wing, especially in 1884 when the issue was the enfranchisement of all workingmen. "He was an old Chartist", he said "and manhood suffrage was one of the points when he was a boy, and they had been fighting for it up to the present time. He thought every man should have a vote."

For some reason he retired from his job at the age of fifty-eight when, having regularly paid the required dues, he was granted a superannuation pension by his union. If ill-health was the cause of his retirement, it did not prevent him from founding the Colchester Trades Council in 1891 and, as its first chairman, presiding over the great expansion of trade unionism that followed. His bearded face and small figure became a familiar sight at the meetings and demonstrations of the next three years. He was elated at the prospect of a united labour movement, such as he had worked for over so many years. "The gospel for working men today was a combination of trade unionism and co-operation; if working men wanted to be lifted up into their proper position, they must join these two Societies and read their newspapers." He now saw Colchester workers as at last well placed to achieve that influence and respect to which their usefulness entitled them. "Trade Unionism had raised the working man in the scale of intelligence and tended to make him a social and intellectual being, it had brought home to both parties in the state the fact that workingmen were the great producers of wealth and that, without labour, drones would perish and empires dwindle. It was a noble thing to see a body of workingmen binding themselves together to uphold the dignity of man and the rights of labour." It was also high time, he thought, to insist that the British state should cease to be the instrument of the propertied classes and should be controlled by the whole people. This point he re-emphasised when in 1892 he denounced, in language unusually strong for him, the use of troops against the miners. "He did not know how to express words strong enough to condemn the action of shooting down our fellow men, the miners in the Midlands. They did not, as working men, pay their soldiers to go and shoot working men." He proposed a success-ful motion condemning the Government's action in sending troops to help the coal-owners.

At the same time years of painstaking work for the betterment of his trade had left him preoccupied with the little gains that could be won within the existing economic order. It was impractical, he thought, to launch an independent labour party and more sensible to follow the leadership of Mr. Gladstone for whom he, like his friend W. G. Blatch, had conceived deep admiration. Free Trade, in particular, had brought many blessings. "No statesman could now hold office for six months if he attempted to reverse that policy. Life and property were never more secure, labour was never better paid, provisions were never cheaper." In 1892 he was elected to the Town Council and in 1894 re-elected, in each case with tacit Liberal support and, when some of his colleagues on the Trades Council tried to break with the Liberal party and support socialist candidatures, Howe broke with them and with the Trades Council itself. That event did not occur until 1895 and during the intervening period he gave his experience and considerable ability to solving the many practical problems arising from the sudden trade union expansion. He chaired meetings, supervised the marshals at the May Day church parades and led the Trades Council representatives when they cross-questioned the Conservative candidate at the 1892 Parliamentary election. When labour candidates contested various local elections, he made sure that they did so on a carefully thought-out and practical programme. When elected to the Town Council himself, he used his position to gain specific improvements, including a fair-wages clause in all Council contracts.

The youthful working-class movement found another valuable ally in the Rector of All Saints, the Rev. T. G. Gardiner.[58] An Anglican clergyman sympathetic to the labour cause was a new phenomenon in Colchester. An Oxford graduate, Gardiner had spent some years in an East End parish before coming to Colchester in 1890. He proved a dutiful Rector, concerned for the upkeep of the church building and determined to draw the laity into parochial work. He quickly became well known for "the striking originality and power of his preaching and the geniality, urbanity and generosity which mark the discharge of all his parochial duties". However, believing in the Church's mission to elevate public life, he took up a number of local causes. He launched a movement to establish a gymnasium for young people, winning support in the most influential quarters, but he also startled polite society with an outspoken attack on Colchester's slums. Even more controversially, he joined the growing labour movement, playing a direct part in the formation of a branch of the Society of Metal Planers and training the leaders of this and other unions in the techniques of wage bargaining by himself playing the part of the employers in mock negotiations.

After investigating the conditions of the female workers in the tailoring industry, he brought down the secretary of the Women's Trade Union Association to try to introduce trade unionism among them. When the Trades Council decided to arrange a May Day church parade, he agreed to take the service in All Saints' Church, though he was careful to get the consent of his Vestry beforehand. His most controversial action was his open support for the boot and shoe workers in their strike in 1892. Though this activity made him notorious in respectable circles, he was no revolutionary but, on the contrary, believed that trade unionism and Co-operation were saving the country from extreme socialism. He saw in the labour movement possible sources of social regeneration, and one of his ideals was the establishment by the workers' organisations of a centre for adult education and other recreations. That was why he gave so much time to the Co-operative Society, shaming its members into promising that they would order clothes only from firms paying standard rates to their tailoresses. He helped to run the Co-operative debating society and always urged the Society not to remain merely a commercial undertaking but to intensify its educational services. He loved this work and, when in 1893 he left Colchester to take a parish in Southwark, he confessed that "there was not a single room in Colchester where he felt more at home than in the Co-operative Assembly Room".

The trade union expansion of the early 1890s was set in motion by a craft which was destined soon afterwards to disappear almost entirely from the town. The boot and shoe makers had been seriously affected by the continuous process of mechanisation in their industry, and especially so in Kavanagh's factory at St. John's Green.[59] When in the 1880s many new machines were installed, 'Society men', that is members of the skilled workers' union, had been employed on them at 25s. a week, a not unreasonable wage by local standards, but gradually they had been replaced by 'boys', non-apprenticed lads of about nineteen to twenty-one years of age, paid at about half the skilled rates. The Union accepted a ratio of one boy to every five men, but soon the boys seem to have equalled in number, and even to have exceeded, the men. A reporter visited one of the boys' workrooms, "where these juvenile employees, intelligently manipulating machines, were doing work formerly done by adult hand labour". The skilled men had already begun to plan some action on this issue when, in January 1892, an unexpected dispute flared up over the relatively minor matter of fines for lateness and absences. An organiser of the union, a militant named Votier, was quickly at the factory and he brought out the lasters, the men who shaped the shoe by fixing its parts on a last and who had been most affected by the recent mechanisation. Kavanagh replied by refusing all negotiations and dismissing all trade unionists, as allegedly he had been planning to do for some time. Thus both sides had acted as if they had been expecting such a conflict. The strikers received 12s. a week in strike pay and also were given financial and moral support by other organised trades at solidarity demonstrations addressed by the Rev. T. G. Gardiner and local union leaders. Kavanagh next held a meeting of his 'boys' and told them that, if the union had its way, he would have to dismiss four-fifths of them. Apparently the response to this was that the boys began to leave his employment and he thereupon gave all his workers a week's notice, closed the factory and said he was booking a passage to South Africa for reasons of health. He remained in the town, however, kept the factory closed and refused offers of arbitration by the Mayor and other prominent people. The stalemate was therefore complete and the Union, while giving strike pay to its members still in Colchester, arranged for some skilled workers and boys to obtain work elsewhere, mainly in London. It also attempted to organise a boycott of Kavanagh's fourteen retail shops in London and Reading, as well as holding a demonstration outside his London warehouse with a band playing the *Dead March*.

Six weeks passed and Kavanagh reopened the factory. Only two of the original strikers returned, pickets from several different unions kept watch at the entrance of the factory, which was now officially 'blacked' by the Union, and several Union members, arriving in the town from elsewhere to take work in the factory, returned home on learning of the dispute. The Union seemed to be holding its position firmly enough for the time, having by now achieved a record membership of 250 out of the 1,100 boot and shoe makers in the town and having won several minor concessions from two other firms, those of Knopp and George. It also vigorously took up the campaign launched by its national leaders to secure the abolition of 'out-work', which apparently was practised even in the vicinity of Colchester's mechanised footwear industry. Kavanagh himself gave way in July on the matter of fines, but not on that of the employment of boys. The blacking of his factory continued and was still in force in the following year when he again made concessions on issues other than the main one. The dispute seems in the end to have petered out, with no clear result that the Union could claim as even a partial victory. For the present the Union remained strong and won a notable success when it forced Knopp, the second-largest employer, to dismiss an allegedly bullying foreman whom he had introduced to counteract workers' resistance to recently installed American machinery. Knopp and the other major employer, George, then joined the new employers' federation and evidently began to prepare for a final confrontation with the Union. For the time being the clash did not occur and the Union branch remained strong enough to give its support to the now rapidly expanding working-class movement.

The first effect of the shoemakers' strike was to stir the other skilled trades. Existing branches, like those of the engineers and tailors, became more active and recruited new members. Unions hitherto unrepresented in the town now formed branches, including the General Union of Carpenters, the Typographical Association which sought to establish a minimum wage of 26s. in Colchester's small but growing printing industry, and the Bakers' Union. By 1893 the patternmakers and the moulders also had organisations. Even the National Union of Elementary Teachers, already represented in the town, showed a new spirit, making a claim to be heard on questions of educational policy as well as on salaries.[60]

The skilled trade most affected by the new militancy was that of the bricklayers. Their union had existed in Colchester for some years, but had been quite powerless to gain any increase in their hourly rate which for sixteen years had remained at 5½d. to 6d. The bricklayers now met and drew up a code of improvements which they asked their employers to implement in the next six months. These included an hourly rate of 7d. for skilled men, a ten-hour day in Summer and a nine-hour day in Winter, a Saturday half-day and special Saturday and Sunday overtime rates. 'Walking time', that is time spent in reaching jobs in outlying places, was to count for some allowance, unskilled labourers were not to be employed on skilled bricklayers' work, and all disputes were to be settled by arbitration. When in the Summer of 1892 the six months' notice elapsed without any concessions being made, twenty bricklayers receiving less than 7d. struck for that rate. As the strike spread with more workers joining it every week, the employers conceded a halfpenny rise in the hourly rate and some of the other changes requested by the bricklayers.[61] At the same time in the engineering industry the unions were increasing their membership and were able to win a 10 per cent rise for skilled men at Paxman's and the Britannia works.[62]

The most striking development, because it was so unexpected, was the spread of unionism among the so-called unskilled trades.[63] The Labourers' Union, the Navvies' Union and the Eastern Counties Labour Federation, which organised mainly farm workers, now established branches in the neighbourhood. The National Vehicle and Traffic Workers' Union held a meeting in the Co-operative Hall to enrol busmen, carmen, cabbies and horsekeepers. The Navvies' Union was the most successful. Charging dues of only 2d. a week, holding smoking-concerts at the Sea Horse in the High Street and recruiting at open-air meetings in various parts of the borough, it quickly reached a membership of 130. It took up the cause of the bricklayers' labourers, seeking to raise their 3½d.-an-hour rate by a further penny to bring them nearer the London rate of 6d. Even women workers, previously neglected by the unions, were invited to a meeting to hear the national leader of the Women's Trade Union Association, supported by a local group of trade unionists, Co-operators and Liberal ladies. Though Howe and other veterans helped when invited, these new 'unskilled' unions soon produced their own local leaders.

The Trades Council, formed in 1891, found itself with a unifying function to perform and it responded to the challenge with spirit. In early 1892 there were some 600 trade unionists in Colchester, but ten months later there were 1,500, and over this expansion the Trades Council presided. It was accepted as the trade unions' official spokesman by the unions themselves, by the Press and by the public. In 1890 the Second International Working Men's Association had made 1 May the occasion for a world-wide display of labour unity, and it was only two years after that when the Colchester Trades Council organised its own May Day church parade. Five hundred members, in their Sunday-best clothes, marched from St. John's Green along St. John's Street, Head Street and High Street to All Saints', where Gardiner took the service. Thousands watched and the Mayor, Wilson Marriage, took the march past at the Town Hall in recognition of the arrival of this new force in the town's public life.[64] Next the Trades Council nominated Howe, Gardiner and Adams for the Board of Guardians on a programme of state old-age pensions, public control of all hospitals, work schemes for the unemployed, more humane workhouse conditions and technical training for orphans; Howe was elected. The unions also supported two women Liberals for the Board of Guardians. Thorrington, representing the now very active Co-operative Society, won a place on the newly established School Board, but the greatest success was Howe's election to the Town Council, though he, like the other Labour candidates, was not opposed by the Liberals. There was even talk of a Labour candidate at the 1892 election, but this was finally rejected as premature. Instead, the Trades Council interviewed the Conservative and Liberal candidates on their attitude to its programme of a steeper Income Tax, increased death duties, nationalisation of mining royalties, an eight-hour day for public employees, and state-provided old-age pensions. The result was a decision to support the Liberal because his answers were considered more satisfactory.[65]

These were hopeful times for the whole working-class movement, which was encouraged by its own economic advances and excited by the new ideas voiced by its own local leaders and visiting speakers. The Kavanagh strike was a dramatic affair, in its early weeks at least, involving confrontation between the pickets and Kavanagh, a mass meeting held provocatively outside the latter's house, and a demonstration of 300 strikers and their supporters through the streets to the Co-operative Assembly Hall where 2,000 people applauded them in. The large May Day church parades, on one occasion including a contingent of chimney sweeps, were watched by thousands of sympathetic townspeople intermingled with country workers up to town for the day. Another impressive occasion was the visit to Colchester by the Navvies' Union branches from East London, the cradle of the new movement. The visitors marched from North Station with Paxman's band at their head and when Colchester supporters, wearing yellow rosettes, joined them, the procession stretched for more than a quarter of a mile; by the time it reached the High Street, it had grown even longer. The elaborate banners of the Londoners particularly impressed one reporter, who also admired their calm assurance. "There was no shouting, no vulgar staring, but every man seemed bent on serious business and all marched like an army, with the same determination, if not with like precision." After a day of meetings, a large crowd escorted the visitors to the station for their 9.00 p.m. departure.[66] It was a time, too, when barriers were lowered. Leaders of the skilled unions willingly gave help to the unskilled workers in their efforts to organise, in their turn the Navvies' Union collected money for the Kavanagh strikers. Urban workers supported the farm workers of the neighbourhood in the Eastern Counties Labour Federation. The Trades Council sent a delegate to declare support for the strikers in the Braintree footwear industry, showed similar solidarity with striking engineers at Chelmsford and sent £54 to the Midland miners' strike fund. It worked with Ipswich Trades Council to establish a regional federation of Trades Councils. Only in their attitude to women's emancipation did Colchester male trade unionists fall short. Some were firm in their advocacy of women's rights and insisted on the need for the organisation of tailoresses. However, women found no prominent place in the local leadership. They provided refreshments for social evenings, and in the Co-operative Women's Guild they had their only, rather timid, voice, but they created no permanent unions in the trades where they worked. This remained the position for many years, as far as working-class women were concerned, the only female presence on the public platform being that of individual Liberal and Fabian ladies sympathetic to some of the labour movement's aims. Finally, this was a time of vigorous discussion. The Co-operative Society, with its Education Fund and its accommodation for meetings, provided the forum for arguments about both immediate and long-term issues. Its Education Committee arranged debates on a wide range of current questions, such as the Eight-hour Day, Temperance, Sunday Closing and public control of schools. Socialism was also discussed and among a succession of lecturers was Tom Mann, who took as his title 'Socialism and Class Struggle'. The Liberal *Essex Telegraph* opened its columns to letters and articles propounding theories to which it was itself opposed, including several on Marxism by the secretary of the newly founded Colchester branch of the Independent Labour Party, the I.L.P.

Political division within the movement certainly contributed to the decline in activity and confidence observable by 1894–5. The Trades Council's endorsement of the Liberal candidate in the 1892 election owed much to the Liberal beliefs of some of its own leading members. Warren Plane, secretary of the Amalgamated Society of Engineers, and G. C. Way, the branch's president, were both Liberals, and Plane sat on the Council of the Colchester Liberal Party. John Howe was less committed, but would not have gained and held his Town Council seat if he had stood independently of the Liberals. These men were determined enough that workers should be represented by members of their own class on all public bodies but thought that this could not at present be achieved by a break with the party from which they expected more concessions than from the Conservatives and to which they were in any case quite sympathetic. Several leading trade unionists canvassed eagerly for Weetman Pearson, the Liberal candidate at the 1892 election, while, in return, Labour representatives were given a clear field by the Liberals when they contested local government seats. So when, in 1893 or early 1894, a Colchester branch of the I.L.P. was started, Liberals were indignant that the new body might now advance its own Labour candidates independently of the official Liberals and perhaps even in opposition to them. In 1894 the I.L.P. did fight the South Ward and, though gaining only 104 votes, precipitated an open breach between its own supporters on the Trades Council and the pro-Liberals on that body, including John Howe who seems soon afterwards to have left the Trades Council, the body which he, more than anyone, had created.[67] The I.L.P. continued to make no little impression by its determination to oppose both parties at local elections and, even more, by its uncompromising affirmation of Socialist principles. It won considerable support from leading local trade unionists, including the Trades Council secretary.

This political division, distressing though it was to the youthful labour movement, was not the main cause of the decline that set in after 1895. More important was the recession in the town's economy which made it more difficult to win, or even to maintain, improvements in wages and working-conditions. Only in the building trade were prospects brighter, because of the current extension of the barracks, and here the bricklayers won the only notable success of 1895. First they gave preliminary notice of their application for an increase of one penny on their hourly rate of 6½d., then, in the absence of any response, struck work, with their union's help moved some of the strikers to alternative employment in London and elsewhere, and quickly won an hourly rate of 7d., firstly from the contractors building the barracks and subsequently from other employers.[68] Next year the building labourers through the Gas and General Workers' Union, to which some sixty out of a possible 200 of them belonged, sought to increase their rate from 4d. to 4½d. an hour, but with what success is unclear. The Trades Council continued active for a few months, but it was significant that its chief preoccupation now was to seek relief for the town's 800 unemployed. The trade depression was intensified by the running down of Kavanagh's factory and its subsequent closure, causing considerable unemployment among boot and shoe workers. Side by side with this development, further mechanisation was proceeding at the two other leading firms, Knopp's and George's, both of which after the Kavanagh strike of 1892 had taken the precaution of joining the new employers' federation. Though Knopp subsequently withdrew because he preferred to deal directly with his own employees, he declared that he was going to mechanise as he thought fit, regardless of any Union objections. George installed new machinery and sought an opportunity to eliminate the union from his works. First, he took no union member into his employment and, as requested by the employers' federation then engaged in a national confrontation with the workers, dismissed all trade unionists among his existing employees. The non-unionists in his factory then struck in solidarity with the dismissed men, Votier again arrived at Colchester to negotiate with George, and again the Trades Council backed the strikers. The union fought hard, realising that its very existence was being threatened by what its secretary called "a deliberate attempt on the part of a capitalistic organisation to break up the union, so that they might crush them unchallenged". There was some sympathy in the town, too, for the locked-out men who were being penalised as the result of a dispute taking place in other parts of the country. The *Essex Standard* was hostile at first. "Striking in the boot trade again", it wrote. "There is nothing like the boot trade for strife between employers and employees. It is almost a disease." However, when the paper's reporter investigated the dispute in some detail, his report showed much sympathy with the strikers' case. Yet George easily emerged victor, installing all the machines he had wanted to and making some of the skilled men redundant. The strikers returned on his terms, including some union men who presumably had to renounce their membership. A month later production was proceeding without restriction and, reported the *Essex Standard*, "the firm were congratulating themselves that they had had the best of the dispute. The great majority of the men, including the cream of the unionists, were back at work."[69] Thereafter, though a branch of the union survived, it had less and less influence, as one footwear factory after another closed down.

Between 1896 and 1900 trade unionism so declined as almost to be ignored by the Press. The Trades Council was dissolved and, when it was refounded some ten years later, its earlier existence had been almost forgotten. When John Howe died in 1904, having spent his last six years in Winsley's almshouses, his obituary in the *Essex Telegraph* recalled "the stirring days when Trades Unionism was very much in the air", almost as if writing of a bygone age. However, over sixty A.S.C.J. members walked in his funeral procession and Thorrington, the Co-operative Society's leader, spoke at the graveside.[70] Their presence testified to the survival after 1895 of the craft unions and Co-operation. The A.S.C.J. and the A.S.E. maintained a quiet presence in the town, and at least one additional craft union, the Painters', founded a Colchester branch at this time. The Co-operative Society, so far from flagging, increased its membership fast:

1886:	1,500	1900:	5,024
1891:	2,406	1903:	5,850
1893:	3,071	1910:	7,762

The Society's extension into the newly developing parts of the borough helped to make it one of the town's largest employers; already by 1899 there were 183 people working for it. Takings for the year rose from £62,000 in 1893 to £129,000 in 1903. By 1911 there was £77,000 in share capital, which "all belongs to the working men and women of Colchester". Educational expenditure was increased, too, with the Co-operative Guild, founded in 1890, very much to the fore. There was no formal involvement in politics because, as one of the Society's leaders said, "probably no community differed more in religion and politics", but in an unobtrusive way the Society remained a solid source of strength for the working-class movement in its dull years around 1900.[71] By that time the 'unskilled' unions had disappeared from the town and, with both the Trades Council and the I.L.P. also dissolved, only the craft unions and the Co-operative Society remained, the two elements that had constituted the working-class movement before the 1892–5 expansion.

The revival of the movement therefore depended very much upon the surviving skilled unions. They too had their problems. The building unions remained fairly strong but were badly hampered by the fluctuations in their industry arising from the spasmodic nature of barrack building in the Camp. In 1905, for instance, after a very busy period, activity had almost ceased and large numbers in all the industry's main trades were thrown out of work. When the Mayor held a meeting to plan a fund for the unemployed, three hundred of the latter tried to crowd into the room but had to be content with sending in a deputation. One of these delegates, a painter, stated that they wanted, not financial relief, but employment from which they could keep their families without charity. "They were not jealous of those in high positions", he said, "but they claimed the right to work." When the Mayor replied that it was impossible for the Council to provide work and that a relief office would be started to which the unemployed could apply, another delegate asked why they could not be employed on road work or in preparing the granite sets for the extension of the tramways. He added that "if the meeting could not help them, they must demonstrate and help themselves". Some concessions were then made. Two of the unemployed were co-opted to each of the ten relief sub-committees, an arrangement unprecedented in Colchester, and some 300 men were given temporary work on river improvement. This employment did not last long and building workers were soon on the streets again with their collecting-boxes.[72] Similar distress must have been experienced in the now disappearing footwear industry, with similar problems for the union concerned. Much therefore depended on the A.S.E. and other unions in the expanding engineering factories, if a trade union revival was to take place. The A.S.E. was led by two cautious Paxman employees, both of them Liberals, who, as advocates of close collaboration with their employers, had not even supported their own union in its 1898 national confrontation with the employers' federation. They secured an agreement with Paxman's by which the union was recognised by the firm in return for a promise to rely on negotiations instead of strikes to settle local disputes.[73] The A.S.E. therefore exercised a moderating influence at this time both in the engineering industry and in what remained of the general labour movement in Colchester. Little or no effort was made to organise the thousands of 'unskilled' workers in the town or to promote independent labour politics. The most important development in the first few years of the century was the spread of trade unionism to some non-industrial occupations, which can only have served to reinforce the prevailing moderation. The Commercial Travellers' Union had established a vigorous branch in the town by 1900 and, a year later, the shop assistants were partly organised. The latter found progress difficult and had to build up support by social gatherings at the Salisbury Hotel or summer outings to Mersea and other resorts, causing a group of well-to-do customers to provide rival social facilities to entice the assistants away from the union. The National Union of Clerks also founded a branch, while the Teachers' Union enjoyed a considerable increase in membership in the now rapidly expanding educational service. Trade unionism was not yet completely respectable, but its activities were so unobtrusive and even timid that they were reported in the Press with little, if any, bias. The public grew accustomed to viewing its local trade union movement as moderate and undemanding.

The 1910 strike at Paxman's surprised the town.[74] It sprang from the increasing impersonality of the firm's management and its abandonment of its past paternalism, to which the workers reacted with remarkable sharpness and resolution, completely ignoring the timidity of their official union leadership. On the Monday after May Day 900 of them struck against the management's reduction of piece-rates, worked out by a 'rate-fixer' or 'speediator' and imposed by a new manager. The men in the machine-shop led the action, leaving their section and marching through the works to bring out the others. They caught sight of the speediator and chased him away, they hooted the manager when he asked them to give him time to consult the directors, and then, in a large body, they marched off through the town, singing "Rule, Britannia" and "Boys of the Bulldog Breed". Spirits were high. Both unionists and non-unionists had struck. The boiler-shop men stated that, though they had no grievance, they were striking to help those who had. The skilled men declared support for the unskilled; if skilled men could not exist on 32s. a week, asked one speaker, how could labourers survive on 18s.? The strike remained solid on the Tuesday and when, on Wednesday, the manager opened the gates and offered work to the unemployed, nobody entered. The public was on the strikers' side. The Pleasant Sunday Afternoon movement gave its weekly collections to the strike fund, which also received two guineas from the Rector of St. Leonard's, the parish where Paxman's was situated. The most disappointing attitude was that taken by the national trade union leaders. The A.S.E. had an agreement with Paxman's to arbitrate over all local grievances and was most embarrassed by its members' action, while the Boilermakers' Society strongly rebuked its Colchester members for offending such good employers as Paxman's. The strikers, however, continued to enforce a complete shutdown and to parade the town daily with their band at their head. At the end of the week the firm virtually gave in, removing the speediator and promising that there would be no piece-rate cuts without a prior conference, while the union guaranteed not to strike without similar consultation.

The public was impressed. The *Essex Telegraph*, which had reported events with sympathy, praised the "true English spirit" of these "honest Christian workmen" and noted how the strike had revealed certain new social realities:

> "To see the imposing processions of the men who had 'come out' was to appreciate the important section of the town's inhabitants which these skilled and orderly and enthusiastically united artisans represent."[75]

Ernest Osborne, who seems to have been the most shrewd of the strike leaders, drew a sterner moral:

> "He would guarantee that never in the kingdom had a dispute been entered upon and carried through in a spirit that this one had been. They came out last Monday in a body

> and, though the gates had been thrown open . . ., yet not
> a man or boy had gone back — and they had taught the
> firm a lesson they had never had before."[76]

Shortly afterwards Paxman's readily conceded a 1s.-a-week increase for its weekly wage-earners.

This event proved to be the first step in the revival of the labour movement. During the strike the labourers had supported the skilled men, though they were not involved in the issues in dispute, and afterwards a few of them joined the new branch of the Workers' Union set up by Tim Smith, a London Socialist who had moved to Colchester a few years earlier. The latter always regarded the Paxman labourers as the base from which he then went on to organise one group of 'unskilled' workers after another. His Workers' Union first secured for the gas-men a 30 per cent rise, special overtime rates, a week's paid holiday and proper washing and mess facilities. Similar gains were then made for roadmen, lamp-lighters, oil-mill workers at the Hythe, some clothing-factory tailors, the East Mill labourers and the unskilled men at Rowhedge shipyard.[77] By 1914 some sixty labourers at Mumford's engineering works had joined the Workers' Union and, when refused a hearing for their claim for a 23s. weekly wage, struck work at their breakfast break, paraded round the town for two hours and then held a protest meeting at the I.L.P. room in St. Botolph Street. The firm, still unwilling to recognise the Union by negotiating with it, offered A.S.E. men 2s. a week extra if they would perform the labourers' work for the duration of the strike, only to be met with a complete refusal and by placards proclaiming "We are British, not blacklegs"; the A.S.E. fitters and turners proceeded to join the strike with demands of their own, so that only fifty of the 300 employees were left at work. When the labourers' strike threatened to spread to Paxman's which, like Mumford's, was engaged on urgent Admiralty contracts, an offer of 20s. was made and this proved enough to bring about a return to work. Mumford's A.S.E. men also won concessions.[78] In the building trades, too, joint action by skilled workers and labourers organised in the Workers' Union secured wage increases, 8½d. an hour for the former and 5½d. for the latter. The current mood even affected the artistes at the Hippodrome who struck for shorter hours, causing the manager to substitute 'bioscope pictures' for his advertised programme. Fifty boys at Barrack Street School, following the example of their London school-fellows, left their lessons and paraded outside other schools, singing "Rule, Britannia" and demanding shorter working-hours and an end to corporal punishment.[79] A renewed attempt was made to organise women workers when the chairman of the local Fabian Society, Patricia Green, set up a Colchester centre of the National Federation of Women Workers but, despite a strenuous programme of meetings and socials, the movement remained in the hands of Fabian and Liberal ladies, since few, if any, working-class women could be persuaded to take office. Another group hitherto unorganised were the railwaymen, and here a member of the I.L.P. was responsible for the growth of the union from a tiny body, so weak that it could not join in the national rail strike, to a position where, in 1914, it counted three-quarters of the 260 local railwaymen among its members.[80] Few sections of local industry were unaffected by this trade union expansion. The fast-growing printing industry found itself obliged to treat with its workers' unions; Spottiswoode's printers caused a sensation in 1911 when they refused to take over printing work sent down to Colchester as a result of a London strike.[81] The older unions were stirred into greater activity. The A.S.E. won recognition by the new Colchester Lathe Co., where improved overtime rates were negotiated, and it secured a 2s.-a-week increase for all local engineering workers.[82] In all these movements the Trades Council, refounded on Tim Smith's initiative in about 1905, was available to help, advise and co-ordinate. Its voice was increasingly heard, too, on social and municipal affairs, including old-age pensions, early closing of shops and hospital admission procedure. It contested seats on the Board of Referees and sought representation on other public bodies, but it left to the I.L.P. the promotion of labour politics, partly because its own membership included supporters of both the Conservative and Liberal parties.

The refounded Colchester I.L.P. had been a major force in the labour movement's twentieth-century revival; not only Tim Smith but several other militant leaders belonged to it. Its origins seem to have been in a purely local organisation, the Colchester Socialist Society, which had, besides Tim Smith, the N.U.R. secretary, a tramways clerk, a newsagent's son, a teacher and a Paxman's blacksmith among its leading members. Started in 1903 or 1904, this Society became increasingly active, holding weekly discussions in the Co-operative Reading-room in Lion Walk and arranging lectures on Socialism in the open air or in public halls. In about 1908 its members decided that they should abandon their local independence and join one of the two Socialist parties, either the I.L.P. or the Marxist Social Democratic Federation. When a member who had belonged to the latter party in London urged the others to form a branch of it in Colchester, Tim Smith persuaded them that Colchester was, in his words, "too aristocratic" to respond to anything more militant than the I.L.P. A branch of the latter was therefore started, which by 1910 had become accepted as Labour's political voice.[83] With a membership of about eighty, half of whom were very active, it maintained a programme of unflagging activity, including weekly party meetings at its rooms, weekly open-air meetings in the High Street and occasional public meetings addressed by, amongst others, Philip Snowden, Keir Hardie, George Lansbury and Tom Mann, whose "electric eloquence" persuaded a large audience in Barrack Street School hall to support an international workers' strike to prevent the outbreak of war. It was not a militant organisation at the start, but it soon moved leftwards after its younger members carried out a revolt against the original leaders. It was rarely unrepresented at municipal elections and in 1910 surprised the public by winning 575 votes in South Ward without "motors or traps". This vote was not enough to gain a seat, but a little later Tim Smith was elected, to the indignation of the Liberal party, whose candidate he displaced. The I.L.P. did not contest the Parliamentary seat but, through its numerous Trades Council members, persuaded the unions to help start a Labour Representation Committee which was preparing to nominate a Labour candidate for Parliament when the Great War broke out. However, its "large united Labour demonstration" on the eve of

War showed that Labour had become a permanent political party in Colchester.[84]

The War had its opponents among local Socialists. George Lansbury, like Tom Mann, had met an enthusiastic response when he urged his audience to boycott the army and join an international strike for peace.[85] On the Sunday preceding the Declaration the Socialist minister of Headgate Chapel denounced war from the pulpit as wicked in itself and calculated to preserve imperialism and promote profit.[86] Such voices were silenced by the wave of patriotic emotion that swept through the town in Autumn 1914.

CHAPTER VI

Social Life

The making of Victorian Colchester, 1815–60

One girl's impression of respectable Colchester at the start of the century survives in the autobiography of Ann Taylor. As a girl of fourteen, she had come to Colchester when her father became Minister of Stockwell Chapel during the Napoleonic Wars. Her memories, she wrote,

> "never present themselves but as bright and warm with a summer's sun . . . It is a nice old town, and the country has just that cheerful pleasantness about it which is inviting to the evening walk or the social ramble. The town, clean, open and agreeable, is situated on a healthful, gravelly hill, descending towards the north and east, commanding from many points a view of the Colne, the meadows through which it winds, and the horizon fringed with woods — 'the High Woods', which formed the most delightful portion of our longer evening excursions. But in this direction I am told that the engineer has been defacing, with his iron lines and brick station houses, one of the prettiest spots and, to our memories, one of the dearest in the whole vicinity. Yet I must not be unjust to the beautiful village of Lexden, terminating a pleasant walk west of the town, or the ornate path through Lexden springs. Innumerable happy associations place them among the brightest of our mental pictures. Large barracks adjoined the town on its southern side, and an air of business and activity was given to the place as a great military station, while the High Street was quite a gay promenade."

Ann found the town as intellectually dull as it was visually delightful. The large Nonconformist community, among whose members she sought new friends, seemed quite devoid of enlightenment and congenial companionship. "No young person" she wrote "was associated in the membership of any Nonconformist church in the town." In the end she did find a few like-minded friends, and together they founded the Umbelliferous Society in which to exchange ideas and recite their compositions to one another. They were interested in the young John Constable, who, though barely embarked upon his career, was singled out for future eminence by this "jury of girls between the ages of fifteen and twenty-one".[1] Ann's circle dispersed and she, too, departed, having made no impact upon a town preoccupied with the worldly amusements then in favour with the officers of the Colchester and Weeley camps and with the resident gentlefolk. However, change was imminent. In 1815–16 de-mobilisation quenched the gaiety as well as intensifying the economic gloom caused by the cloth industry's collapse. The pace of the social round perceptibly slackened as the officers left the neighbourhood. The races on Lexden and Mile End Heaths, so well supported during 1750–1815, now sank into obscurity. Only at St. Dennis's November Fair was the old programme of public breakfasts and dinners, theatre and dances, repeated in a form little different from that of the past half-century, except that the Three Cups replaced the White Hart as host, but it was now always uncertain whether enough of the right people would attend. In 1824 "upwards of 200 fashionables" were at the theatre, but in 1831, it was reported, "the public week has been duller than usual", with less than forty at the public breakfast, about twenty at the dinner and 150 at the ball. Another poor season in 1834 led the *Essex Standard* to declare that "the fashion for fairs, balls and plays is evidently passing away".[2] The theatre in general was losing custom. During the War it had been so well patronised that in 1812 a move was made to a new building in Queen Street with a capacity of 1,200, but, despite visits by Ellen Tree in *As You Like It* and by other leading figures, several seasons were close to being failures and by 1843 William Wire could write that "the theatre passed its prime some years since; in fact, this is not a theatre-going town now".[3]

Meanwhile, amid the deepening post-war slump, the Reform conflict grew sharper and the poor, especially in the villages, more sullen. Frivol-ity was increasingly out of place, and a new seriousness among the well-to-do made them responsive to the current Evangelical movements and to the call for more missionary work among the people. Leaders of local society and their ladies took up good works. The Smyths of Berechurch Hall, the Rounds of East Hill House and Birch Hall, the Papillons of Lexden Manor were of a more sober stamp than the great families of the previous century. Georgianna Rebow of Wivenhoe Park was a busy social worker, very different from a predecessor of the 1770s, Mary Rebow, whose correspondence shows her, by comparison, as an amiable but frivolous girl. Since ownership of property, especially in land, con-ferred high standing, these families set standards of public behaviour to which the less eminent were also drawn. There was still much self-indulg-ence, religious indifference and neglect of public duty, but the ideals destined to inspire Colchester's Victorian middle class were already being given the stamp of upper-class approval. It should be added, however, that some ordinary people, especially Nonconformists, had been in advance of their social superiors; it was their principles of sobriety, earnestness and social concern that were now spreading to the gentry.

Moral seriousness was most observable in Evangelical religion. Ang-licans presented a steady stream of candidates for confirmation, 2,208 at St. James's in 1814, 1,600 in 1818 and 1,830 in 1822. When the Bishop of London consecrated the new Lexden church, it was announced that 350 of the 550 seats were to be free.[4] There were new churches at St. Botolph's and Shrub End and major improvements at St. Leonard's, St. Giles's, St. Peter's and St. Martin's. The Roman Catholic church was built in Priory Street in 1837. Among Nonconformist chapels, Stockwell was several times enlarged, Lion Walk increased its seating, while the Wesleyan Chapel in Maidenburgh Street was replaced by a new building in Culver Street. In 1839 the Primitive Methodist Chapel, where C. H. Spurgeon is said later to have been converted, was built in Artillery Street and in 1844 a schism at Lion Walk led to the opening of Headgate Congregational Chapel. Even greater zeal was needed in the sustained effort to provide places of worship in the growing suburbs, where Nonconformists took the lead since Anglicans already possessed churches in every parish. In 1812 Lion Walk was holding services in Harwich Road district and by 1844 had built a chapel there. At Mile End the Baptists seem to have been the pioneers, but by 1828 the Wesleyans were claiming strong support at their chapel, probably situated in Mill Road where Chapel Cottages now stand.[5] At West Bergholt the Wesleyans were also represented, along with the Baptists and the Congregationalists. At Lexden, as at Mile End, the Baptists were overtaken by the Wesleyans, who met first in a cottage and from 1859 in their new chapel, still standing in Straight Road. At Shrub End, Lion Walk opened a chapel in 1843, only a few years before the new Anglican church was built. The Hythe received special attention because of its growing population and the supposed immorality of its waterside community. Lion Walk had a group there in 1822 and a permanent building from 1846. The Wesleyans were less successful, despite sustained efforts, having to close their Hythe chapel and their Magdalen Street chapel in the 1840s. Finally, in Greensted, Lion Walk maintained a preaching station in 1851 and there was a small Primitive Methodist group as well. This record, which is probably incomplete, is an impressive one, especially as times were hard for the tradesmen and artisans who were the strength of Colchester Nonconformity. Several ministers also served rural north Essex. The Wesleyan minister took services in the Tendring Hundred and the St. John's Green Baptist minister at Lawford and Weeley Heath, while Lion Walk actively supported the Essex Congregational Union's mission to found new rural chapels.[6]

Religious observance increased rapidly. In 1829 Eld Lane Baptists claimed congregations of 800, the Wesleyans 700, Stockwell Congregationalists about 1,200, Lion Walk about a thousand and St. John's Green Baptists 400. Nonconformists at this time claimed higher attendances than the churches, but a new generation of Anglican clergy soon redressed the balance, so that by 1851 there were four people attending church for every three at chapel.[7] The Rev. Horace Roberts raised the congregation at the new church of St. Botolph's from seventy to over a thousand, with 200 children at Sunday school.[8] Equally vigorous were the widely respected Vicar of St. Peter's, William Marsh, and J. T. Round, who, after teaching at Balliol, became Rector of St. Runwald's. It was consistent with the new evangelicalism that laymen began now to play a prominent part in religious life, as well as taking the message into a variety of secular movements. Horatio Cock, a wealthy surgeon, bridged the years between the old outlook and the new. After an earlier life of conventional comfort he undertook a wide range of good works, stinting himself to find money for beneficence. He became a Hospital Governor and a leading worker for the Benevolent Society and Lying-In Charity, but was even more zealous in religious causes, as President of the Bible Society and active patron of the Church Missionary Society, the Society for the Propagation of the Gospel in Foreign Parts and, for good measure, the Methodist Mission. "In his domestic circle and family connections might be seen everything of mildness and affectionate behaviour. To instruct his household and train them in the ways of godliness was his unceasing endeavour. The return of the Sabbath was to him a delight and witnessed his constant attendance, and his family's, in God's sanctuary; and his own house was one of daily prayer and praise."[9] One of his numerous Nonconformist counterparts was J. A. Tabor, a member of Lion Walk and the author of its history, who gave sustained service to the town's religious and civic life. Pious laymen were active particularly in the auxiliary religious bodies which founded branches in Colchester, like the Bible Society, the S.P.C.K., the Wesleyan Missionary Society and at least half a dozen others.

A counterpart of religious zeal was the religious bigotry which not infrequently found public expression. The *Essex Standard* reported Nonconformist schisms with some relish and with no concealment of its prejudices. In 1840, for instance, it wrote:

> "We understand there is a 'screw loose' in the Baptist meeting house, or rather dissension in the congregation. No marvel truly — for where look we for dissension but among dissenters? The story is that the Baptists are again tired of their minister; and they who treated their former kind-hearted zealous pastor, Mr. Francies, so vilely, are now quarrelling with his successor, Mr. Rust . . . We suppose Mr. Rust has been tickling the 'itching ears' a little too sharply. A further communication on the wranglings and recent unseemly interruptions of religious services at the Independent meeting house, East Stockwell Street, has reached us, which we shall endeavour to find room for next week."[10]

Nonconformists replied with often bitter attacks upon the Anglican establishment, especially on the Church Rate which required them to pay for the upkeep of buildings belonging to a denomination not their own. The intense feeling thus aroused sharpened social as well as denominational divisions; the two sides, already partly drawn from different economic circles, tended increasingly to spend their leisure and take their pleasures separately. Both Anglicans and Nonconformists showed a foolish intolerance towards Roman Catholics. Sir G. H. Smyth resigned his Colchester Parliamentary seat over Catholic Emancipation, to his supporters' strong approval. In 1842 the President of the largely Nonconformist and Liberal Mechanics' Institute threatened to resign if a Roman Catholic priest lectured to that body in a way which the President found objectionable.[11] The supposed 'Popish' sympathies of Lord John Manners, Conservative candidate in 1852, elicited unpleasant attacks from the Liberals and Nonconformists and also led to a remarkable rift among Conservatives, some of whom started a weekly newspaper expressly to put out of business the *Essex Standard*, the owner of which was Manners's chief critic.[12]

Amid this religious zeal middle-class gentility throve. It tended to see itself as the upholder, not of gaiety and splendour as in the previous century, but of decency and Christian refinement. The social scene in Autumn 1825 exemplified the post-war mood. The local paper reported the first concert by the recently formed Colchester Music Society before "a select party" and, in the same week, "a sale of ladies' useful and ornamental work" at the Cups in aid of the Bible Society and Church Missionary Society. The New Florists' Society held its annual show and the Botanical Society entertained "a highly respectable company" in the Botanical Gardens, a six-acre park behind Greyfriars, East Hill. Colchester Philosophical Society was starting its new series of lectures and was busily expanding its museum. The Conservative Reading-room was open in Head Street and two similar institutions in High Street, each being maintained by a club of subscribers.[13] The voluntary bodies involved in these activities were themselves a phenomenon little in evidence before 1800. They served as a medium that was to be characteristic of nineteenth-century Colchester, providing means by which the town's middle class created its own social life and its own respectable circles. They can also be seen as the secular counterpart of the contemporary participation by the laity in religious activity.

Pleasure in property and in its accompanying privileges was as central to the outlook of the well-to-do as were religious zeal, good works and refined taste. Those with wealth or high income felt fully entitled to the Parliamentary and municipal franchise and, generally, they sought to exclude others from these rights precisely because they were poor or propertyless. Such opinions, though more plausibly presented, underlay the middle-class opposition to Colchester Chartism, and they were held as firmly by many Liberal employers as by Conservative gentlefolk. Well-to-do people assumed the right to exclusive control of the town and they expected the obedience of their economic inferiors. When at the Municipal Enquiry of 1835 the Commissioner cross-questioned leading officials with some firmness, the Corporation protested that this "ungentlemanly conduct excited among the assembled crowd the coarsest ribaldry and produced rancour and hostility towards the members of the Corporation, who are persons that the lower classes ought to have been taught to respect".[14] James Hurnard, the Quaker poet, noted how wealth led its possessors to expect the deference of others:

"We have great bankers, too, who love obeisance,
Great men who cannot see beneath chins
Or notice meaner people right or left,
And tread upon the earth that soon will cover them
As though they had forgot from whence they sprang".[15]

Nor was it too expensive to keep up a position. Servants' wages were low, country girls were counted fortunate to gain such employment and most middle-class families enjoyed leisure, comfort and standing by keeping domestic staff. In 1841 George Stokes, Mechanics' Institute President, in his High Street house, and the Rev. James Round, Rector of St. Runwald's, each employed one male and five female servants. Roger Nunn, a doctor in Queen Street, had a governess living in and three servants; the Grammar School headmaster kept two and a High Street pawnbroker one.[16] New houses were becoming available in or near Lexden Road. When in 1837 Beverley Lodge paddock was offered for sale, the estate agent couched his advertisement in these terms:

> "This delightful spot presents every possible inducement
> for the erection of a villa or ornamental cottage residence,
> which in this superior neighbourhood will secure imme-
> diate tenants in a situation of first-rate respectability".

By 1859 a trade directory noted that "there are many first class houses and terraces for a mile out of town, and this road as far as Lexden forms the principal promenade".[17]

One man, who aspired to a grand house in Lexden, found a place in James Hurnard's poem:

> "Like several of our Lawyers, in his childhood
> He was a hunger-bitten charity-boy,
> And swept a lawyer's office for small wages.
> These men become important personages,
> And when they offer to shake hands with you
> They do you honour with a pair of fingers;
> This boy was soon promoted to a stool,
> And so at length became himself a lawyer.
> He was a little active bustling man,
> Extremely neat and dapper in apparel,
> Ignorant of books except his books of law,
> But with a fund of hearty cheerfulness,
> And with a ready boldness of behaviour
> That made him popular with the Tory squires,
> Although his brother kept a barber's shop.
> Self-confidence, however, bore him onward . . .
> Ere long as he advanced in his profession
> He built himself some handsome offices
> In the Church-Lane, which made his brethren jealous,
> And moved into a mansion which he bought
> At lovely Lexden, near by Colchester,
> And kept his horse and gig and livery servant . . .
> He gained the status of Councillor
> And bye and bye the dignity of Alderman
> And strutted grandly in a scarlet cloak."[18]

The more forward-looking among the well-to-do also wanted a Colchester where public cleanliness and elegance would match their own domestic comfort and respectability. Despite their dislike of rising rates, they supported moves to improve and gas-light the main streets, curb and pave the

side-walks, replace disagreeable public buildings and remove inconveni-
ent features from the town centre. A letter to the Press in 1840 complained:

> "In every town we enter may be seen new Churches, new
> Hospitals, new Exchanges, new Town Halls . . . to meet the
> cultivated taste or the extended wants of their inhabitants.
> In our town of Colchester, the last twenty years have wit-
> nessed the erection of a Hospital, a Church, a Provident
> Asylum for decayed tradesmen, and a Corn Exchange . . .
> but we appear now to have come to a standstill, and this
> with (at least) one material defect in the list of our public
> buildings — we refer to our antiquated, inconvenient, ugly,
> patched and tumble-down Town Hall — which (being held
> up by the houses on each side) is a standing mass of all the
> barbarous architecture which each successive carpenter to
> the Corporation has chosen to load it with; formerly the
> Town Theatre, now the Town Gaol, it is at once an incum-
> brance and a disgrace. There can be but one opinion on the
> propriety of an effort being made to erect a Hall worthy of
> our ancient town and affording those conveniences in
> which the present one is injuriously deficient, a Hall, an
> Assembly Room, Courts and Offices, and in addition to
> these, a Public Library, Museum, etc."[19]

The completion of a new Town Hall and a new Corn Exchange led the
Essex Standard to exclaim: "This is emphatically an age of *improvement*,
which, like a mighty tide, is rolling onwards with a power that is wholly
irresistible".[20] Two years later a scheme was announced to develop the
Lord's Land, north of Crouch Street, as a planned spa-like precinct,
comprising an elegant bath-house, surrounded by lawns, and a crescent
of detached houses, set amid spacious gardens. This dream never became
reality, but one improvement was finally carried out when the cattle
market was removed to the bottom of North Hill. The *Essex Standard*
rejoiced that "the High Street will no longer present the spectacle of
crowds of cattle blocking up the way and making the air vocal with their
cries and redolent of their odour. We shall rejoice more in the remembrance of such a scene than in its actual realisation."[21]

The social life of the poor is less easily pictured; even where it emerges
into the public view, it is often through some court case or other such
event reported in the Press. The poor were not articulate about their
enjoyments, except for James Carter and John Castle who unusually left
autobiographies. Post-war life was hard for the workers, with wages low
and unemployment never far away. The old ceremonies of the clothworkers, such as the Bishop Blaize processions, had ceased along with the
cloth trade, and the various artisans who predominated after 1800
apparently had no craft cultures of their own. The tailors were an ancient
calling, but James Carter shows how they had neither time nor spirit for
more than "the balderdash, the ribaldry and the worse-than-childish
squabbling which usually formed the staple of the shop-board conversation".[22] Carter was no prig, being well aware that such ignorance arose
from bleak working-conditions, precarious employment, constant fear of
ill-health and lack of intellectual opportunity, of all of which he gives first-

hand evidence. Similar information about the silk-weavers comes from John Castle who was one of them.[23] Their livelihood was more insecure than that of the tailors, and they lacked even the stimulation of sharing a work-place with fellow-craftsmen. To the complaint that low wages and long hours stunted initiative and mental activity, the Victorian answer was that self-help would still enable the prudent to become their own masters or otherwise to shape their own lives, but the careers of Carter and Castle showed how illusory such prospects were. Carter ruined his health in attempting to build up his business, though he did, almost uniquely, continue to pursue his intellectual interests by sheer effort of will. Castle was a brave, cheerful and religious man, whose struggles for his comrades' welfare gave him self-respect and moral strength, but, though the Colchester Co-operative Society, which he largely founded, was destined to become the centre of adult education for the town's working people, he personally had too little time left over from his work to reach James Carter's high level of self-education. The small minority who did learn to use their intellects probably owed this success to the stimulus of religion or politics. Carter records how, through a sudden interest in politics and international affairs, his workmates bought a weekly paper to read aloud and how strong arguments arose as a result.[24] Castle, too, gained much from his close association with the group of ex-Chartists who helped him form the Co-operative Society.

For most workingmen, and many working-class women, the public house remained their social centre, to the disgust of many moralists who often complained about the increasing number of such resorts. In fact, proportionately to the population, their number kept falling. The new beerhouses were often in parts of the borough where suburbs were coming into being without amenities of this kind, like Parson's Heath, Lexden Heath, Old Heath and the Hythe. Fairs provided brief holidays for many people, and this too was a subject of criticism. A correspondent of the *Ipswich Express*, describing the town's Stock Fair in July 1842, wrote that "the gingerbread portion of the community, together with the more sturdy railway men, flocked down in the evening and, amid noise and confused mirth, squandered their money either in trifles or debauchery".[25] To some workingmen the Friendly Societies gave new facilities for social intercourse. These had originated in the eighteenth century but had multiplied by early Victorian times. On the one hand there were the Oddfellows, a national society governed by standard rules, and the Essex Provident Society, managed by local gentlemen for the poor's benefit, and on the other hand, a wide range of self-governing clubs, many of them attached to inns. Almost all societies had an annual dinner. William Wire recorded in his diary, "Attended my Benefit Club feast, a very good plain dinner for which 2s. 6d. was paid the meeting before".[26] At the self-governing public house clubs the members were accused of indulging in so much drinking that the funds were often endangered. For the poorer freemen there was also some fellowship in the political clubs which were organised in the public houses by the candidates.

There was little other entertainment, especially for women. Cricket and other organised games were not at that time played by the Colchester poor, who lacked the necessary leisure, energy, income and playgrounds, but they did enjoy the countryside and they offered firm resistance when the local gentry and clergymen tried to put a stop to their annual picnic at Lexden Springs on the grounds that, being held always on Good Friday, it was offensive to churchgoers and morally harmful to the holidaymakers. The occasion was said to be one of noise and roughness, but a local gentleman who visited it to see for himself gave a different picture when he described it many years later:

> "Instead of roughs and rowdies I found a vast concourse of respectable and well-conducted people, including not only the working classes, but a fair proportion of the sons and daughters of substantial ratepayers, engaged in friendly social intercourse or in old-fashioned sports and pastimes, which to me seemed quite harmless and innocent and which I feel persuaded would so have appeared to even the strictest of Anglican clergymen had the day been Easter Monday instead of Good Friday. I did not go as a reporter to prepare sensational paragraphs . . . I simply wished to ascertain the truth for myself, and what I witnessed was an ideal old-fashioned holiday, with the manifestation of better manners, more mutual consideration and kindly feeling, and more innocent happiness, than I have seen displayed in any popular gathering since."[27]

The poor were fond of bathing, usually in the river at a spot near North Bridge, and there was discontent when this was polluted by the outflow from the Middleborough sewer. For lack of other diversions they were apt to flock to unusual or sensational events. Many watched when in 1823, for stealing a few cheap articles, a man was whipped at the cart-tail for 200 yards. The entry of a circus into the town, the arrival of the first railway train and every Parliamentary Nomination Day drew thousands of spectators.

The railway brought single-day holidays within reach of all but the very poorest. On Easter Monday 1846, half-price fares were charged for an excursion train to London, which, with its ten open cattle-trucks fitted with seats, left Colchester at 7.00 a.m. and returned from London at 6.00 p.m.; such was the interest that hundreds had to be turned away. In September of the same year 1,500 people visited London in thirty-five carriages, drawn by two engines, at 6s. and 4s. for covered and open-air accommodation respectively. An accident on the Romford embankment delayed the departure from London and there was a further delay at Stratford while the mail train passed, all to the passengers' vociferous indignation. Such excursions soon became commonplace. The Great Exhibition was visited by thousands of Colcestrians, mostly using the frequent special trains run that year at a halfpenny a mile. People now attended London conferences or rallies of their Temperance organisation or Friendly Society. A special train ran from Wivenhoe and Colchester for the People's Welcome to Garibaldi, and it was full.[28]

Between high and low life were other circles, not clearly defined, where intellectual seriousness reigned. William Wire's diary affords glimpses of this unobtrusive part of Colchester's social life. Wire, a tireless anti-

quarian, devoted much of his time to the town's past, especially to the
Roman period, evidence of which was constantly being brought to his
attention during the building operations of the 1840s. He refers to friends
and acquaintances from a variety of social circles, political parties and
religious denominations who shared his own wide interests. Dr. Duncan,
after whom the north-east postern gate in the Roman wall is called, writes
to invite him to an archaeological lecture, and the Rev. H. Jenkins,
Rector of Stanway, tells him in one letter of his excavations on the
Gosbeck's site and in another maintains that the Temple of Claudius was
on or near the site of the Norman Castle. With another friend Wire
discusses whether Camulodunum was Colchester. He receives from an
Ipswich friend some drawings by Philip Morant of the Lexden earth-
works, borrows from a lawyer some documents about the Colchester
Volunteers of the Napoleonic Wars period and reads a diary written by an
eighteenth-century Colcestrian. He inspects old town maps at the house
of the Editor of the *Essex Standard* and he buys a rare Prospect of Colchester. He presents some objects to the new Sudbury Museum, lends
others to the Society of Antiquaries and, with a friend, visits Professor
Henslow at Hitcham to see his botanical collection. He notes various
disservices to the town's historical past, such as the destruction of part of
the Balkerne Gate by the proprietor of the adjacent inn to enable his
customers to watch the trains at the new railway station, the scandal of the
cow-sheds built against the Castle wall, and the haphazard way in which
items are being collected for a proposed Colchester museum. He
accompanies the recently formed Essex Archaeological Society on a visit to
Coggeshall's antiquities and himself conducts a British Archaeological Society party around Colchester. He tries to trace lost paintings by Dunthorne,
Constable's friend, and collects subscriptions for a reprint of a Colchester
Civil War tract. He visits churches at Langenhoe, Feering and Little
Horkesley to see carvings or do brass-rubbings. From friends he receives
information on matters of interest to him, the flora and fauna of north-
east Essex, the site of Colchester's former Jewish synagogue, the successive owners of the recipe for the eringo-root sweetmeat, a Colchester
speciality, the location of a military whipping-post on Lexden Heath, and
details of the Goldhanger Red Hills. Contemporary events interest him,
too. He notes the enclosure of part of Magdalen Green, the opening of
Wesleyan schools in Culver Street, and the first steps towards the long-
delayed removal of Middle Row in High Street. He attends lectures on
Phrenology and on Machinery, and meetings on Early Closing, Corn Law
Repeal and the preservation of local footpaths. From an old Chartist
friend, Stephen Clubb, he hears about a machine he has invented for
stripping barley of its skin for the making of puddings. All the time he is
on the alert to scrutinise the upcast from current building operations in
the hope of finding archaeological evidence or he is buying objects of the
Roman period and looking for possible Roman sites. Despite personal
troubles his life was busy, useful, varied and studious. He communicated
with people from a wide range of social, religious and political back-
grounds, with Anglicans and Nonconformists, gentlefolk and shopkeepers and artisans, clergymen and laymen, but, with one exception, all
males. Yet, in case from this a picture is formed of a united community of

intellectuals transcending divisions of class or creed, it is worth adding that, in Wire's opinion, Conservatives and Anglicans formed the Colchester Literary Institute expressly to crush the largely Liberal-Nonconformist Mechanics' Institute. Furthermore, Wire's own failure to achieve recognition during his lifetime for his outstanding service to the town's Romano-British archaeology was probably due in part to his social inferiority and his Chartist past.[29]

Wire was not the only man of humble origin to build for himself a life of scholarship. One of his friends, who accompanied him on the visit to Professor Henslow's museum, was John Brown, for twenty-five years a stone-mason on East Hill, who, after saving enough money, acquired a farm at Stanway to give himself the conditions in which to pursue his intense interest in Geology. He left no known diary, and less is known of him than of Wire. He contributed articles on his subject to learned journals, gave items to the British Museum and in his will left £300 to the Royal Geological Society. There was quite widespread popular interest in current scientific and technological matters and this was reflected in the Mechanics' Institute programme. In the year in which Wire heard a lecture on Machinery delivered by the chief engineer of the recently opened London–Colchester railway, the Institute's members were able to hear others on Mechanics, Astronomy, Agricultural Chemistry and Physiology.[30]

Mid-Victorian times, 1860–90

After 1860 social change was slow. To the satisfaction of polite society, Colchester remained the large country town which it had been ever since the cloth industry's extinction, and its economic security now seemed to be assured by the prosperity of its agricultural neighbourhood. The challenge of industrialism still consisted of the railway, the St. Peter's Street silk-mill and little else. Technical change was proceeding quietly in tailoring and shoemaking, but not so as to obtrude or awaken anxiety about its social consequences. When, after 1875, the agricultural slump seemed to endanger Colchester's market-town economy, the Camp's 3,000 occupants provided alternative custom for many of the threatened tradesmen.

The railway had not brought with it the industries and the radical politics which a few Liberals had hoped for. Even as the line was being constructed, one of the latter expressed his disappointment:

> "It is confidently expected that the line will be opened in the course of the year 1842. But what astonishes our minds is that the inhabitants of Colchester appear to be perfectly unconcerned about the undertaking. As to any commercial movement, or any attempts at internal improvements, or the construction of improved streets, or building of new houses, a railway in the moon would just as powerfully affect the *mind* of the Colchester folks and stir up a spirit worthy of the age in which we live. The fact is, there is very little public spirit, and that little, we fear, has been exhausted in the late subscription for a new Town Hall.

Instead of being the first in a series of improvements to follow in rapid succession, we fear it will be an isolated moment of the liberality of the present generation, unless, as we fervently hope, the railway will infuse some fresh spirit into our townsmen, by introducing amongst us a new order of individuals, who will give an impetus to business, despite the old-fashioned notions that cling to our townsmen, who think they have an hereditary right to command and control the business of the town, because their fathers *lived before them*. These are the remnants of Tory exclusiveness, and we fear that most of the indifference that prevails at the present time may be traced to the blighting influence of Toryism now rampant in the Borough. May we have a speedy deliverance; then we may hope that Colchester will be blessed with a revival in her commerce, and possess an influence commensurate with her population."[31]

In the event, the railway led to no appreciable growth of commerce or industry nor to any Liberal advance, but to an improvement of travelling-facilities for the comfortably off, who were liberated from their rural isolation and enabled to travel for business or pleasure with speed and cheapness. Within a year of the railway's opening, the *Essex Standard* reported:

"A good day's work. Railroads for ever. A legal gentleman of Colchester left that town by mail train for Warwick, which he reached by 11 o'clock, and went on to Leamington to complete his business . . . returned to London via Coventry, reached town by 6 o'clock, dined and kept three appointments during a stay of 2½ hours, returning to Colchester by the mail train to a late tea at 11 o'clock, after which he finished the labours of the day by communicating, through the same night's up-mail, to his friends at Leamington his safe arrival."[32]

The town's respectability remained unaffected. The Great Eastern Railway's own 1865 *Guide* presented Colchester as an ancient town, keeping pace with civic progress but avoiding industrialisation:

"We look with a feeling of almost reverence upon a town which existed before the Christian era, and was a place of importance and a seat of power when nearly all the rest of the country was a wilderness. As we glance down its main streets . . . we see in its elegant shops, hotels and public buildings, the freshness and taste of the present day mingled with the memories of the past."

The *Guide* then noted the new public buildings and the foremost antiquities and observed that "the commercial aspect is of limited character, there being no manufactories in the town".[33]

So Colchester remained a congenial place for those who found industrialisation distasteful and who could afford a secluded residence with spacious garden. The railway's advocates had envisaged "the beautiful slope from Braiswick and Mile End studded with villa residences",[34] but at this time most middle-class development occurred on or near Lexden Road. "It is superfluous", wrote the *Essex Standard*, "to remark that houses on the Lexden Road are in great demand."[35] Land between Crouch Street and Maldon Road was offered for sale in 1865 with the recommendation that houses there would enjoy the double advantage of rural seclusion and proximity to Crouch Street shops.[36] By that date Beverley Road and the Avenue had also been opened. The residents of this neighbourhood, now reinforced by Army families, were cared for by numerous servants. At Lexden House, Edward Round, banker, and his family kept a cook, lady's maid, housemaid and footman, while elsewhere in the town, at East Hill House, Margaret Round had an even larger staff, including a butler. Thomas Catchpool, J.P., Quaker proprietor of the High Street iron foundry, lived, not in the ever more crowded town centre, but up Lexden Road, at Highfields, where he had a resident staff of three. Nearby, at Sussex Lodge, an army major was looked after by a batman and two female servants, while in St. Mary's Terrace, an army widow kept a butler, lady's maid, cook, housemaid and kitchen-maid.

The social round was a busy one. At East Hill House, "the finest mansion in the borough", the philanthropic widow, Margaret Round, presided over "many of those pleasant gatherings of the *élite*, which have so much to do with the social life of a community".[37] At such social occasions the gentry of town and country regularly met the Army's upper ranks. St. Dennis's Fair had ceased to be the fashionable season, but in a single week of 1877 the annual county ball was held in the Town Hall, with dancing until 5.00 a.m., and at the Camp 300 guests from Colchester and North Essex joined the officers and their families at a Grand Military Ball. A few weeks later the Essex and Suffolk Club was opened in the High Street, with a ladies' suite and a billiards-room, the entrance fee being £5 and the annual subscription £3; this was the second such establishment, the Colchester Club having been opened a few years before. The theatre was slow to regain respectability, but the building in Queen Street was used for amateur dramatics by town and military groups; among the performers was Baden-Powell who got into trouble for using army bandsmen in musical sketches for the local Conservative Club.[38] Large and fashionable audiences were reported at two lectures by Oscar Wilde on 'The House Beautiful', in which the speaker said that "he had often been asked what was the most artistic colour. One colour was not more beautiful than another. It was ridiculous to make one colour fashionable. What would be said of a paragraph stating that B Flat would next year be the fashionable note?"[39] Music was less well supported. A Promenade Concert by the Town Band attracted only a handful of listeners; "our townsmen were never famous for their appreciation of native talent and they have made no advance in that direction", wrote the *Essex Standard*.[40]

Cricket at last obtained proper accommodation. In 1861 the *Essex Standard* had reported that "the match between Colchester and Ipswich was played at Bentley, in consequence of no ground being available for the purpose in the former town. Is there any other town in England, greater or smaller, and whether or not numbering as Colchester does

some of the finest players in the county, which cannot boast the possession of a cricket ground?" However, the Colchester and East Essex Club
had just been founded, among the members being "some of the first
gentleman players of the district", and in 1865 it obtained a twenty-one-
year lease on a large field facing Wimpole Road, part of the old barrack
ground, at £30-a-year rent. A 'match pitch', seventy by twenty-five yards,
was levelled and laid with turf from the long-established ground at Wivenhoe Park. There were hopes that an all-Essex side would be raised to
entertain leisured people from all over the county, and a professional
bowler was engaged who was to bowl to the bigger subscribers only. The
club also played Colchester's first-ever Rugby match here, against the
Garrison. However, by 1877 the pitch was finally judged to be too
powdery, despite all the treatment given it, and its location had proved
too remote from most members' homes; it was also immediately adjacent
to the Contagious Diseases Hospital and unprotected against the incur-
sions of small boys from the neighbourhood.[41] So in 1878 a move was
made to Cambridge Road where lawn-tennis courts as well as a cricket
pitch were laid out, though a critic thought that "the area is somewhat too
circumscribed and that a hard-hitting batsman would have little difficulty
in putting the ball outside the boundary".[42]

It all makes a pleasant picture, but even the well-to-do remained in too
close proximity to their humble fellow-townsmen not to be aware that
many of the latter lived lives altogether different from their own. The
contrast was clear between comfort and deprivation, between respectability and degradation, between cultural opportunities and cultural
deprivation. While a minority enjoyed facilities for discriminating
shopping, playing cricket or hearing lectures, the pace of progress was
slow in the provision of relaxations for the poor. Elementary schools were
not expected to arrange games, lacking as they did playing-fields and
sometimes even playgrounds. Out-of-school facilities for sport were few.
"There was no place even for children to play, except the Castle Bailey,
and that had been very near being turned into a Cattle Market", wrote
the *Essex Standard* in 1868. That paper's proprietor, John Taylor, was
singled out for commendation because, uniquely, he sometimes opened
his garden for youngsters to play in. The Ragged School's attempt to
counteract vandalism and alleged immorality among boys and girls was a
most interesting undertaking, but its duration was limited and its value
lay in the provision of elementary education rather than of wholesome
relaxation. The Band of Hope probably contributed more to the latter
purpose, though few of its members came from the 'Ragged' class. Many
youths probably used their leisure in much the same way as those whose
case came before the Colchester Bench in January 1872:

> "Mr. Barnes ... wished to request the Bench to give instruc-
> tions to the police with reference to the extraordinary
> number of idle boys about the town, and especially at the
> Hythe, who indulged in that outrageous habit of throwing
> stones at old men and others. A few days ago he was down
> at the Hythe and saw twelve boys pelting an old man, who
> tried to earn a living by carting water. The old man went
> up to him and showed him that he had just received a

severe blow under the eye from one of the stones, and asked what he was to do, as he could not run after the boys. The old man told him that it was the constant habit of the boys to stone him . . . Mr. Savill said the same thing was carried on in Roman Road . . . Mr. Barnes remarked upon the damage that was done to property by these idle boys. Mr. Tabor agreed that the boys were most outrageous; and added that this was not to be wondered at, when it had been a fact, proved before the Bench, that thirteen or fourteen boys had been at the Anchor public-house on Sunday evenings, drinking, gambling and so forth."[43]

Though such gossip about juvenile vandalism doubtless arose from the behaviour of a minority, as did that about the growth of prostitution among young Colchester girls, the leisure time of most young people was certainly aimless and boring.

For working-class adults the horizons were hardly more spacious, and this was annually reasserted at the Guy Fawkes celebration. Though William Wire believed that the large crowds in the High Street wanted only to enjoy the fireworks, there were always some roughs looking for trouble and by 1875 the situation had become even worse, according to a Press report:

"It is a matter of regret that the Gunpowder Treason Plot celebration did not this year pass off without a collision between the police and the public. During the morning hundreds of urchins paraded the streets, dressed in the usual grotesque style, and there were also two or three parties of men and big lads who levied 'blackmail' upon the townspeople. Later in the evening a noisy crowd took complete possession of the town and so committed themselves that the police had to take eight of the ringleaders into custody . . . The Head-Constable said . . . During the evening of the 5th a great disturbance, which commenced about nine o'clock, occurred in the town, and he sent 14 constables out with a view to endeavour to quell it. In Maldon-road, where fireworks were being thrown in all directions, the constables were stoned and struck. The mob then passed through several streets to the Castle Bailey, where they pulled down the palings and fences. They then started in another direction and in St. Botolph's-street broke the window at the residence of Mr. A. T. Osborne, and at the Woolpack Hotel. Lamps were broken, and also the windows at the Gardeners' Arms, St. Giles' Church and other places."[44]

Such mob violence, when directed by interested parties, could obstruct free speech and endanger free political activity. The Chartists easily overcame it at their 1838 rally, but Josephine Butler's meetings had to be closed almost before they had begun, and at a Mayor's meeting to discuss the starting of a Public Library, a seemingly unlikely occasion for violence, an organised mob tried to intimidate the project's supporters.[45]

Rowdyism was confined to a minority, probably a very small one. Most poor people's social life presents a depressing rather than a melodramatic picture. In 1884, when electric lighting made a premature appearance in some of the smarter shops, a reporter visited the east end of the town and wrote the following story about a fortune-teller living there:

> "Stretching from nearly the centre of the town of Colchester to the river quays is a long tolerably wide thoroughfare, known in different portions of its length by three names, Magdalen Street, Barrack Street and Hythe Hill . . . There are miserable little tottering hovels, low public-houses, whose customers teem out in the evening from the adjacent courts and alleys; here is a general shop, with nothing for sale but rotten oranges and clothes pegs — the landlord has just cleared everything out for last month's rent. A little further off is a shoemaker's establishment, with no commodities apparently but auctioneer's bills and theatre placards. One cottage occupant labels his door 'Shaving Saloon', fixes a barber's pole to the doorpost and offers to draw teeth at 6d. a-piece, inserting in his window as a pledge of his prowess enough incisors and grinders of the genus homo to fill a quart mug . . . The inhabitants of the street and environments are many of them the residuum of the population. One room for a family is all the accommodation many a house affords; here, in a garret, sleeps the lazy idler of the street; next door is a lodging house, the haunt of those who beg by day and thieve by night. Shoeless children run about the street from morn till after dark; hatless women gossip and quarrel at the entrance of the courts, and at night fight with their besotted husbands going home from the 'Roaring Lion', turned out ten minutes after eleven. Now and then a juvenile-looking policeman walks up and down the pavement, a terror to the children, the scoff of the adults. Sometimes the Salvation Army perambulates the street, but the diversions of the place are mainly confined to drunken sprees outside, or drunken quarrels within.
>
> It is at the bottom of one of the numerous courts leading from this long thoroughfare that an old hag, with unkempt hair and forlorn mien, who has a considerable notoriety in the town, finds a home. Her fame has been handed down, not from generation to generation, but from shop assistants to novices for a dozen years. She plies, to her, the lucrative trade of a fortune teller. During the day she passes most of her time in bed; at night she lights her tallow candle and waits for customers. And of these she has no lack . . . One can hardly understand how three-fourths of the female shop-assistants in the town can for a moment listen to the garrulous old dame. The electric

light in the establishments in which they are employed
surely should drive away ideas worthy only of barbarous
times."[46]

One must not generalise about the triviality of working-class life.
Another facet was the continuing pleasure taken in the countryside. An
'Old Colchester Inhabitant' wrote during these years:

"Around the town the walks so rare,
With pleasant views and sweetest air,
If for Berechurch you wish to make
Or by the field to Lexden take,
Through meadows green and fields so gay,
Should you for High Woods steer your way,
Where'er you go, which way you take,
A pleasant walk you always make;
And the big field so large and free
With pleasant breezes from the sea.
In winter time, if frost and snow,
Down to Bourne Pond in troops we go,
All pushing on with quickening paces,
Surrounded by such smiling faces.
There some are skating with full pride,
While others keep the humble side;
Tho' now and then some get a fall,
Yet, oh! such sport for one and all."[47]

These, however, were pleasures that added nothing to rates or taxes.

Another contrast was that between the respectability in polite society and
the network of prostitution in the poorer areas of the town.[48] Though
prostitution occasioned only brief, usually embarrassed, references in the
Press, these were sufficient to show that it was never absent from the town
during the century and that it was increasing even before the Camp's
establishment. In 1842 Holy Trinity vestry sent to the Colchester Bench a
resolution that "the awful extent of female prostitution in this town is a
matter of deep regret to the inhabitants of the parish". The arrival of the
troops at once caused a further increase, as girls came into the town from
other places and some innkeepers took up the business; there were
customers enough because the younger soldiers were not allowed to
marry. Protests were soon being made at the unseemly conduct of the
men as they waited for their girls to emerge from the silk-factory or even
from the Ragged School, hitherto regarded as a triumph of Christian
reclamation. Some of this may have been innocent enough, but by 1867
prostitution was sufficiently organised to occasion a petition from clergymen of all denominations against the relicensing of inns that kept
brothels, as a result of which thirteen inns, all but one near the barrack
gates, had their licences withheld until investigations could be carried out
into their record. In 1869 Colchester was affected by the third of the Contagious Diseases Acts, which sought to limit venereal disease in certain
military towns by means of the medical examination of prostitutes and the
compulsory treatment of those found to be diseased. A senior policeman
could bring a girl before a Magistrate who could require her to undergo

examination and, if found to be suffering from venereal disease, to be confined for up to nine months' treatment in the Lock Hospital, built in 1869 on the east side of the new Colchester cricket ground. The police responsible for the Act's implementation were not from the borough constabulary but from the London Metropolitan force and they usually operated in plain clothes. Nobody was immune from accusation and at least one girl, apparently unconnected with prostitution and free of disease, was brought before a Magistrate; only girls from poor families appear to have been accused. Prostitutes could volunteer for examination and treatment, and many did so, thereby acquiring a sort of official licence to practise. It was this implicit regulation of vice by public authority, as the critics saw it, which chiefly inspired the opposition to the Contagious Diseases Acts. However, for scores of women shut up in the Lock Hospital for boring months on end, the reality was one of initial humiliation and of ultimate coarsening. Generally forbidden visits even from philanthropic ladies and living under national bureaucratic control, they were friendless and quite helpless. On release, some at once returned to their old calling and, when the official Chaplain of the Hospital appealed for £100 for a reception-centre in which those discharged could be taught other skills, that sum could not be raised. Their only help came from an inadequate private scheme, which remains obscure because the Press and its readers found the whole subject distasteful, but it was probably the result of a typically courageous initiative by Mrs. Margaret Round. Meanwhile, the brothels continued to trade, their proprietors being virtually protected as long as they helped to implement the Acts; only rarely did their existence receive mention, and that too only through some accident that led to a Court case.

In 1870 the issue was briefly brought to public attention at a by-election. The Liberals accepted as their candidate Sir Henry Storks who, when Governor of Malta, had imposed the Contagious Diseases Acts and was now required at the War Office to perform a similar service in British military centres. He found his path to Parliament barred by a determined opponent, Josephine Butler, a suffragist and an advocate of improved female education, who had recently devoted herself to the protest against the Acts, which she saw as sanctioning a vice, threatening personal liberty and offering indignities to women while sparing men who might have been exposed to disease. Her plan was to draw attention to the Acts by persuading Colchester Liberals to desert their official candidate. Her ally, Baxter-Langley, was at first advanced as an Independent to draw votes from Storks but, when he had gained enough publicity, he withdrew, after issuing an appeal to Liberals to deny their votes to "a man who declares a SIN to be a NECESSITY"; for Storks believed prostitution to be regrettably indispensable to an army. How many abstained is unclear, since Liberal support in the town was in any case falling because of suspicions that the Government wished to reduce the armed forces, but the Liberal vote did drop by about 600, Storks was defeated and several hundred known Liberals were among the abstainers.

As the organiser of the anti-Storks campaign, Josephine Butler was made the chief target by the brothel-keepers, who sent their roughs to besiege her hotel and to attack her as she left Baxter-Langley's meetings and the single meeting which she addressed in person at a schoolroom in Osborne Street. The mob's hatred revealed a depth of degradation which contrasts sharply with the respectable face of Victorian Colchester. The *Essex Standard*, though deploring her campaign in rather obscure language, nevertheless corroborated her own account of the violence. After one of Baxter-Langley's meetings had been broken up, it reported, "the platform was then taken possession of by some of the roughest of the mob who danced about almost fiendishly", before parading round the town in triumph. Equally revealing was the prudish or self-interested blindness of leading Liberals and of pro-Liberal working-class leaders, who refused to recognise the threat to personal liberty presented by the Acts. The working-class Liberals not only failed to reject Storks as candidate but vigorously campaigned for him and passed a resolution deploring Baxter-Langley's opposition to the election of Storks who, whatever his purpose in trying to enter Parliament, was standing as Mr. Gladstone's supporter. The newspapers' solemn reticence about the real issues was hardly breached. The *Essex Standard*, in unusually cramped language, commented that "a subject was, unhappily, at one time threatened to be introduced" and rejoiced in having given no space to reporting on the disagreeable themes involved. The Liberal *Halstead Times* regretted that Baxter-Langley had "flooded the borough with filthy literature on a disagreeable subject . . . on a matter of sanitary expediency". The speed with which this remarkable contest was forgotten is a measure of the uncomfortable feelings aroused by it. The brothels continued to do business. When the earthquake shook Colchester in 1884, there were those who thought the event to be God's punishment for the wickedness of the town. The Minister of Stockwell Chapel answered them with these words: "They all knew that the sins of Colchester were great, and he did not desire to diminish the blackness of the picture but they must all see that, if this had been intended as a punishment, it had been misdirected, since it had fallen on the steeples of our sanctuaries and upon our schools, and not upon the houses which he dared not name, nor upon persons who traded upon immorality".[49]

Though these glaring contrasts were to be found in Colchester society, religion did serve as a partly unifying force, though without lessening class differences. Evangelicalism was by now an influence in most middle-class homes and in many poor ones, too. Church and chapel activity was widely reported in the Press, and public speakers often discussed secular issues in terms of Christian principles. Many laymen became strongly committed to their own denomination's interpretations and policies. When St. Albans Diocesan Conference met in Colchester, the *Essex Standard* issued a circular promising to include a full account of the proceedings in its next number and to publish the same information in a special booklet, an impressive display of confidence in the public's interest in the minutiae of ecclesiastical affairs. Massive evidence of Christian self-assurance was to be seen in the continued building or rebuilding of churches and chapels. Anglicans restored, enlarged or reseated St. Leonard's, All Saints', Greenstead and St. Peter's in the 1850s, Holy Trinity in 1866 and again in 1886, and in the 1870s St. James's, St. Mary's-at-the-Walls, St. Michael's, Berechurch, and St.

Nicholas's. Completely new buildings were erected at Mile End in 1854, Ipswich Road in 1863, Belle Vue Road in 1869 and Old Heath in 1879, all four being in growing suburbs where accommodation for worship was inadequate or non-existent. Lion Walk was rebuilt in 1863 in a style at that time little associated with Congregationalism, in the 1870s St. John's Green Baptist Chapel was rebuilt and a new Quaker Meeting House was opened in Sir Isaac's Walk, and in the early 1880s Eld Lane Baptist Chapel was restored and a new Baptist chapel opened at Parson's Heath. This account omits many minor alterations. To the impressively large total expenditure involved should be added the money spent by most denominations in building, improving and maintaining their schools, which they saw as an extension of their Christian mission.

Clergymen were powerful forces in local life. At Stockwell Chapel two able ministers in their turn filled the building with eager worshippers. Joseph Herrick, after surmounting the troubles of his youthful ministry, by his combination of modern knowledge and homely language assembled a devoted and thinking congregation so large that the chapel had several times to be enlarged. "Sabbath after Sabbath, and at week-day services, might be seen the intellectual and ignorant, the aged and the young, the wealthy and the poor, all alike looking intently and silently upon that well-known tranquil face."[50] When he died at his work in 1865, he was succeeded by Thomas Batty, "young, possessed of a vigorous constitution, overflowing with zeal", who took his Christianity into the field of public service, campaigning for a Public Library, supporting the Hospital and playing a principal part in establishing the Albert School of Art.[51] Canon Irvine, who came to St. Mary's-at-the-Walls in 1872, besides infusing new spirit into his own parishioners, came almost to dominate Anglican policy in the town "with an imperious will, that could brook neither contradiction nor defeat". He had been a Liberal when he first arrived, but soon became a strong Conservative. Highly educated and a brilliant controversialist, he made atonement for his assertiveness by subsequent contrition and extensive benefactions from his own pocket. His service to elementary education was perhaps decisive, ensuring as it did an almost untroubled passage from an entirely denominational system to one in which church schools co-existed with publicly provided ones. When the establishment of a School Board had first seemed imminent because of Anglicans' inability to meet the rising costs of their schools, he struggled to prevent it and offered a personal donation of £1,000 to the Church schools, yet, when the Board was set up, it was he who took the initiative in devising, along with the Nonconformists, a non-sectarian syllabus for religious instruction, a then rare feat of inter-denominational co-operation. He served on the Board and also helped promote the Albert School, but reserved his chief effort for the Hospital, the welfare of which was very dear to him.[52] Irvine, Herrick and Batty were above the average of their colleagues in intellectual power but not in devotion. The Rector of St. Giles's welcomed the help of a new curate, "not that he himself might be relieved from work, but that much more could be done".

Within the denominations most of the cost and almost all of the management were provided by substantial citizens and neighbouring gentry.

Few, if any, workingmen filled any position of importance, except possibly among the Primitive Methodists, while very few women of any class were at all prominent. Yet for a growing number of working people their social life had much to do with their place of worship. Church and chapel were developing a network of societies and secular activities; the press frequently reported their tea meetings, concerts, discussions, outings, cricket matches and similar social occasions. Typical was the Mutual Improvement Society at Culver Street Wesleyan Chapel. All meetings began and ended with prayer, and three of the meetings each year were entirely devotional. The programme began in the Autumn and ended in the Spring, and included lectures, papers given by members, elocution lessons, competitive recitations, discussions, dissolving views and socials. Before each meeting the library was opened for borrowing.[53] The Society usually had large attendances and it enjoyed a long existence. Thoughtful workingmen were attracted by such facilities and there is evidence that many of them were strongly affected by evangelical Christianity at this time. Most of those who towards the end of the century emerged as the local trade union and Co-operative leaders appear to have been convinced and thoughtful Christians, and through such channels the working-class movement in the pre-1914 period came to be shaped in no small degree by religious influences, especially those emanating from Nonconformity.

Religious zeal had its less attractive aspects. Side by side with missionary work among the poor went a determination to direct their private lives in a manner consistent with conventional propriety. One example of many was the attempt to keep young people away from the fair and the theatre. A letter to the Press, headed 'Theatricals' and signed by 'Christiana', read as follows:

"Sir, Perhaps one of your numerous correspondents will be able to inform that large portion of the Colchester community who take a deep interest in the children of the poor whether it be true that the admission to our theatre has been reduced to the low price of 3d. to the gallery. The trade's right to do so no one can for a moment dispute, but everyone is at liberty to comment most freely on the evils which will inevitably follow to the numerous children of the humbler classes of this community. Its effects upon the girls must be most injurious, and in too many cases, alas, fatal to their morality — not from what is represented at the theatre, but from the society into which they are thrown there. The reduction of the price to 3d. brings it within the power of almost any girl to go; and if they cannot muster the 3d., they will at such a price be almost sure to find some boy or lad to take them, and the first step to ruin has in tens of thousands of instances been a visit to the gallery of the theatre . . . Although at the Girls' Evening Ragged School, in Osborne Street, there was kindly got up by the ladies on Tuesday week a treat of cake, magic lantern, etc., instead of there being a full attendance (as there would most certainly otherwise have been) between

thirty and forty girls were absent, known to be at the
theatre . . ."[54]

Four months later the committee of the Ragged School made a statement
declining to accept any financial donation from the proceeds of an oper-
atic entertainment to be held under the Mayor's patronage at the Theatre
specifically to help the Schools. The grounds of the refusal were
"that among the most fruitful nurseries of vice among the children of
the poor are low priced theatres and that the object of Ragged Schools
is to reclaim the little outcasts of society from the practice and evils of
vice".[55]

Late Victorian and Edwardian times, 1890–1914

Till the 1880s Colchester had remained a country town. C. H. Spurgeon,
who grew up near the Hythe, is said to have greeted news of the 1884
earthquake with the words, "Well, I am glad to hear that something has
moved the old town at last". Lady Southwalk's memoirs, describing the
Colchester elections of the 1880s at which her husband was a Liberal
candidate, depict a place which, socially, had hardly changed since
Victoria ascended the throne.[56] Hares could sometimes be seen running
down Lexden Road into the town in those years. Even after 1900
paintings by local artists still give the town a semi-rural appearance, but
contemporary photographs show High Street traversed by trams and
motor-cars and lined with shop-fronts in the current fashion. In 1907
R. A. Beckett, in his *Romantic Essex*, described how the town's more
antique features were being threatened by the advance of industrialisation and modernisation:

> "As you approach Colchester over the breezy heaths of
> Fordham and Bergholt that overlook the valley of the
> Stour on the one hand and that of the Colne on the other,
> your first distant view of the town will very likely be a dis-
> appointment. Its noble situation is undeniable; the bold
> yet wide hill, on which it stands, compelling the river to
> curve right round it in its progress towards the further
> marshes and the sea, and the railway to take an even wider
> sweep. But its ancient tiled roofs and church towers are
> intermingled with the chimneys of factories and the cold
> blue slate of the newer streets; and the whole town is
> dominated from its most commanding height not by
> the grey fretted spire of a stately cathedral but by a brick
> structure of doubtful architecture which you learn to be
> a water-tower.
> This impression is not at once removed from the mind of
> the visitor when he enters the town and saunters through
> its principal streets. Here and there he will come across
> interesting old houses and a well-preserved inn or two of
> the coaching age; but signs will be abundant that the mere
> sentiment of antiquity has not been allowed to stand in the
> way of commercial progress. Old houses are still being
> pulled down to make room for others more fitted to

stand in the streets of a thriving provincial town, which
is just what Colchester at first sight proclaims itself to
be."

After describing some of the town's antiquities, the author concludes
his Colchester chapter with these words:

"From this point the romantic interest begins to fade; Colchester settles down to its trade returns and annual oyster-
feast, and pulls down any ancient monuments without
compunction. Musing on these things, I found myself one
starless summer night wandering again round the old
Roman gate. Overhead rises the ugly modern water-tower.
Pushing open a heavy iron gate, I tread amid rank grass to
the edge of a reservoir. In the stillness I hear, every few
moments, a musical gush of water, driven up at regular
intervals by the machinery in the pumping-station below
the hill. While Colchester sleeps, this indispensable work
goes on . . .
The spell of a magic Past, carelessly hidden beneath a
prosaic Present — this is the spell of Colchester."[57]

Colchester had retained many natural amenities and historical buildings, partly because large industries had not ravaged its town centre.
Several important firms had started there but, except for the foundries in
the High Street and in Culver Street, these had either been closed, like
the St. John's Street and the Castle Bailey foundries, or had found more
spacious sites, like the two largest of the town's breweries and Knopps'
footwear factory. St. Botolph's goods station fortunately caused several
footwear and tailoring firms, as well as the Britannia ironworks, to settle
in its vicinity. Other firms preferred the Hythe area where, besides its rail
and river facilities, there was space for extensive development. Nor was
the town centre disfigured by the presence of a railway and there was no
welcome for proposals that, because North Station was so far away, a line
should be laid from Maldon to a new station in Crouch Street or that a
branch of the G.E.R. should leave the main line at Stanway, proceed to a
station in the middle of the town and go on past the Hythe to rejoin the
G.E.R. at Ardleigh. This escape from the worst abuses of industrialisation
was not due to the intervention of public authority, which in any case
lacked effective powers at the time; indeed, some Town Councillors
probably thought that economic considerations should always take pre-
cedence and agreed with the Paxman's spokesman when he said he
"should like to see the day when the outskirts of the good old town
bristled with tall chimnies".[58] If, however, public authority could, or
would, do little to defend the amenities, there were individuals who
deplored, and sometimes resisted, the less happy accompaniments of
Colchester's development. William Wire wrote in his diary in 1843:

"When I was walking up Balkon Hill, I saw that a portion
on the North side of the Balkon Fort had been destroyed
in order to build additional rooms to the King's Head to
command a view of the railway. What a pity that one of
the best-preserved remains of Roman times should be
destroyed to administer to the sensual pleasures, as it may

be considered only as a decoy to induce persons to enter
the house to drink."[59]

There was also concern at the loss of open spaces. The heathland around
Colchester had been enclosed without protest earlier in the century, and
some people had even rejoiced that in consequence there would no
longer be places in Stanway or West Bergholt where unspecified immorality, crime and incendiarism could breed. The town's own open spaces had
some strong defenders. When the Botanical Gardens behind Greyfriars
were sold for housing, the *Essex Standard* regretted that "this once attractive spot" had now to be "surrendered to the builder and the leveller".
The same paper commiserated with Old Heath residents at their open
spaces being taken by the Army as a practice-range, though, as it turned
out, the Army's need for such facilities may well have retained for the
town some amenities that would otherwise have been lost to later devel-
opers. There was also a movement to preserve local footpaths, in which
William Wire and James Hurnard were involved. In 1875 some North Hill
residents combined to oppose the removal of trees in St. Peter's churchyard, and the *Essex Standard* tried to save a plantation to the west of
Abbeygate Street, which relieved the drabness of the Scheregate neighbourhood. When 'Jumbo', Colchester's much-needed water-tower, was
opened in 1883, it was deplored because, besides being out of scale, its
utilitarian architecture was so placed as to dominate the ancient High
Street, though its ill-repute in respectable circles may have been due to its
champion having been a leading radical.[60] Pollution had its opponents,
including a committee of doctors whose report on public health in 1865
had contained the following paragraph:

"A number of chimneys exist which pour forth volumes of
smoke, to the sore injury of the inhabitants and to the destruction of our gardens . . . It is no trifling thing to be
obliged to keep our dwelling-house windows closed during sultry weather and it limits the ventilation of our
homes . . . It is now impossible to grow roses and flowers
as formerly in Colchester. Approach the town any morning before the fires are lighted, and remark the clear
atmosphere; and approach the town at 4 or 5 o'clock in the
afternoon, and contrast the foul, sooty atmosphere, and
you may estimate the amount of pollution by smoke."[61]

If there was satisfaction at the town's retention of many pleasant
features, there were some who viewed industrial and population growth
as reassuring evidence that the town was at last moving into the main-
stream of progress. When in 1892 Wilson Marriage opened Castle Park,
the *Essex Telegraph* commented:

"In the matter of improvement it would seem as though
Colchester has now taken a decided step forward and has
developed a spirit of progress that is very satisfactory,
though rather startling when the conservatism of the
Borough is remembered. The cause of this is easy to be
seen. With the extension of the town and the introduction
into it of a large increase in the industrial population,
there has grown up that demand for progress in municipal

affairs that is making itself felt in all centres of commercial activity."[62]

The Press was quick to report the innovations of the age. In 1898 it described, among a score of such events, the Council's new electricity undertaking, the first cremation in the cemetery and a cinema show in the Cups.[63] Next year another experiment caused the *Essex Telegraph* to write that "the enterprise of the Great Eastern Railway is doing much towards making Colchester a suburb of the great Metropolis". It was referring to 'the supper train', which every Sunday morning left Liverpool Street at three minutes past midnight, full of Colcestrians returning from the London theatres; courteous waiters served five-course suppers at 2s. 6d. in a tastefully decorated dining-car; the fare was half-price and the journey was the swiftest of the day. The train waited at Colchester station to take businessmen to London early on the Monday morning.[64] In July 1904, when the first trams ran, an observer wrote, "the appearance of the trams alters the hitherto somnolent character of the Colchester streets, and gives them a busy and lively aspect". However, only two years had passed when it was noted that "tramway rides are not as popular as they were. The novelty has gone."[65] One reason for this was the arrival of a new form of transport. The first motor-car is said to have appeared in the streets in 1896, and two years later J. H. Clamp, a St. Botolph Street furniture dealer, bought from the Coventry Horseless Carriage Company a motor-van capable of speeds between 4 and 14 m.p.h.; a reporter did the thirty-four-mile journey to and from Clacton in only three and a half hours. Mr. Clamp's rural business increased appreciably. By 1907 there were enough private cars for the Colchester Motor Club to be formed with thirty members. General Booth travelled in a motor-car when he came to inspect the Salvation Army barracks.[66] Motorcycles were also on the streets. The G.E.R.'s motor-omnibuses to Mersea and Nayland, when they first ran in 1905, were not well patronised because of the breakdowns and delays, but within a year the service was reported to have been much improved. Soon the G.E.R. had Norfolk's as rivals on the Nayland route and Berry's on the Mersea route. By 1914 Moore's had opened their Colchester–Tiptree–Kelvedon service. Anxiety was expressed at "the numerous motor car cases that nowadays occupy the time of our Bench" and there was even greater cause for concern when, in the course of a few weeks in 1913, one car skidded into a tram in Lexden Road, another cut a waggon in two on North Hill, while a third killed a child at Mile End.[67] Popular entertainment was expanding, too. The theatre had recovered respectability in the 1880s, and Colcestrians had been able to enjoy performances by Lillie Langtry, Mrs. Patrick Campbell, Gladys Cooper and Charlie Chaplin. In 1908 "a large and fashionable audience" watched Ellen Terry in Shaw's *Captain Brassbound's Conversion*.[68] The Theatre Royal met competition from the Hippodrome, which presented plays as well as variety shows, and, by 1910–11, from the Headgate Electric Theatre, later the Cameo, and the Vaudeville Electric Theatre, later the Empire, situated close to the present Mersea Road roundabout. The advertisements and reviews of current plays and films in the pre-War years testify to the wide and varied programme of popular entertainment available to Colcestrians all the year round at prices within the capacity of thousands. Such developments transformed social life for the ordinary public and there was little regret among them at the passing of the Victorian era. When in 1907 some £4,000 was raised towards a fund to make Colchester a cathedral city, there was no small concern that, in the event of such a change, Colchester would cease to be "a progressive town" and would again become a backwater.[69]

This expansion of popular entertainment would have gone for little, had not real incomes risen for many working-class families. The improved standard of living was reflected in the rapid increase in Friendly Society membership. The Oddfellows and the Foresters had been represented in Colchester in the 1840s, with the former at first overshadowing the latter, but workingmen seem then to have been in a minority among the members. As wages began to rise, more and more workers joined until in 1913 these two societies had some 6,000 members between them in the town, and there were thousands more in the smaller organisations. There still remained, too, a number of local bodies offering Friendly Society benefits. All these acted as social clubs. The annual galas at Wivenhoe Park, Lexden Manor or some similar large estate were the occasions given most prominence in the Press, but there were other events during the year which helped to occupy the leisure time of members and sometimes of their families.

The workers' improved position was especially evident on Bank Holidays, the 1871 legislation having been accepted in Colchester from the start. Good Friday, Easter Monday, Whit Monday and Boxing Day had long been customary holidays here, but the first August Bank Holiday occasioned a flag on the Town Hall, the decoration of private houses, music from a military band and a Friendly Society gala in Lexden Park; it rained heavily for almost the whole day. Next year the weather was fine, over 5,000 attended the Friendly Society gala at Wivenhoe Park, every train to the coast from the two stations was filled to capacity and relief trains were run.[70] The railway had reached Walton in 1867, just in time to enable thousands of working-class families to spend Bank Holiday at the seaside without first facing a hard struggle to get there. As 'An Old Colchester Inhabitant' wrote:

> "To go to Walton! What a fuss —
> Must hire a trap or take the bus!
> Now at the station pay the fare,
> Step in the train and soon get there,
> And as the charge is now so low,
> In summer time in troops we go."[71]

Almost all annual outings now had the seaside as their destination. In Summer 1871, the choirs of both St. Paul's and Lexden churches went to Walton by rail, while the employees of Moy's coal firm and of the *Essex Standard* newspaper still preferred to travel to that resort by "the van" and "the bus" respectively. That summer Clacton was also looking for patrons, but few day-visitors were expected to face the omnibus journey from Weeley railway station to this new watering-place. Instead, Clacton's promoters saw their resort as one "which would attract by its taste and elegance" and they were reported to have expressed "considerable pleasure" when the proposed Thorpe–Clacton branch line was abandoned in 1872. Yet so many were crowding on the Weeley–Clacton omnibus service that the building of a branch railway could not indefinitely be delayed. In 1882 the Mayor of Colchester attended the new line's opening, and Clacton quickly became as popular with Colcestrians as Walton. Several thousand of them booked for the various coastal resorts at Whitsun 1896; about a thousand of these travelled on the Sunday.[72]

Workingmen gradually gained more access to sporting facilities. When in 1865 Colchester and East Essex Cricket Club acquired the Wimpole Road ground, the formation of a Working Men's Club, with access to the facilities, had been suggested but not, apparently, carried out. Cricket was then still a pastime for young gentlemen, and was stated to be so in the Press, the other teams being those of the Garrison, the Grammar School and its Old Boys, some of the larger private schools, and the Liberal and Conservative parties. From 1880 onwards, however, when the Wimpole Road ground had become the public Recreation Ground, clubs were started at each of the three ironworks, Britannia, Paxman's and Mumford's, as well as at the Colchester Manufacturing Company and the Co-operative Society; clubs were subsequently formed at other workplaces, including Spottiswoode's, the printers, where there were two teams. Football followed the same path. In 1854 Colchester Grammar School played Dedham Grammar School before a large crowd, and for twenty years these and a few other schools, together with the Garrison, were almost alone in having a regular programme of matches. When in 1875 "lovers of football" formed Colchester Football Club, they met at the George and their leading players were mostly past pupils of the Grammar School and similar schools. The report of their first anniversary began, "Colchester Football Club. This prosperous *coterie* of young gentlemen held its annual meeting and dinner at the George Hotel . . ." They had no pitch of their own, however, and had to hire the Cricket Club's ground in Cambridge Road. When the latter was sold for building, the Football Club had to move from one unsatisfactory place to another until in 1909 it acquired its present Layer Road ground.[73] Meanwhile, football had become less exclusive. There was a Paxman's team by 1873 and, in the 1880s, at least three others, the Excelsiors, the Crusaders and St. Peter's Institute. Then with the opening of six pitches on the Recreation Ground, more clubs were formed; in 1887 only forty-one matches were played there, in 1893 there were 123 and by 1904 as many as 218.[74] Some clubs had their own pitches, while in the Camp "the Abbey Field was alive with football every afternoon". Soon after 1900 the teams playing in the local leagues included the Town Club, Excelsiors, Crown, Corinthians, Rovers, Victor Rovers, Grammar School, Old Colcestrians, Olympic, Athletic, Eccentrics, Shrub End, St. Botolph's, St. Peter's, St. Nicholas's, St. Nicholas's Choir, Stanway All Saints, Headgate, Culver Street, Black and White, Mid-Week, Thursday Excelsiors, Colchester Thursdays, Mumford's, Paxman's, Benham's Athletic, Post Office and the Co-operative Employees. A number of these clubs had second elevens, and there were less established sides not competing in official leagues, as well as about a dozen representing different units in the

Garrison. There was a Thursday League for groups enjoying a Thursday Early Closing holiday, and also a Junior League. Paxman's Athletic Club, with the advantage of a ground in Land Lane, off East Hill, besides entering teams in local leagues, enabled hundreds of its young men to play football in its inter-departmental tournament, so that on the lighter evenings of April and May the pitch was in constant use; there was a similar tournament in cricket. Such widespread participation in the game could not fail to affect the original Town football club, which in its early days, according to its official history, "was considered — shall we say — rather exclusive". From the 1890s the club began to draw its players and supporters from wider social circles, and the new popular enthusiasm sometimes caused ungentlemanly clashes. In 1897, after a drawn match between the Town club and its chief rival, the Excelsiors, the supporters of the two teams fought in Maldon Road. This was not the only violent occasion, for a local paper wrote that "the game has become of late years so frequently a cause of tumultuous outbursts . . . that the clubs have found it necessary to put up warning notices on the fields".[75] The crowds grew in size — on one Easter Monday a 3,000 attendance was reported — and, as the Saturday half-holiday was gained by more and more people, the Club was assured of a good gate every week.

The new spirit of independence among the working-class community affected religious life. Almost all the forty places of worship developed clubs and activities designed to sink roots into the social as well as the spiritual life of their congregations, including discussion groups, libraries, football and bicycle clubs, Temperance Societies, Bands of Hope, Mothers' Meetings and Church Lads' Brigades. The Sunshine and Social group of the Eld Lane Young People's Christian Endeavour had eighty members, St. Stephen's Women's Social Club about 130 and St. Paul's Social Club, which had its own reading-room, billiards-room and coal club, a hundred. Another link with the working-class public were the Pleasant Sunday Afternoons held in several of the Nonconformist chapels around 1900. Ministers of all denominations needed to be, and clearly were, indefatigable. Their reward lay in the size of their congregations and their own high standing among the public generally. In 1903 Lion Walk claimed increasing attendances at its services, had 1,012 scholars and teachers in its Sunday schools and maintained four branch chapels.[76] St. Mary's-at-the-Walls was equally active, with its choir of forty, its Church Lads' Brigade, Bible classes with 400 scholars, and a Mission in Maldon Road.[77] Opportunities for worship were frequent; in 1914 St. Botolph's, St. Giles's, St. James's, St. Leonard's and St. Martin's each held a service daily.

There were few misgivings among the religious bodies at the end of the century. Church and chapel enlargement went vigorously ahead, not in the already well-served town centre so much as in the growing suburbs. Near the Hythe, the Primitive Methodist Chapel in Artillery Street and the Wesleyan Chapel on Hythe Hill were improved, and in 1904 the Wesleyans built the Wimpole Chapel and Sunday schools at a cost of £5,500, while St. Botolph's Church kept a mission, made of iron, in Canterbury Road, which in 1905 it replaced with a £750 brick building. In the growing area around Maldon Road, St. Mary's-at-the-Walls erected an iron chapel of ease in 1903, and a Baptist Chapel was also started in Burlington Road. So high was the level of activity among all denominations that one is astonished to read the few comments that indicate doubt about the future of Christian devotion in the town. The most striking of these were made in an article in the *Essex Telegraph* in 1914 on the history of Stockwell Chapel, which, having described past struggles and successes, forecast the chapel's possible closure in the light of the elderly composition of the congregation:

> "Sad to say, there is room for improvement at Stockwell. In church work, the scarcity of young men of zeal and courage, zealous for the preservation of the institution, thankful for the liberty of free and uninterrupted worship, is a matter of grave concern. As the veterans have passed away, those remaining have been seriously handicapped, new energy not being easily obtained. The generations which were treated most harshly, would be ashamed of the apathetic youth of today."[78]

However, such signs of faltering were rare and the general impression is of participation by thousands in the work of church and chapel.

One trend may be seen as implying some dissatisfaction with the older denominations, without involving any rejection of Christianity itself. From 1880 the evangelical initiatives came, in several cases, from less orthodox sects. The Colchester Society of the New Church, whose Swedenborgian predecessors had made a short appearance in the town earlier in the century, was re-formed in 1882 and by 1914 maintained two branches, one in Priory Street and the other in George Street at the Oddfellows' Hall. Lexden Mission was formed in 1882, the Gospel Band in 1884 and the Railway Mission in 1892. Christian Science arrived in 1907. In 1902 was formed the Colchester branch of the Telegraph Messengers' Association, designed "to help Post Office messengers to live true, straight and honest lives for God and man" and to provide a room where the lads could enjoy wholesome company and receive advice from their benefactors.[79] Overshadowing all of these was the Salvation Army, which had appeared briefly in 1874 and had returned in 1882, putting up large, red posters bearing the message "Declaration of War. Attack on the Citadel of Sin. No Compromise with Beelzebub. The first guns loaded with redhot Gospel shot will be fired prompt at the time fixed." They took the former skating-rink in St. John's Avenue for their barracks and, despite initial hostility, soon won a prominent position in local life; when General Booth first came in 1896, the Mayoress attended the gathering.[80] Statistics are unobtainable, but the impression created is that in the new movements plebeian influence was stronger than in the older denominations. Many poor people certainly attended revivalist meetings, such as those conducted by Gipsy Smith in the Corn Exchange in 1901, where "every night the doors are besieged before the appointed hour and at their opening the tides of humanity pour in like a flood and occupy every inch of space".[81]

Seen from the present day, Colchester society of 1900–14 seems to be one of poverty, social deprivation, class division and intellectual restriction. Compared with mid-Victorian times, these first years of the new century were seen by contemporaries as the age of Youth, of emergent woman, of working-class independence and advance. There was vigour, variety and free discussion. "Is God good?", the subject for discussion in January 1914, at St. Mary's-at-the-Walls parish room, would have been an impossibility at any secular, not to say religious, gathering twenty years earlier.[82] Above all, hope pervaded virtually all public activity and an increasing number of private lives as well. In the week when the nine-teenth century gave place to the twentieth, 'Mark Downe', in the *Essex Standard*, welcomed the new age as one in which science and technology would transform the lives of all Colchester people. His picture of the Col-chester of 2000 A.D. was a fantasy which could not conceal his underlying confidence.[83] He wrote:

"This week at the beginning of the Twentieth Century, we may appropriately look forward and picture the Colches-ter that will be 100 years hence.

Let us, then, conjure up a vision of the Colchester that is to be, the Colchester of 90,000 inhabitants in the auspici-ous year of grace 2001 . . . But what a growth! What a number of pleasant country walks that we once knew are now in this year 2001 transformed into suburban resident districts, with paved streets, lighted by electricity or acety-lene gas, or here and there by the newly invented phos-phorescent light, which stores up the sunshine in the day and gives it out in the form of a pleasant white effulgence at night . . .

Lexden, it will be observed, is no longer a village, but merely the west end of the town. Alas, the famous Springs that we read of in the old guide books, have been prosa-ically drained off into underground pipes to supply power for the district electric light station and to ensure a dry sub-soil for the cottage dwellings on either side of Spring Hill . . . Southward the suburban villas reach to Stanway and Berechurch, covering many an acre of what used to be agricultural land. Northwards the sea of roofs stretch to Braiswick and Milend; eastwards it stretches far beyond Greensted parish . . . How fine these central streets look with their splendid avenues of trees on either side — and what a forest of tall chimneys away there to the far east. Yes, that is the manufacturing district . . .

Airships, even in 2001, are a trifle risky, except on the still-est days of summer . . . But it is too windy and too cold on this January day, otherwise we might do well to hire a flyer and survey the town from aloft. However, there is no need to trouble about that. The trams are constantly run-ning at halfpenny fares, or we can get a motor at any of the electric supply stations for the modest fee of 2d. an hour. How easy is locomotion in these twentieth century times. From Milend Public Library to the Berechurch arboretum is but a quarter of an hour's ride in the tram, and each of the railway companies — either the Great Eastern from the North Station or the new line from Central Station near Headgate — will take us to London in very little over the half hour. There is a proposal for the County Councils to take over the railways in a few years, in which event it is expected that the fare from Colchester to London will be reduced from 2s. 6d. to 1s. at the most, but we must be content with the half-crown fares for the present, and certainly the accommodation in the saloon cars is not bad, and the electric locomotors are far preferable to the smoky old steam engines . . . which filled your eyes with smut if you looked out of the window.

You are surprised, are you, to notice, as you lean comfortably back in the velvet-lined saloon car of the tram that there are none of those telegraph poles and wires that used to disfigure the streets? Has telegraphy become a lost art, you inquire? No, but posts and wires have been done away with for some decades, even in the remotest districts of the country. Both telegraphs and telephones nowadays work on the wireless principle . . . every householder is his own telegraphist and has in his entrance hall a transmitter and receiver, by means of which he can converse at any time with any of his friends in any part of the United Kingdom, or if he wishes to hear the performance at any one of the London opera-houses, he has only to signal to the booking office, transmit the fee by telegraphy cheque system and the necessary rapport is established as the curtain rises. On Sundays he can, if he desires, listen to the choir at Westminster Abbey or the preacher in St. Paul's Cathedral and, of course, if he gets tired by the sermon, he can unswitch and go to sleep . . .

Never were relics of the past so valued as now . . . when they have been so rapidly diminishing, and such a thing as a Roman pot or a British coin is hardly ever discovered, the whole site of the ancient Camulodunum having long been completely entombed beneath modern dwellings. A good deal of the old Roman wall has gradually tumbled away, St. Botolph's Priory ruins have all but succumbed to the devastations of time, and only in the Castle, the remaining fragments of the Town Wall and in some of the Churches is to be seen in situ the actual handiwork of the ancient builder.

Commodious as the Town Hall at first was, it has already been found hardly adequate to the requirements of the rapidly growing borough . . . The old Library building has been annexed to increase the accommodation of the municipal offices, and a handsome new Central Library erected in connection with the magnificent Technical College on the north side of High Street . . . Branch libraries quite equal in size and importance to the central institution have been erected in four of the principal suburban districts.

Another interesting institution, started in the middle of the 20th century, is the famous Colchester Natural History Museum. This is quite distinct from the Museum of antiquities at the Castle, and fierce was the opposition when it was inaugurated, and great was the outcry about 'fancy expenditure', but the number of visitors annually brought into the town by this and the other attractive features of the place has amply repaid the heavy outlay. It has not been found necessary to extend the area of the cemetery . . . due to the establishment of the Corporation Crematorium.

In education we have in Colchester kept pace with the times. It need hardly be said that there is none of the old class distinction . . . The schools are now attended by all classes . . . They are well staffed and well equipped in Colchester, all the latest improvements having been introduced in the matter of classrooms, gymnasia, laboratories, swimming baths, and so forth.

One thing remains unchanged . . . human nature. There are still the same feelings of love and hate, still the same political strifes and bickerings, still the same sectarian differences and intolerances . . . and on the other hand still the same displays of friendship and goodwill and the same public-spirited desire amongst a few for the welfare of the old town . . .

If any of your readers think I have drawn too fanciful a picture, all they have to do is to cut out this column and keep it till the year 2001, and they will see."

NOTES AND REFERENCES

There is insufficient space to list all the sources on which this study is based. The references, which are given, are mainly those for the longer *verbatim* quotations and those concerned with the more important matters described or discussed in the book. In many cases I have omitted sources which readers can easily discover for themselves.

ABBREVIATIONS

Newspapers

Chelmsford Chronicle	Ch.Ch.
Colchester Gazette*	C.G.
Essex and Suffolk Times	E.S.T.
Essex and West Suffolk Gazette	E.W.S.G.
Essex, Herts. & Kent Mercury	E.H.K.M.
Essex Standard	E.S.
Essex Telegraph	E.T.
Halstead Times	H.T.
Ipswich Journal	I.J.
Northern Star	N.S.
Suffolk Chronicle	S.Ch.

* The second newspaper of that name, starting in 1877, is recorded without abbreviation.

Other

Benham's Colchester Directory	Benham
Colchester Central Library	C.C.L.
Essex Record Office	E.R.O.
Essex Review	E.R.
Goody's Colchester Almanack	Goody
Kelly's Directory of Essex	Kelly
National Society for Education	National Society
Official Guide to the Great Eastern Railway (Colchester Line), 1865	G.E.R., 1865
Pigot's Essex Directory	Pigot
Victoria County History of Essex	V.C.H.
White's Directory of Essex	White

CHAPTER I: THE TOWN'S ECONOMY

1. V.C.H., 2, pp.403–4
   E.S. 25.3.1893

2. Ch.Ch. 15.3.1791, 12.6.1818
   I.J. 7.11.1812
   C.G. 12.4.1817
   Pigot, 1832, p.276

3. Brown, A. F. J., *Essex People*, 1972, pp.120, 122, 125

4. *Ibid.,* pp.120–128

5. White, 1848, p.74

6. C.G. 19.2.1820
   Essex Farmers' Journal, Dec., 1836, pp.554–5 (article by G. E. Fussell)

7. E.T. 11.2.1905
   Benham, 1897, pp.157–9

8. *Autobiography of Sir George Airy*, 1896, pp.17–18
   Cromwell, *History of Colchester,* 1825, pp.294–5
   E.S. 21.1.1842, 22.8.1845
   G.E.R. 1865, pp.163–4
   H.T. 2.9.1882

9. House of Commons, Select Committee on the Silk Trade, 1832
   E.S. 9.10.1886

10. Pigot, 1839, p.108
    V.C.H., 2, p.484
    E.S. 16.5.1845
    N.S. 2.3.1844, 13.4.1844

11. V.C.H., 2, p.496
    C.G. 24.1.1835
    E.S. 6.1.1843, 8.3.1844, 17.12.1852
    See also John Booker, *Essex and the Industrial Revolution*, 1974, Ch.1

12. C.G. 24.1.1835
    Pigot, 1839, p.106
    E.S. 13.1.1837, 13.12.1844, 6.6.1845, 24.1.1846, 13.8.1847, 15.6.1945

13. The chief sources used in this paragraph and the following one are the 1851 Census and White's *Directory of Essex*, 1848
    Also C.G. 20.9.1823; E.S. 13.9.1844

14. Brown, *op. cit.*, pp.167–8
    E.S. 25.4.1845

15. E.S. 9.2.1844, 12.4.1844, 19.4.1844, 10.5.1844, 19.6.1846

16. For this and other sections on the Hythe, see Cockerill and Woodward, *The Hythe, port, church and fishery.*
    C.G. 4.1.1817, 10.5.1817, 23.6.1823
    E.S. 1.3.1844, 5.2.1847
    Pigot, 1839

17. E.S. 10.4.1846

18. C.G. 22.3.1814, 8.7.1820, 25.7.1835
     E.S. 22.9.1837, 25.12.1840, 8.1.1841, 12.4.1902

19. E.S. 10.4.1846
     Brown, *op. cit.*, p.171

20. E.S. 7.10.1842, 23.12.1842, 22.4.1846, 27.11.1846, 5.2.1847

21. The evidence for this and the following two paragraphs is to be found
     mainly in the *Essex Standard* of April 1846 to August 1847.
     Also E.S. 6.7.1855, 9.11.1855

22. E.S. 10.1.1840, 14.2.1868, 10.12.1898

23. G.E.R., 1865, p.159
     E.S. 23.2.1877
     C.M. 30.8.1879
     H.T. 6.11.1886

24. E.T. 9.7.1880, 8.1.1910
     Marriage and Sanders, *The Port of Colchester and the Navigation of
     the River Colne,* Appendix F

25. Marriage, E., & Son Ltd., *The annals of one hundred years of flour
     milling,* 1940
     E.S. 22.1.1875

26. E.S. 28.3.1855, 12.7.1867, 16.6.1869, 31.5.1878
     E.T. 27.10.1914
     H.T. 5.2.1887
     Benham, 1897, pp.157–9

27. E.S. 13.10.1865

28. E.T. 15.12.1894

29. E.S. 14.6.1867, 20.12.1867, 30.7.1869

30. For the history of Paxman's, see *Essex County Standard,* 'Paxman's
     Centenary', 1965, article by Dr. Geoffrey Martin. Also *Paxman's
     World,* Spring 1955, pp.4–5
     E.W.S.G. 4.10.1867
     E.T. 16.1.1866
     E.S. 6.8.1875, 18.6.1976
     Goody, 1878, p.28

31. E.S. 6.12.1861, 1.2.1867
     E.W.S.G. 15.10.1852
     Benham, 1897, pp.146–8
     Meggy, East Anglia, 1865, p.71
     V.C.H., 2, pp.487–8

32. E.S. 30.7.1869, 9.4.1875, 12.3.1887, 19.3.1887
     E.T. 30.9.1882, 20.4.1907
     Colchester Gazette, 16.3.1887
     V.C.H., 2, pp.487–8

33. Woodward, *Colchester as a military centre*

34. E.S. 4.2.1882
     E.T. 6.10.1894

35. E.S. 23.4.1898

36. Benham, 1897, pp.157–9
    E.S. 8.1.1887, 1.1.1898, 13.12.1902, 10.4.1920
    H.T. 5.2.1887
    E.T. 7.3.1891, 23.6.1894, 24.12.1912

37. E.T. 17.10.1896

38. E.S. 5.3.1898
    E.T. 20.4.1907

39. Kelly, 1878, p.88
    E.S. 2.1.1886, 12.3.1887, 19.3.1887
    E.T. 5.7.1890, 6.2.1892
    Colchester Gazette, 16.3.1887
    C.M. 5.3.1886

40. *Industries of the Eastern Counties, c.*1890, p.182
    E.S. 7.4.1895, 23.4.1898
    C.M. 8.1.1876, 22.4.1876
    E.T. 16.3.1895, 6.4.1895
    Colchester Gazette, 16.3.1887

41. E.S. 19.3.1887

42. V.C.H., 2, pp.487–8
    E.T. 31.10.1908, 16.6.1914

43. V.C.H., 2, pp.483–4
    Information of the late Mr. Samuel Blomfield
    Benham, 1897, pp.150–1
    E.T. 27.6.1914

44. E.T. 9.7.1904, 11.1.1908, 10.1.1914, 17.1.1914

45. Benham, 1897, p.148
    E.S. 19.8.1933, 25.11.1933
    E.T. 13.10.1894

46. *Paxman's Centenary, op. cit.*
    Benham, 1907, 1908
    E.S. 9.10.1886
    E.T. 26.9.1903, 7.5.1910

47. Kelly, 1900–1914
    Essex Standard, Industry Supplement, April 1960
    E.T. 10.12.1914, 15.12.1914

48. E.T. 24.6.1905, 3.1.1914
    E.S. 27.2.1926

49. E.T. 6.3.1897, 4.3.1899
    E.S. 17.8.1907

50. Wheeler, *Report on the River Colne,* 1894, p.3
    E.T. 18.6.1880, 6.8.1880
    E.S. 3.8.1895, 24.8.1895, 6.8.1910, 28.2.1914

51. E.T. 22.8.1908

CHAPTER II: THE TOWN'S GOVERNMENT

1. E.S. 10.6.1831, 24.6.1831
2. S.Ch. 9.9.1820
   C.G. 7.9.1822
3. Ch.Ch. 27.3.1818
4. C.G. 13.3.1825
   E.S. 25.1.1834
5. E.S. 3.10.1834, 5.12.1834
6. S.Ch. 22.7.1826
   E.S. 29.4.1831
7. E.S. 19.4.1834
8. C.G. 19.1.1822, 20.7.1822, 18.1.1823
   S.Ch. 18.7.1829
   E.S. 14.11.1834
9. Drew, *The Fire Office*, 1952, pp.14–16
   E.S. 16.7.1921
10. Ch.Ch. 18.8.1809
    Cromwell, *History of Colchester*, 1825, pp.301–2
11. *Ibid.*, pp.304–5
    E.R.O., D/P 200/8/2
12. Cromwell, *op. cit.*, pp.302–3
    C.G. 10.8.1822, 18.10.1823, 11.9.1824
    E.S. 24.10.1885
13. *Abstract of Returns relative the expense and maintenance of the poor*, 1818
14. Report of Poor Law Commission, Appendix (B.2)
15. E.S. 8.4.1831, 6.5.1831
    Poster issued by Tufnell before the election
16. E.S. and C.G., April to May, 1834, *passim*
17. E.S. 24.11.1837, 11.11.1842
    E.S.T. 17.11.1837, 5.1.1838
18. E.W.S.G. 3.12.1852
    E.S. 10.3.1876
19. E.W.S.G. 2.3.1855
    E.S. 22.10.1852, 8.8.1862, 6.2.1863, 26.2.1887
20. E.S. 2.5.1845, 26.2.1887, 30.1.1897, 15.3.1963
21. E.R. 56, pp.1–8
    E.S. 9.2.1855
22. E.S. 22.8.1845, 18.6.1847, 6.6.1885
23. E.S. 4.2.1842, 8.1.1847, 11.5.1855
24. E.S. 17.10.1834, 2.5.1851
    Brown, *Essex People 1750–1900*, p.164, 180
25. E.S. 5.7.1854

26. E.S. 13.10.1865

27. E.S. 20.10.1865, 18.8.1871

28. E.S. 3.1.1872, 1.3.1872

29. I am indebted to Dr. John Penfold for help on the history of the Hospital. Newspaper references to Hospital affairs are too numerous to list here, but the annual reports, often summarised in the press, are a major source. See also E.S. 3.8.1878 and the 1908 *Souvenir of the Opening of the New Children's Ward.*

30. E.T. 21.3.1900
    E.S. 29.9.1883
    H.T. 3.1.1880, 21.10.1882

31. *The Re-opening of Colchester Town Hall,* 1971
    E.R. XI, p.34
    E.S. 29.1.1887, 6.11.1897

32. E.T. 22.10.1892

33. E.S. 17.5.1902

34. E.S. 28.12.1849, 1.1.1887, 4.1.1896, 3.10.1896
    E.T. 30.9.1882, 5.6.1909, 11.10.1913, 7.3.1914
    H.T. 2.9.1882

35. E.S. 19.9.1885
    E.T. 30.7.1904, 6.8.1904, 7.3.1914, 6.6.1914

36. Kelly, 1899, p.119

37. H.T. 14.6.1884
    E.T. 10.3.1906

38. E.T. 9.11.1912

39. E.T. 7.2.1903

40. E.T. 4.3.1899

CHAPTER III: EDUCATION

1. E.R. 49, pp.125 foll., article by L. C. Sier
   I.J. 8.2.1812
   E.S. 19.2.1841
   C.G. 22.5.1818

2. Blaxill, *History of Lion Walk, 1662–1937,* p.36
   C.G. 22.7.1820
   E.T. 9.11.1912

3. E.S. 19.2.1841

4. *Returns on Education of the Poor* (1819), Colchester section
   Education Enquiry Abstract (1835), Colchester section

5. I.J. 7.3.1812
   E.K.H.M. 19.3.1839, 10.10.1839
   E.S. 27.12.1850
   Brown, *Essex People* 1750–1900, 1972, p.164

6. Ex inf. National Society
   Ex inf. Mrs. Betty Richardson (for Mile End Rector's appeal)
   E.S. 28.3.1845

7. E.S. 28.3.1845, 11.10.1865

8. E.R. 49, pp.125 foll.
   Ex inf. National Society
   Blaxill, *op. cit.*, p.36
   E.R.O., D/ACM 12
   E.S. 3.1.1845, 26.11.1869
   Ex inf. Dept. of Education

9. *Education Enquiry Abstract* (1835)
   E.S. 23.12.1870, 6.11.1872

10. Annual reports of the Education Committee of Council
    National Society, *Church Schools Enquiry,* 1846–7
    E.S. 11.5.1859, 9.6.1871, 29.3.1872

11. Annual reports of the Education Committee of Council
    Ex inf. National Society

12. E.W.S.G. 4.10.1872

13. E.S. 20.12.1872

14. Annual Reports of the Education Committee of Council
    E.S. and E.T. 1891–2 *passim*, especially E.T. 5.3.1892

15. E.S. 12.1.1895, 11.1.1896
    E.T. 13.10.1894
    Kelly, 1899, pp.125–6

16. E.T. 29.2.1908, 25.4.1908
    Borough of Colchester, *Education Year Book*, 1910

17. *Ibid.*
    Ex inf. Dept. of Education
    E.T. 25.4.1908

18. E.S. 8.3.1913

19. E.S. 11.12.1857, 11.6.1869, 5.1.1907
    E.T. 28.5.1892

20. E.S. 5.1.1907
    E.T. 29.2.1908, 8.5.1909, 8.3.1913

21. E.S. 12.4.1834
    C.G. 7.3.1835, 28.3.1835, 16.5.1835
    Autobiography of Sir G. B. Airy, 1896, pp.17–18

22. E.S. 10.11.1843, 10.4.1845, 21.6.1850

23. E.S. 12.4.1834, 2.6.1837, 18.5.1849, 20.6.1851
    E.S.T. 21.12.1839
    Report of the Commission on Charities (Essex), 1835, p.531

24. E.S. 1851–3, *passim*

25. E.S. 24.6.1853, 28.5.1869
    E.W.S.G. 2.12.1860, 21.10.1870

26. E.S. 2.2.1877

27. E.S. 23.8.1871, 30.8.1871, 13.9.1871
28. E.S. 30.7.1875, 6.2.1892, 3.8.1901
29. *Report of the Enquiry into the Charities of Colchester*, 1886
    E.S. 22.5.1897, 25.12.1897
30. E.S. 7.11.1896, 6.11.1897
31. E.S. 10.6.1899
    E.T. 3.8.1901, 1.2.1908, 2.7.1910
    Sadler, *Report on the Secondary & Higher Education in Essex*, 1906,
    p.229
32. For the history of this school, see Brown, A. M., *Colchester County
    High School, The First 50 Years*
33. *Ibid.*
    Ex inf. Dept. of Education
    E.T. 5.11.1910
34. Sadler, *op. cit.,* pp.250–2
    E.S. 28.3.1885, 4.4.1885, 28.9.1895, 16.10.1897
    E.T. 16.7.1912
35. E.S. 4.11.1899
36. E.S. 22.5.1897
    E.T. 25.1.1896
37. E.T. 5.11.1910, 16.7.1912
38. Cromwell, *History of Colchester,* 1825, pp.342–9, 357–8
    Brown, *Essex People*, 1972, p.144
    White, 1848, p.86
    C.G. 12.1.1822, 8.2.1823, 21.6.1823
    E.S. 18.1.1834, 26.12.1834
39. Hurnard, *A Memoir*, 1883, pp.119–20
    E.S. 27.4.1833, 20.1.1837
    Rules of Colchester Mechanics' Institute, 1838
40. E.S. 21.12.1833, 21.10.1852, 23.1.1863
    I.E. 29.10.1839
    E.S.T. 16.2.1839
41. *Rules,* 1838, *op. cit.*
    E.S. 15.1.1841, 14.7.1848, 11.12.1848, 9.7.1852
    Brown, *op. cit.*, p.180
42. E.R.O., T/B 70/2
    E.S. and E.T., 1858–9
43. E.S. 27.9.1839, 14.7.1848
    Rules of Colchester Literary Institute, 1848
44. Regular reports of the Literary Institute's activities were published in
    the local press
    Kelly, 1862, 1878, 1890
45. *Catalogue of the Library of the Colchester Literary Institution*, 1886
46. E.S. 6.3.1861, 5.3.1898
    E.T. 4.3.1899, 2.3.1901
    H.T. 31.8.1901

47. Sadler, *op. cit.*, pp.252–3
     Ex. inf. the late Mr. George Pateman
     E.S. 1.2.1896, 29.1.1898, 14.3.1914
     E.T. 21.12.1895, 29.10.1904, 21.12.1907, 11.10.1913
48. E.S. 19.4.1913
     E.T. 1914 *passim*
49. Lewington, *A Brief Account of the Colchester Co-operative Society,*
     1977
50. E.S. 3.2.1875, 25.2.1899, 2.11.1907
     E.T. 31.3.1894, 9.3.1901, 2.4.1910

CHAPTER IV: POLITICS

 1. *The Colchester Poll*, 9 March 1820
 2. C.G. 11.3.1820
     S.Ch. 19.6.1819
     Proceedings of the late elections for Colchester & Essex, 1820
 3. C.G. 1.1.1820, 15.1.1820, 25.6.1825
 4. Sel. Cttee. on *Depressed State of Agriculture*, 1821, pp.106 foll.
     I.J. 7.5.1825
 5. Ch.Ch. 4.9.1807
     C.G. 7.9.1822
     E.COL.1 (942.074), E.COL.1 (329.942) in C.C.L.
 6. E.H.K.M. 3.1.1825
     I.E. 18.7.1843
 7. E.COL.1 (942.074), E.COL.1 (329.942) in C.C.L.
 8. S.Ch. 3.2.1826
 9. E.S. 6.3.1862, 16.7.1921
     Ch.Ch. 6.11.1812, 20.3.1818
10. E.S. 6.3.1862
     Hurnard, *The Setting Sun*, 1878, pp.136–7
11. Ch.Ch. 3.4.1818
12. Ch.Ch. 12.6.1818
     E.S. 6.3.1862
13. Ch.Ch. 6.11.1812, 6.3.1818, 12.6.1818
     E.S. 6.3.1862
     Proceedings of the late elections, 1820, *op. cit.* p.13
14. Harvey, Book of Press Cuttings in C.C.L.
     Coller, *People's History of Essex,* 1861, p.181
15. *The Sickle, The Colchester Courier* (Copies in E.R.O.)
16. S.Ch. 2.4.1831
     E.S. 6.3.1862
17. S.Ch. 30.4.1831
     E.S. 6.5.1831

18. E.S. 1831–2, *passim*
19. Poster, issued 6.5.1831
20. *Ibid.*
21. E.S. 2.6.1832
22. E.S. 16.6.1832, 30.6.1832, 8.2.1834
23. E.S. 7.1.1832, 26.12.1834
    Poster issued 27.4.1831
24. E.S. 11.6.1832, 22.10.1832
25. E.S. 19.4.1861
26. Hurnard, *op. cit.*, pp.135–6
27. E.S. 30.6.1843
    Poster issued 5.7.1852
28. S.Ch. 6.1.1849, quoting *Daily News* article
29. E.H.K.M. 25.11.1834
    S.Ch. 20.12.1834
    E.S. 26.12.1834, 10.12.1841
30. E.S. 14.7.1848
31. *Ibid.*
    I.E. 18.7.1843
32. E.S. 14.7.1843
    I.E. 1.2.1842, 15.2.1842, 11.7.1843, 18.7.1843
    Brown, *Essex People,* p.174 (Diary of Wm. Wire)
33. E.S. 14.7.1848
    S.Ch. 23.10.1847
    I.E. 27.7.1847
    E.T. 12.8.1899
34. E.S. 31.5.1865
    E.T. 13.1.1894
    Harvey, Book of Press Cuttings in C.C.L.
35. Hurnard, *op. cit.*, pp.132–5
36. E.S. 8.12.1838, 16.2.1839, 16.11.1839
    E.M. 10.10.1839
37. E.S. 14.1.1832, 14.4.1832
38. C.G. 9.4.1836, 25.6.1836
39. E.S. 31.12.1831
    S.Ch. 3.1.1835
40. E.S. 25.1.1838
    S.Ch. 19.11.1831
41. E.S. 14.1.1842
42. E.S. 26.7.1861, 14.4.1871, 9.10.1886
43. E.W.S.G. 26.7.1861
    E.S. 28.1.1866
44. E.S. 13.1.1843, 24.3.1843, 21.3.1845

45. E.S.T. 18.1.1840
    E.S. 6.1.1843

46. Cromwell, *History of Colchester,* 1825, p.379

47. E.S.T. 24.8.1839

48. E.S. 17.11.1837

49. E.S. 11.2.1832

50. Seaman, *Valedictory Address,* 1850 (in E.R.O.)

51. Cromwell, *op. cit.*, p.387
    C.G. 26.10.1822

52. E.T. 20.8.1859

53. E.S. 21.3.1866, 6.4.1866

54. E.S. 11.11.1870

55. E.S. 16.10.1886

56. E.S. 3.7.1886, 17.7.1886, 16.8.1890, 26.5.1900
    E.T. 18.3.1893, 10.1.1914

57. E.S. 6.2.1874

58. E.T. 2.4.1880

59. E.S. 22.3.1872, 25.1.1890
    E.T. 16.8.1890

60. Kelly, 1899

61. E.S. 2.11.1849
    E.T. 10.1.1894
    Blaxill, *History of Lion Walk,* 1938, pp.48–9

62. H.T. 22.11.1884
    E.T. 28.5.1892, 25.6.1892, 29.1.1898

63. E.S. 6.7.1895

64. E.T. 22.1.1910, 3.12.1910
    E.S. 1.11.1902, 6.4.1907

65. E.S. 21.12.1838

66. E.S. 26.7.1867, 30.8.1867

67. Butler, *An Autobiographical Memoir,* 1928, pp.80–4
    E.S. 27.3.1874

68. Hurnard, *op. cit.,* pp.129–30

69. E.S. 7.8.1867

70. E.S. 3.4.1886, 17.4.1886

71. E.S. 21.12.1895

72. E.T. 15.4.1893, 21.10.1893, 22.12.1894, 4.8.1914

73. E.T. 19.9.1908, 9.11.1912, 26.7.1913
    E.S. 26.7.1913

74. H.T. 20.1.1906

CHAPTER V: WORKING-CLASS MOVEMENTS

1. Ch.Ch. 3.6.1885
   E.R.O. Q/RSf1
2. E.R.O. Q/RSf2
3. Brown, *Essex People 1750–1900*, 1972, pp.108–10
4. E.S. 24.5.1834
5. E.H.K.M. 27.5.1834
6. E.S. 19.9.1834
7. E.S. 28.7.1837
8. S.Ch. 20.8.1836
9. C.G. July to Oct. 1835
10. E.S.T. 2.2.1838
11. There are numerous reports of the activities of the Colchester Work-
    ing Men's Association in the 1838 file of the *Essex and Suffolk Times*
12. E.S. 9.2.1838
13. E.S.T. 16.2.1838
14. E.T. 16.8.1890
15. E.S.T. 2.3.1838
16. E.S. 6.7.1838
17. E.S., E.S.T., Ch.Ch., S.Ch., Sept. 1838
18. E.S.T. 3.11.1838
19. E.S.T. 24.11.1838, 1.12.1838, 15.12.1838
20. E.S.T. 29.12.1838
    E.H.K.M. 11.12.1838
21. E.S.T. 8.12.1838, 1.6.1839
22. E.S. 16.8.1839
    I.E. 13.8.1839
    E.S.T. 6.4.1839
23. E.S. 22.11.1839
24. N.S. 30.4.1842
25. N.S. 26.3.1842, 25.6.1842
26. E.S. 7.4.1843
27. E.S. 30.6.1843
28. N.S. 2.3.1844, 13.4.1844, 20.4.1844
    S.Ch. 24.2.1844
    E.S. 9.10.1846
29. E.S. 30.7.1847
    S.Ch. 30.10.1847
30. S.Ch. 13.10.1847
31. E.S. 14.7.1848
32. N.S. 1.4.1848, 8.4.1848

33. E.S. 21.4.1848, 28.4.1848
     S.Ch. 15.4.1848
     I.E. 11.4.1848
     Essex Herald 25.4.1848

34. S.Ch. 10.6.1848
     E.S. 26.5.1848, 23.6.1848

35. E.S. 25.4.1851
     S.Ch. 12.4.1851, 26.4.1851

36. *Notes to the People*, Vol. 2, p.884
     People's Paper 4.4.1857, 19.9.1857
     E.T. 12.3.1859

37. E.T. 13.1.1894

38. *Ibid.*
     E.S. 13.1.1894

39. E.S. 26.11.1921

40. N.S. 2.3.1844, 13.4.1844, 20.4.1844
     S.Ch. 24.2.1844

41. E.S. 9.10.1846
     E.W.S.G. 22.7.1853, 12.8.1853, 19.8.1853

42. E.W.S.G. 22.4.1853, 6.5.1853
     E.S. 20.5.1853

43. Brown, *Essex People 1750–1900*, 1972, p.176 (Diary of Wm. Wire)
     E.S. 28.6.1844, 21.6.1861, 18.3.1870, 15.12.1871
     E.W.S.G. 18.4.1867, 28.3.1872

44. E.S. 17.11.1865
     E.T. 16.1.1866

45. E.S. 7.4.1843, 16.10.1846, 14.6.1861, 15.2.1867
     I.E. 13.10.1846
     E.W.S.G. 13.4.1854

46. Amalgamated Society of Carpenters and Joiners, Annual Reports
     E.M. 29.3.1879
     E.T. 2.4.1898

47. E.T. 23.9.1882

48. E.W.S.G. 5.7.1872, 12.7.1872
     E.S. 10.7.1872

49. E.S. 2.8.1872, 9.8.1872, 25.3.1874
     C.M. 17.11.1877

50. Amalgamated Society of Tailors, Annual Reports
     E.T. 5.9.1891, 26.5.1894

51. Brown, *op. cit.*, pp.128–32 (Diary of J. Castle)
     *One Hundred Up, The Centenary Story of Colchester Co-operative
     Society*, 1961
     H. W. Lewington, *A Brief Account of the Colchester Co-operative
     Society*, 1977
     E.S. 21.1.1863

52. E.T. 20.4.1901
53. E.T. 2.4.1892
54. E.S. 6.4.1866
55. E.S. 17.1.1868
56. E.S. 1.6.1877
57. *Census of Great Britain*, 1871, Enumerators' Returns for Colchester
    C.M. 6.7.1879
    E.T. 7.11.1891, 19.12.1891, 2.4.1892, 28.5.1892, 16.9.1893,
    7.5.1904, 14.5.1904
58. E.T. 13.9.1890, 20.9.1890, 23.1.1892, 23.4.1892, 12.11.1892
59. E.S. and E.T., Jan. to Aug. 1892, *passim*
60. E.T. 28.5.1892, 10.9.1892
61. E.T. 21.5.1892, 11.6.1892, 18.6.1892, 25.6.1892, 30.7.1892
62. E.T. 20.8.1892
63. E.T. 1892–3 *passim*
64. E.T. 7.5.1892
65. E.T. 21.5.1892, 28.5.1892
66. E.T. 9.7.1892
67. E.T. 30.6.1894, 7.7.1894, 21.7.1894, 13.10.1894, 27.10.1894
68. H.T. 18.5.1895, 22.6.1895
    E.T. 6.4.1895
    E.S. 6.4.1895
69. E.S. 16.3.1895, 23.3.1895, 13.4.1895
    E.T. 23.3.1895, 30.3.1895, 6.4.1895
70. E.T. 14.5.1904
71. Lewington, *op. cit.*
    E.T. 9.2.1901, 4.6.1904, 22.8.1911
72. E.T. 7.1.1905, 21.1.1905
73. E.T. 7.5.1910
74. E.T. 7.5.1910, 10.5.1910
75. E.T. 10.5.1910
76. *Ibid.*
77. Ex inf. the late Timothy Smith
78. E.T. 23.5.1914, 30.5.1914
79. Ex inf. the late Timothy Smith
    E.T. 16.9.1911, 23.3.1912
80. Amalgamated Society of Railway Servants, Annual Reports
    E.T. 2.7.1898, 3.3.1914
81. E.T. 25.2.1911
82. E.T. 28.5.1912
83. Ex inf. the late Timothy Smith
    E.T. 11.4.1908, 7.7.1908, 26.9.1908, 1.1.1910

84. E.T. 3.3.1914
85. Ex inf. the late Timothy Smith
86. E.T. 4.8.1914

CHAPTER VI: SOCIAL LIFE

1. Gilbert, *Autobiography of Mrs. Gilbert, 1874*, Vol. 1, *passim*
2. E.S. 24.11.1831, 21.11.1834
3. Brown, *Essex People*, 1972, p.172
   E.S. 22.3.1913
4. C.G. 7.8.1818, 1.7.1820, 20.7.1822
5. Important sources for the history of Colchester's churches and chapels are:
   Cockerill and Woodward, *Colchester Churches*, 1973
   Blaxill, *The Nonconformist Churches of Colchester*, 1948
   White and Kelly, Trade Directories
6. Essex Congregational Union, Annual Reports
7. E.R.O. Q/CR 3/1,2: 1851, Census, ecclesiastical returns
   C.G. 18.3.1837
8. E.S. 18.4.1845
9. Dakins, *Sermon at the Death of Horatio Cock*, 1832
10. E.S. 6.3.1840
11. Brown, *op. cit.*, p.166
12. J. B. Harvey, Book of Press Cuttings (in C.C.L.)
13. C.G. Oct.–Nov. 1825
14. C.G. 10.5.1834
15. Hurnard, *The Setting Sun*, 1878, p.169
16. Census of Gt. Britain, 1841, enumerators' returns
17. Kelly, 1859, p.55
18. Hurnard, *op. cit.*, pp.235–6
19. E.S. 3.1.1840
20. E.S. 13.6.1845
21. E.S. 8.8.1862, 15.8.1969
22. Brown, *op. cit.*, p.111
23. *Ibid.*, pp.120–8, 131
24. *Ibid.*, p.111
25. I.E. 26.7.1842
26. Brown, *op. cit.*, p.171
27. E.S. 6.3.1864, 18.4.1914
28. E.S. 17.4.1846, 24.9.1846
29. Brown, *op. cit.*, pp.164–185

30. *Ibid.*, p.169
    White, 1848, p.128
31. I.E. 11.8.1846
32. E.S. 17.5.1844
33. G.E.R., 1865, p.159
34. E.S. 19.8.1842
35. E.S. 10.2.1864
36. E.S. 22.2.1865
37. Census of Gt. Britain, 1841–71, enumerators' returns
    E.S. 9.10.1886
38. E.S. 17.4.1872, 28.8.1872, 5.1.1877, 16.3.1877, 26.5.1900
39. H.T. 22.3.1884
40. E.S. 29.7.1864
41. E.S. 14.8.1861, 27.1.1865, 9.3.1877, 16.3.1877
42. E.S. 24.5.1878
43. E.S. 2.2.1872
44. H.T. 13.11.1875
45. E.S. 4.3.1870
46. *Suffolk Times*, 11.7.1884
47. An Old Colchester Inhabitant, *Recollections* (Newspaper cuttings in possession of Mr. John Bensusan-Butt, to whom I am indebted for this source), ll.201–18
48. Much information about the Contagious Diseases Acts episode has been obtained from the unpublished thesis of Mina Trustram, "State Regulation of Vice", 1977. Other information is contained in Josephine Butler's *An Autobiographical Memoir* and in the contemporary Press.
49. *The Earthquake in East Essex*, 1884, p.60
50. E.S. 3.2.1865, 10.2.1865
51. E.T. 16.5.1914
52. E.T. 2.1.1897
53. Colchester Wesleyan Mutual Improvement Society, Programme 1886–7
54. E.S. 3.1.1855
55. E.S. 9.5.1855
56. E.S. 24.4.1897
    E.T. 10.1.1914
57. Beckett, *Romantic Essex*, 1907, pp.44–5, 60
58. E.S. 9.10.1886
59. Brown, *op. cit.*, p.169
60. E.S. 27.6.1851, 13.3.1861, 24.3.1875, 29.9.1883, 15.1.1898

61. E.S. 13.10.1865

62. E.T. 22.10.1892

63. E.S. 26.2.1898, 19.3.1898, 31.12.1898

64. E.T. 25.3.1899

65. E.R. 13, p.250
    E.S. 14.4.1906

66. E.S. 29.1.1898, 6.7.1907

67. E.S. 31.8.1907, 5.4.1913, 17.5.1913

68. E.T. 15.8.1908

69. E.S. 20.7.1907

70. E.S. 7.8.1872, 8.8.1873

71. An Old Colchester Inhabitant, *op. cit.*, ll.193–200

72. E.T. 30.5.1896

73. E.S. 3.5.1854, 25.3.1863, 30.11.1864, 1.10.1875, 22.4.1882, 24.7.1909
    C.M. 6.5.1876

74. E.T. 10.3.1906

75. Clark, *Colchester Football Club*, 1924
    E.S. 6.1.1897, 3.4.1897, 3.5.1913

76. E.T. 14.2.1903

77. E.T. 10.10.1908

78. E.T. 16.5.1914

79. E.T. 24.1.1903

80. E.T. 10.10.1896, 27.8.1912

81. E.T. 20.4.1901, 27.4.1901

82. E.S. 31.1.1914

83. E.S. 5.1.1901

THE POPULATION OF THE BOROUGH OF COLCHESTER, 1801–1911

The following figures are compiled from *The Victoria History of the County of Essex,* Vol. II (1907) pp.353–4.

1801	11,520	**1861**	23,815
1811	12,544	**1871**	26,345
1821	14,016	**1881**	28,374
1831	16,167	**1891**	34,559
1841	17,790	**1901**	38,373
1851	19,443	**1911**	43,452

INDEX